Thomas

Liturgical Resources
for the Year of Mark

ORDINARY TIME, YEAR B OF THE LITURGICAL CYCLE

the columba press

First published in 2008 by
the columba press
55A Spruce Avenue, Stillorgan Industrial Park,
Blackrock, Co Dublin

Cover by Bill Bolger
Origination by The Columba Press
Printed in Ireland by ColourBooks Ltd, Dublin

ISBN 978 1 85607 627 2

To my classmates, All Hallows, 1983

Acknowledgement

I would like to acknowledge the help and feedback I have had from so
many people – priests in parishes, musicians, liturgists, scripture scholars, and most importantly many who 'sit in the pews' – to the materials
printed here during the time that I was putting together this collection
of resources. I would also like to thank Dr Francisca Rumsey of the Poor
Clare Monastery in Arkley, and my colleague here in Lampeter, for
proofreading the manuscript.

Table of Contents

Preface

'And Jesus said to them, "Therefore every scribe who has been trained for the kingdom of heaven is like the master of a household who brings out of his treasure what is new and what is old".' (Mt 13:52). This saying always puts me in mind of the priest who has to preside week after week at the Sunday Eucharist of the community. Here he is expected to act as the host of the family gathering of the New People, the New People formed as sisters and brothers of the Lord around the Lord's Table, and he is expected to provide fare for them.

The fare is what this book is about. On the one hand, it is old because the liturgy itself is the great link with the past: with our tradition, with the meal practice of Jesus, and with all the memories of God's bounty. On the other hand, the liturgy must be ever new: we are not engaging in a pageant but celebrating our identity now as a people transformed, consecrated to become the Body and Blood of the Anointed One. So out of the wealth of our memory as the church we have to be always bringing out treasure for the household that is both new and old. Without the new, the liturgy becomes fossilised; without the old, the liturgy is cut adrift from its origins and its promises.

If this book helps you to recall the old in the midst of the new, and to think of new ideas in the midst of the old, I shall have achieved my aim. In putting these resources together I have tried to keep the average congregation in mind, aware that each local church has to look back and appropriate the riches of the past, but also be open to explore new ideas for celebration and to accept new challenges from our reflection on who we are and where we must go as the People of God. This balance of old with new, in celebrations that strive to express authentically who we are, is the challenge facing us in a world where cultural change becomes ever more rapid. Today, we have to avoid twin temptations: one of 'just going with the flow'; the other of 'jamming on

the breaks.' The first temptation imagines that liturgy can exist
without the tradition; the second imagines we can isolate liturgy
from the world around it. The former temptation plays down
the importance of the Communion of Saints, the latter a robust
belief in the Incarnation. It is always worth recalling what
Picasso is reported to have said about tradition: 'Tradition is
having a baby, not wearing your grandfather's hat!'

T.O'L
Lampeter
Corpus Christi 2008

Psalm Numbers

In the *Lectionary* and *Missal* the numbers given to the Psalms follow that given in the Latin *Ordo Lectionum* which, being in Latin, naturally follows the Vulgate numeration. The Vulgate numeration followed that of the Old Greek translation ('The Septuagint') as this was seen as 'the Psalter of the Church.' However, most modern books, apart from Catholic liturgical books, follow the numeration of the Hebrew text of the Psalter.

Since this book's primary referents are the books of the Catholic liturgy, the Septuagint number is given first and the Hebrew numeration is then given in (brackets). The same convention as is used in the English translation of the Liturgy of the Hours. See *Breviary*, vol 1, pp 640*-641* for further information.

For example: The Psalm that begins 'My heart is ready' is cited as Ps 107(108).

For convenience here is a concordance of the two numeration systems:

Septuagint	Hebrew
1 – 8	1 - 8
9	9 - 10
10 -112	11 - 113
113	114 - 115
114 - 115	116
116 - 145	117 - 146
146 - 147	147
148 - 150	148 - 150

The Sequence of Gospel Readings:
An Overview

The purpose of this table is to show at a glance the sweep of readings through Mark in Year B. We must remember, of course, that this sweep is always interrupted by Easter. It also shows at a glance that there is no sequence in the first readings; each being chosen as having some relationship with the gospel of the day.

Sunday	Gospel	First Reading
	Lectionary Unit I	
1 – Baptism	Mk 1:6b-11	Isa 55:1-11
2	Jn 1:35-42	1 Sam 3:3-10, 19
	Lectionary Unit II – Stage I	
3	Mk 1:14-20	Jon 3:1-5, 10
4	Mk 1:21-8	Dt 18:15-20
5	Mk 1:29-39	Job 7:1-4, 6-7
6	Mk 1:40-5	Lev 13:1-2, 45-6
7	Mk 2:1-12	Isa 43:18-9, 21-2, 24-5
8	Mk 2:18-22	Hos 2:16-7, 21-2
9	Mk 2:23–3:6	Dt 5:12-15
	Lectionary Unit II – Stage II	
10	Mk 3:20-35	Gn 3:9-15
11	Mk 4:26-34	Ezek 17:22-4
12	Mk 4:35-41	Job 38:1, 8-11
13	Mk 5:21-43	Wis 1:13-5; 2:23-4
14	Mk 6:1-6	Ezek 2:2-5
	Lectionary Unit II – Stage III	
15	Mk 6:7-13	Amos 7:12-5
16	Mk 6:30-4	Jer 23:1-6
17	Jn 6:1-15	2 Kgs 4:42-4
18	Jn 6:24-35	Ex 16:2-4, 12-5
19	Jn 6:41-52	1 Kgs 19:4-8
20	Jn 6:51-58	Prov 9:1-6
21	Jn 6:61-70	Jos 24:1-2, 15-8

| 22 | Mk 7:1-8, 14-5, 21 | Dt 4:1-2, 6-8 |
| 23 | Mk 7:31-7 | Isa 35:4-7 |

Lectionary Unit III – Stage I

24	Mk 8:27-35	Isa 50:5-9
25	Mk 9:29-36	Wis 2:12, 17-20
26	Mk 9:37-42, 44,46-7	Nm 11:25-9
27	Mk 10:2-16	Gn 2:18-24
28	Mk 10:17-30	Wis 7:7-11
29	Mk 10:35-45	Isa 53:10-11
30	Mk 10:46-52	Jer 31:7-9

Lectionary Unit III – Stage II

31	Mk 12:28b-34	Dt 6:2-6
32	Mk 12:38-44	1 Kgs 17:10-16
33	Mk 13:24-32	Dan 12:1-3

Lectionary Unit III – Stage III

| 34 – Christ the King | Jn 18:33b-37 | Dan 7:13-4 |

The Sequence of Second Readings:
An Overview

The purpose of this table is to show at a glance the sweep of readings through the epistles in Year B. We must remember, of course, that this sweep is always interrupted by Easter.

Sunday	Second Reading
1 – Baptism	1 Jn 5:1-9
2	1 Cor 6:13-15, 17-20
3	1 Cor 7:29-31
4	1 Cor 7:32-35
5	1 Cor 9:16-9, 22-3
6	1 Cor 10:31-11:1
7	2 Cor 1:18-22
8	2 Cor 3:1-6
9	2 Cor 4:6-11
10	2 Cor 4:13-5:1
11	2 Cor 5:6-10
12	2 Cor 5:14-17
13	2 Cor 8:7, 9, 13-5
14	2 Cor 12:7-10
15	Eph 1:3-14
16	Eph 2:13-8
17	Eph 4:1-6
18	Eph 4:17, 20-4
19	Eph 4:30-5:2
20	Eph 5:15-20
21	Eph 5:21-32
22	Jas 1:17-8, 21-2, 27
23	Jas 2:1-5
24	Jas 2:14-8
25	Jas 3:16-4:3
26	Jas 5:1-6

Proclaiming Jesus in Year B

Background

Of all the books of the restoration of the liturgy inspired by Vatican II, the lectionary seems to be one that draws fire from all quarters in the Catholic Church at present. Conservatives attack it simply on the grounds that they imagine some gilded age – a slippery moment in real time – prior to the new Order of Mass in the vernacular. Liberals attack it as they claim they would like readings with 'relevance to today' – an equally slippery moment in the human historical continuum. Between these groups lie many preachers/celebrants who criticise it for (1) giving too many readings; (2) readings which are 'difficult' to preach upon; (3) readings which do not 'make sense' (e.g. do not have a readily recognisable 'theme'); (4) readings which do not provide a 'thought for the day'; (5) that there are Old Testament readings included at all; or (6) that the gospels do not fit with 'the epistles' (i.e. the second readings).

By amazing contrast, outside the Catholic Church the lectionary seems to be winning more friends by the day. Churches that are familiar with the notion of a lectionary and a liturgical year who want to up-date their lectionary are often opting for the Roman lectionary – restyled 'the common lectionary' – on the basis that it is as good as any such work is likely to be. Other churches, either discovering the value of a liturgical year or of using a lectionary, or both, are coming to it as if it were a preaching tool of excellence. And, a few lections from the Catholic canon apart, the lectionary has been adopted as it stands, usually not out of some vague desire for ecumenical conformity – a typically Catholic concern – but because of its intrinsic worth.

The simple facts are, firstly, that without lectionaries any celebrant/worship leader is likely to fall back on a canon within the canon which is little more than a collection of 'pet texts' – then the breath of the Christian memory is curtailed; and, second, given the content of the Christian canon any attempt to create a broad lectionary is going to involve compromises, swings and roundabouts, and will always leave some loose ends. But as lectionaries go, ours appears to be as good as anyone can come up with at the moment. Given that the lectionary was created in just a few liturgically busy years in the late 1960s, this is a great tribute to its creators.

Seasons, themes, and continuous reading
In the history of Christian lectionaries there have been two ways of creating lectionaries. The first, and simplest, is to opt for continuous reading (*lectio continua*) of texts as this allows biblical books to be appreciated whole, and it avoids any 'temptation' to skip over bits that are unpleasant. Given that the gospels are episodic in structure this method is ideally suited: read one story/incident today, then move to the next tomorrow or next Sunday.

However, given that the liturgical year is fundamental to Christian liturgy – a component of practice already established by the time the Acts of the Apostles was written – the method of continuous reading could never hold unrivalled sway. How could one read a parable text on Easter Day just because it was the next reading in a sequence? The very fact that the rudiments of the liturgical year predate the gospels we possess has meant that the nature of the day – for example, if today is the day of Pentecost – determines the reading if there is a reading that is linked to that day. So at Christmas we need to hear of Bethlehem; at Easter of the resurrection; and on 6 August of the transfiguration. Such lectionaries using readings appropriate to the time being celebrated as known as 'eclogadic lectionaries.'

Alongside these two major dynamics in creating lectionaries there is a third, lesser, factor: the appropriateness of a particular scriptural passage to a celebration either of a saint or topic. Thus the Common of Doctors in the 1570 Missal had Mt 5:13-19 as its gospel, while the Mass in Time of War had Mt 24:3-8. As with eclogadic lectionaries, the choice of reading is being determined by what is being celebrated on that day. This reaches its logical conclusion in the readings at weddings, funerals, and other major celebrations; but the celebration of 'special Masses' often leads to choices whose 'fit' is tenuous or to superficial 'links' between a piece of text and a situation. However, given that the celebration is about a special event, and this has to be referred to in the homily, there is a certain inherent demand that one somehow finds a 'suitable' reading.

Ordinary Time

Although every lectionary has to have an eclogadic element (for Christmas and Easter at the very least), it is still desirable that as wide a range of texts as possible be used in the liturgy; hence the creation of any lectionary that covers the year has to be a compromise between the two selection methods.[1]

The compromise worked out for the 1970 lectionary was complex, elaborate, and on a scale never before attempted in Christian liturgical history. It is this sophistication – once the inevitable need for a compromise is recognised – that has recommended it to so many groups in their several searches for a lectionary. So on certain days in the year when key moments in the Christ-event are to be celebrated, the readings are the same each and every year: the Passion according to John in the Good Friday Liturgy is the best example. Then there are the eclogadic choices for Christmas and Easter, and to a lesser extent for Lent and for Advent: but varied over a cycle of three years for the Sundays and other major feasts. Then outside these special seasons we have 'ordinary time' and here the criterion is continuous reading and by spreading the material over the three-year cycle a greater variety of gospel material is now used than ever before. The simple device of using Matthew in year A, Mark in B, and Luke in C, now seems so obvious that we forget that it

---

1. In terms of planned liturgical time, the third method can be ignored as it would destroy the whole rationale of a lectionary: thus the current lectionary's assumption that on saints' feasts – very special festivals excepted – that the readings 'of the day' rather than those from the Commons are used.

was a revolution in 1970. Today one has to speak to groups who have just adopted the lectionary to hear expressions of 'what a brilliant idea' it is to devote a year to each of the three synoptics (knowing that John is well represented in the seasons' sections). Which gospel is read in any calendar year is determined by the simple method of dividing the date by three: if the remainder is 1, then it is the first year of the cycle and Mt; if 2, then the second year and Mk; and if the date is perfectly divisible, the year 3: Lk. So 2006÷3=668 'and two over', hence it is 'year 2.' From an ecumenical perspective this was an inspired way of determining the cycle as there is no 'Vatican inspired Year Zero' telling people that a particular year is Year A – it is simply a matter of AD and maths! For most people, this is about as much as they know about the structure of the lectionary in Ordinary Time: each year we read one evangelist. Is there anything more to be said?

Three Christologies

To appreciate the lectionary we must note that once the option of continuous reading was taken, there were still many other decisions as to what would and would not be included in the continuous reading. There were three key factors facing the selectors: (1) that even in Mk – once the chapters, after 11:1, relating to the final week in Jerusalem are omitted since they are used in Lent/ Holy Week – there is too much material to distribute over the available number of Sundays unless very large sections (often made up of several stories) were read each Sunday; (2) there are passages in the triple tradition so alike each other that they would be given undue prominence and *de facto* be read each year, and so these have to be curtailed; and (3) there are parts of each gospel text that for a variety of reasons are so problematic (e.g. corrupt texts, duplications, interpolations) that they are best omitted from public reading or pruned of erratic verses. Hence the selectors describe their work in the 1981 edition not as 'continuous reading' but more precisely as 'semi-continuous'.

If we take Mk as an example we have 'continuous reading'

up to the time Jesus arrives in Jerusalem and then some snippets from the Jerusalem discourses. The result was that the selectors had a total of 405 verses[2] from between Mk 1:1 and 10:52 available to them for Ordinary Time. However, they used only c. 190 of these (i.e. just under half the text), plus 20 verses from Mk 12-13, and 70 verses from Jn. This selection was not just a case of pruning and dividing out what was left: knowing that they had to select, they deliberately adopted a policy of presenting the pieces of the gospel as part of a larger plan to show the gospel writers' intentions. They assumed that each of the synoptics 'presents us with a recognisable' and, we might add, distinctive 'portrait of Christ and a *particular approach* [their italics] to his teaching' and hence the gospels are presented separately over the three years (*Introduction to the Lectionary*, 1982, p xlvii). Their aim in this process of selection was outlined as 'allowing the main lines of the structure and theology of each ... to be grasped by preacher and reader [which] should allow the message of each ... to penetrate gradually into the consciousness of the faithful' (*ibid.*). They then provided the three schemata they envisaged acting as the scaffolding over each year. But then (possibly recognising that neither (1) what a text's audience hears is static over time or cultures, nor (2) does biblical scholarship stand still) add that 'such schemes are not definitive, but it is hoped that they will be a help' (*ibid.*).

The three schemes (labelled Tables I, II, and III) are to be found on pp xlviii-liii in the *Introduction to the Lectionary*. We get a flavour of how they work by taking Mk as an example. It declared that it sees Mk's 'main interest' as 'the person of Jesus himself'. This is seen as progressively revealed in the text as the journey towards Jerusalem moved forward and based around the climactic question 'who do men say that I am?' (Mk 8:29). It

2. Using Nestle-Aland's numbering in the Greek text which, in effect, stands behind our translations rather than Vatican *editio typica* of the Clementine-Vulgate or the two editions of the *Nova Vulgata* (1979 and 1986): the 1969 *Ordo Lectionum* provided only text references; while the *Nova Vulgata* has had almost no impact on the lectionary actually in use today.

sees Peter's 'You are the Christ' as at 'the heart of Mark's gospel'. In taking this position, the lectionary is following the mainstream of contemporary exegetical thinking about Mk today – indeed since the lectionary appeared there has been an increased emphasis among scholars on the need to view each gospel as an entire unit as opposed to seeing them as quarries for the traditions that lie behind our texts.[3] The lectionary then explains the inclusion of the 57 verses from Jn on Sundays 17 to 21 as adopting a single unit from Jn's, 'the sermon on the "Bread of Life"' which it sees as fitting 'well into [a particular] part of Mark's gospel, which is concerned with Jesus' revelation of himself and is known as "the Bread section".' And, as dovetailing of texts goes, this is about as neat as anything we might find: on Sunday 14 we have Mk 6:30-34 which is followed in the gospel text (6:35-44) with the feeding miracle of the five loaves and the two fish, which is supplanted in the liturgical reading by the bread/feeding/eating sermon from Jn. The compilers do not explain the rationale for selecting Jn 18:33b-37 for Christ the King; but this to my mind is rather pleasant for while in mathematics consistency is virtue, in theology its systematic invocation often spells death to that imaginative process without which faith is impossible.[4]

The scaffolding sees the readings on the 34 Sundays as forming three Units, divided again into Stages, and then with a key point for each Sunday's passage. So Mk is read as revealing the figure of Jesus the Messiah (Unit 1), then 'the Mystery of Jesus' progressively revealed (Unit 2), and then the Mystery of the Son of Man (Unit 3). Unit 2, for example, is then seen as Jesus revealing himself to the Jewish crowds (Stage 1), then to his disciples (Stage 2), and then manifesting himself (Stage 3). Then to take a Sunday within Stage 2, e.g. Sunday 11: Mk 426-34, we have it described as 'Parables of the Kingdom'. It is this keynote that then acts as the criterion for which snippet of the Old Testament

---

3. See, for example, the essays in R. Bauckham ed., *The Gospels for All Christians* (Grand Rapids, MI/Cambridge 1998).
4. Nor do they explain the choice of Jn 1:35-42 for Sunday 2.

is chosen (Ezek 17:22-24) and thus the Psalm (Ps 91:2-3, 13-16). This method of selecting the Old Testament reading is based upon the hermeneutic that 'the Old prefigures the New, the New fulfils the Old.' While this hermeneutic is controversial today, it is impossible in a short note like this to even open up the question: suffice to note that was the rationale behind the selection, and noting the key point made in the schema often provides a focus for reading the Old Testament passage. This link between the gospel and the Old Testament reading brings up the question of the relationship of both to the Second Reading: the simple answer is that there is none. Just as the gospels are read 'semi-continuously' (with the First Reading and Psalm in tow), so the epistles are read 'semi-continuously' over the three years (see Table IV, p liv). The only exception to this during Ordinary Time is on Sunday 34 in each year when the Second Reading is linked to the feast of Christ the King. So whenever one finds a common theme in all three readings: either it is so common it could be found virtually anywhere, or it is a coincidence, or else it is in the mind of the reader and accommodated in each of them.

The scaffolding can best be seen as a grid:

Year B: The Year of Mark

Unit	Stage	Sunday
1 The Figure of Jesus the Messiah		1 2
2. The Mystery progressively revealed	1. Jesus with the Jewish Crowds	3 4 5 6 7 8 9
	2. Jesus with his disciples	10 11 12 13 14
	3. Jesus manifests himself	15 16 17 18 19 20 21 22 23
3. The Mystery of the Son of Man	1. The 'Way' of the Son of Man	24 25 26 27 28 29 30
	2. Final revelation in Jerusalem	31 32 33
	3. The fulfilment of the mystery	34

No lectionary – since it must be a work of compromises – will ever be free of critics; but justice demands that if we accept the basic liturgical premises that have inspired Christian reading at the Eucharist since at least the early second century, then we should acknowledge our lectionary as about as good as any rite within the whole of Christian liturgy has ever had. My own view is that it is not only as good as any, but I know of none better in the last 1800 years for which we have evidence in Greek, Syriac, and Latin. Yet, despite its use for 40 years in the Roman rite, its genuine exploitation in the formation of Christian consciousness is minimal.

Lastly, one consequence of the excellence of our lectionary has been its adoption by others outside the Roman rite or even any connection with Rome. This is a fact that must now be a factor in the thought of anyone brashly calling for a new or different lectionary: it could be that if the Roman rite were to change its Sunday lectionary unilaterally, it would be, by that change, actually sundering the unity of Christian worship – a unity created by groups recognising in this lectionary an encapsulation of their view of scripture's place in worship.

Sunday

The church celebrates the paschal mystery on the first day of the week, known as the Lord's Day or Sunday. This follows a tradition handed down from the apostles, which took its origin from the day of Christ's resurrection. Thus Sunday should be considered the original feast day.

General Norms for the Liturgical Year and Calendar, n 4

Lectionary Unit I

This unit consists of just two Sundays which are seen to open the year/the gospel by focusing on the figure of Jesus the Messiah. This is expressed on the Feast of the Baptism (Sunday 1) with Mark's account; and then the call of Andrew and his companion from John's gospel (Sunday 2). The two events taken together provide the witness from heaven and earth to Jesus being the Promised One.

The Baptism of Our Lord

Note

This feast's history really begins in 1970 when it was chosen as the last moment of the Christmas cycle. It has no conceptual link with Christmas, except, it could be argued, that in the eastern rites it is part of Epiphany and so could be seen as an extension of Epiphany (and it is so linked in the current western Liturgy of the Hours). However, that is not how it is presented in the eucharistic liturgy where it is celebrated as a distinct 'event' in the life of Jesus. So how should we approach this feast?

First, it is now approaching mid-January and for everyone in the congregation, the president included, Christmas is long in the past, people have been back at work for weeks, schools have re-opened, people are already thinking of a 'Spring Break', and even chatter about the New Year seems a little dated. So looking back to Christmas or referring to this as the close of Christmas is just adding noise to the communication.

Second, this is about the baptism of the Christ by John, it is not a celebration of baptism as a sacrament or even the concept of baptism within the Paschal Mystery. Such thoughts belong to Easter, and the Easter Vigil in particular, not to this day. So this is not a day for having a baptism during the Eucharist. Such a celebration just confuses the understanding of what is being re-called and fills the understanding with muddle. Indeed, if it is the community's practice to celebrate the baptism of new members of the gathering during the Eucharist, then this is one of those Sundays which should not be used for baptisms.

Third, when we look at the position of the baptism of Jesus within the gospel kerygma we note that it is the public announcement of the beginning of the work of the Messiah. It marks a beginning of a period, not a conclusion. The basic structure can be seen in Mark (after the opening of the gospel comes the work of John which comes to its conclusion in his baptism of

Jesus and the glorious theophany of approbation): 'Thou art my
beloved Son: with thee I am well pleased' (Mk 1:1-11). The other
synoptics maintain this structure except that they add the pre-
lude of the Infancy Narratives; while in Jn 1:29-34 the testimony
of John the Baptist is concluded by his reference to the theophany of the Spirit descending on Jesus like a dove. In all the
gospels, this 'event' is then followed by the messianic ministry
(what we often refer to as the 'public life'). So the baptism of the
Lord by John had a distinct place in the preaching of the church,
it marked the 'visible' anointing by the Father in the Spirit for his
work. It is the great beginning.

Fourth, the baptism of Jesus now has a definite place in the
liturgy of the church, it is now a moment in our common memory
and celebration of the Lord. So it would be appropriate to look
on it as the beginning of Ordinary Time, and, in particular, a celebration of Jesus as 'the Messiah,' 'the Anointed One,' 'the
Christ'. So the tone of these notes is that of beginnings, not of
conclusions.

Introduction to the Celebration
Today marks the beginning of the public life and ministry of
Jesus Christ as he set out to do the Father's will and announce
the arrival of the Kingdom of God. And the moment of the beginning of the messianic work of Jesus is marked by the moment
of his baptism in the Jordan. He is acclaimed on earth by the
prophet John and links himself to John by being baptised by
him. He is acclaimed from heaven by the voice of the Father and
the presence of the Spirit. As the people who have heard his
preaching and accepted his call, who have confessed him as the
Christ, and set out to follow his way, let us pause and consider
the words addressed to Jesus: 'Thou art my beloved Son, with
thee I am well pleased.'

The Asperges
Use Option A (the Rite of Blessing and Sprinkling with Holy
Water) and then first form of the opening prayer; if you choose

Option B (a Rite of Penance) then these kyrie-verses are suitable:

Lord Jesus, you are the Son of the Father. Lord have mercy.

Lord Jesus, upon you the Spirit descended in the form of a dove. Christ have mercy.

Lord Jesus, you are the Beloved of the Father. Lord have mercy.

Headings for Readings
First Reading

This is a prophecy of the new world that will be ushered in when the Messiah, the Holy One of Israel, comes among God's people; we believe that this time of the Lord began with the baptism of Jesus in the Jordan.

Second Reading

One can use the option for Year B, but Acts 10:34-38 (the reading for Year A) is to be preferred because is the only passage in the New Testament outside the gospels that mentions today's feast.

However, if you use the Year B option:

In this reading we hear an answer to the question: what does it mean to call Jesus 'the Christ'? Jesus is the one sent by the Father and he sends the Holy Spirit into our lives.

Gospel

The Father addresses Jesus: 'You are my Son, the Beloved; my favour rests on you.'

Prayer of the Faithful
President

My friends, today we recall that Jesus is the Christ, the beloved Son of the Father, and because he has come and shared our humanity we can stand now with him and ask the Father for all we need.

Reader (s)

1. On this day when Jesus began his ministry we pray that his body the church will be faithful to the gospel he entrusted to it. Lord hear us.

2. On this day when Jesus was baptised by John we pray that people everywhere will recognise him as the Lord's anointed. Lord hear us.

3. On this day when Jesus was manifested to his people we pray that the People of God will have the courage to manifest him in our world. Lord hear us.

4. On this day when the Spirit descended on Jesus we pray that the Spirit will descend on all who are in darkness or who are despairing. Lord hear us.

5. On this day when the Father pointed out his Son standing in the midst of the creation, may we remember that the environment is God's gift to us. Lord hear us.

6. On this day when Jesus heard the voice of the Father we pray that all who have died may be called to be beloved sons and daughters. Lord hear us.

President

Father, we have been made your children of adoption in baptism; so as you look upon your beloved Son, look also on us, and grant our needs for we pray to you in Jesus Christ, our Lord. Amen.

Eucharistic Prayer

Preface of the Baptism of the Lord (P7), (Missal, p 410).

Invitation to the Our Father

The beloved Son of the Father made us his sisters and brothers, and so we can pray:

Sign of Peace

The Messiah announced the new relationship of peace when he welcomed people to his table. Let us celebrate this new relationship now in the sign of peace.

Invitation to Communion

This is the Beloved of the Father, who now invites us to share his life at his table.

Communion Reflection

The hymn given in the Breviary, 'When Jesus comes to be baptized' (vol 1, p 371), for Evening Prayer I of this feast is appropriate as a reflection today.

Conclusion

Solemn Blessing 3 for the Beginning of the New Year (Missal, p 368) is appropriate as for most people what is most obvious about this time is that is the beginning of the new year – and we should within our Eucharistic assembly formally ask God's blessings on the coming year.

COMMENTARY

First Reading: Isa 55:1-11

This reading from Isaiah can be replaced with that given for Year A. Isa 55:1-11 is the concluding prophecy of Deutero-Isaiah's book: it began with the cry 'Comfort, comfort my people, says your God' (Isa 40:1); now it ends with this solemn statement that the Lord is in full control of the destiny of his people. As it is read within the church it is the announcement that the time of the Messiah has now begun; that is the reign of the Christ which begins with the baptism in the Jordan.

Psalm: Is 12:2-6

This text from Isaiah has so many psalm-echoes that one could easily forget that it is not found within the Psalter. It is a hymn of thanksgiving that was composed after the time of (First-) Isaiah and inserted as a finale to chaps 2-12. The original meaning of the phrase 'you (plural) will draw water from the wells of salvation' is obscure, but has become fixed in the memory of the church as a prophecy of Christian baptism and it is, presumably, for that reason it was chosen for use here.

Second Reading: 1 Jn 5:1-9
The use of Year A (Acts 10:34-38) is preferable. The reading from
1 Jn can be seen as adding another early witness to the
Trinitarian theology found in the gospel. Like many sections of
this letter, today's reading is a very well developed piece of catechesis on the identity of Jesus and his mission. The significant
feature is the manner in which the beliefs of the community are
inseparable from its life as the community of the baptised. The
whole passage, with its short phrases and careful use of repetition, is likely to have been a text that was intended to be committed to memory; and given the references to baptism in the passage it may be that this was part of a baptismal catechesis.

First Reading > Gospel Links
The link between Isa 55 and the gospel is complex. The first
reading looks forward to the joy of the messianic times; then the
gospel account of the baptism of Jesus is seen as the beginning of
these times.

Gospel: Mk 1:7-11
This presentation of the baptism scene is earlier than that in
Matthew, but it is one of those passages in the synoptics where
all three have very similar perspectives. One point to remember,
however, is that here in Mark the baptism scene is the far more
stark opening to the whole gospel than in either Matthew or
Luke where there are already the manifestations of the identity
of Jesus that form part of the infancy narrative. In Mark the
baptism scene is far more obviously the answer to the question:
who is this Jesus whose gospel we are beginning to hear? He is
the one who is uniquely the Son of the Father and the bearer of
the Spirit.

HOMILY NOTES

1. Today is a day of celebrating beginnings in the liturgy: the
    beginning of the preaching and the public ministry of Jesus
    which is announced with the great cry from heaven of the

Father's joy in the work of his beloved Son. Yet Mark expects that as you hear this opening blaze of heavenly light and glory, you know and remember that his story will end in the darkened Friday of the crucifixion. We also are now at a beginning: the beginning of a year. The initial excitement of New Year is over, the champagne has been corked and drunk; so we can now stop and reflect that a new period of our lives in the world is beginning.

2. The public ministry of Jesus today is that which is carried out by you and me, the individuals that go to make up the Body of Christ, the church. Preaching the truth, doing the truth in love, bearing witness to the Father, caring for the poor, being attentive to the Spirit, recognising the presence of God in respecting the environment, seeking justice and peace, offering thanksgiving to the Father in the liturgy – all these are the public works of the Son carried out by his people. Now is the time to take stock and ask: are we being attentive to this public ministry with which we are charged?

3. There is no end to the variety of public ministry to which we are called in imitation of Christ, to do the will of the Father, being empowered by the Spirit. However, let us take three examples.

4. Bearing witness to the truth. We live much of our lives being buffeted by propaganda of one sort or another: whether it is formal propaganda intended to create great lies that oppress people, to advertising, to manipulating numbers to prove a point, to putting a spin on a story. There is even the realisation that if you repeat an idea often enough, people will become so familiar with it that they will assume it is some basic fact. Do we simply acquiesce with this, or do we seek to get behind the bald headlines, strap-lines, and tags? Do we confront the part we may be playing in the propagation of falsehoods out of selfishness or the desire for power? Honesty is the obedience that we owe to the structure of the creation, doing the truth is a holy activity because God is the source of all truth. The lie, big or small, is the witness to all that is not of

God and has no place in the kingdom; as we see in just three
words in the name Jesus gave Satan: 'The Father of Lies' (Jn
8:44).

5. Caring for those who suffer oppression. The oppressed are
all those who are in need and cannot escape from that situation by their own exertions: be it illness, or poverty, or
ignorance, or as a result of injustice. We believe in a God who
forgives and gives us chance after chance, and who challenges us to do to others as we would have them do unto us.
To acknowledge the goodness of God to us is to accept that
we have an obligation to show that same goodness. This care
is not something 'added on' to being a Christian, but what
makes us a holy people. God is holy in his action towards us:
he loves us in our needs; we act in a holy way in imitation of
God when we seek to act with love to those in need. Thus a
holy people can pray: forgive us our trespasses as we forgive
those who trespass against us.

6. Respecting the creation. Because the environment in which
we live is material does not mean that we can look on it with
indifference or as something simply to be used and discarded.
We believe that the whole of the creation is God's gift and
that all that was made was made through the Word: it is 'shot
through' with the character of the Word who in the fullness
of time took on our humanity for our salvation. But if the
world is God's gift and bears the traces of the Creator within
it, then we must respect it and use it with care, conscious that
it is here to sustain life not just for us but for all the generations to come. We live in world where we march through
the creation like vandals, but this is incompatible with acknowledging the Father, or calling ourselves disciples of the
Son, or claiming that the Spirit enlightens us.

7. In all of these it is often quite acceptable 'to mouth the truth':
to talk for example of being less exploitative or less consumerist, but when this starts to become actual in deeds it
starts to become painful. It is one thing to say one abhors
falsehoods; it is another thing to actually point them out. It is

easy to fret over care for the elderly or the poor, another thing to actually visit an elderly relative or give enough money to groups that work with the homeless. Here Christianity confronts us with the reality of the Cross. Ours is not a polished philosophy of rhetoric and good intentions: the public witness to the Father's will ended for Jesus in his death, his humble obedience right to the bitter end. It is the willingness to embrace this reality of the pain inherent in doing the good in the midst of a sinful world that sets us apart. It is only in grasping this reality of what acting with truth and goodness cost, and that building the kingdom makes demands on us, that we become the beloved daughters and sons of the Father.

8. To recall the scene of the baptism of Jesus is to resolve anew to being his public witnesses in the world.

Second Sunday of Ordinary Time

Introduction to the Celebration

We have assembled here because each of us has heard, in one way or another, the call of Jesus to come to him and see the life he offers us. And because we have heard that call to become disciples, we are now thanking the Father for his love in creating us, in caring for us, and sending his Son among us. This theme of being called to be disciples runs through our reflections and prayers today.

Now, let us reflect that we have been called by Jesus to be disciples, let us ask for the strength to continue in his way, and let us ask pardon for those times when we have followed other paths and other ways.

Rite of Penance

Lord Jesus, you call us to come to you. Lord have mercy.

Lord Jesus, you call us to share your table. Christ have mercy.

Lord Jesus, you call us to live as disciples. Lord have mercy.

Headings for Readings

First Reading

This reading tells us of the call of the prophet Samuel who had been given a specific task in the household of God. Samuel's response was a generous willingness to listen to what the Lord was going to ask him to do.

Second Reading

We are not just a group of individuals: we are the body of Christ, the temple of the Holy Spirit, and we belong to one another.

Gospel

This reading tells us of the call of two of the disciples: they accepted Jesus's invitation to come and see where he lived.

Prayer of the Faithful
President
As a gathering of sisters and brothers in Christ, let us pray to the
Father for the strength to become disciples and the wisdom to
discover our individual vocations.
Reader (s)
1. For ourselves, for the strength to set out on the road of discipleship. Lord hear us.
2. For ourselves, for the wisdom to discover our individual vocations. Lord hear us.
3. For all Christians, for the energy to renew our discipleship in
the face of trials. Lord hear us.
4. For those of our sisters and brothers for whom discipleship
has become tiresome, for the grace to discover the relationship
with God afresh. Lord hear us.
5. For ourselves, and all humanity, that we will respect the integrity of the creation which God has given us as our earthly
home. Lord hear us.
6. Specific local needs and topics of the day.
7. For our sisters and brothers who have died, that they may inherit the promise of discipleship in the banquet of the kingdom.
Lord hear us.
President
Father, you call us to yourself in Christ Jesus; hear your people
now for we pray to you in union with that same Jesus Christ,
your Son, our Lord. Amen.

Eucharistic Prayer
No Preface or Eucharistic Prayer is particularly appropriate.

Invitation to the Our Father
Jesus has called us to be his sisters and brothers, and so in union
with him we can pray:

Sign of Peace
We can only learn how to be disciples when we learn to live in

peace with our sisters and brothers. Let us now express our willingness to renew our efforts to live together in peace by exchanging a sign of peace.

Invitation to Communion
John the Baptist pointed out the Lamb of God and Andrew and
Peter became disciples; now the Lamb is in our midst, let us too
hasten to become disciples.

Communion Reflection
Ordinary Time should have a simplicity to mark a contrast with
the solemnity that has surrounded Christmas, so have a structured silence. Begin it with the invitation: 'Now let us thank the
Lord in silence for the gift of his relationship with each of us that
allows us to say "I am a disciple".' Then measure a minute on
your watch, and conclude the silence with 'Let us pray'.

Conclusion
Solemn Blessing 17 (Apostles) fits with today's gospel, insert the
names 'Andrew' and 'Peter' in the first intercession.

Notes
Given today's emphasis on invitation and response as being at
the heart of discipleship, the profession of faith should reflect
that structure by using the renewal of baptismal promises formula from Easter Sunday (Missal, p 220-1)

COMMENTARY

First Reading: 1 Sam 3:3-10, 19
The first three chapters of 1 Sam set out the credentials of
Samuel as a prophet uniquely chosen by God. First, there is the
story of his birth, then his apprenticeship with Eli, and now
comes his actual calling and his response of willingness to take
on the task of prophet (this is mainly in vv 9-19). The opening
section of the book then concludes with his recognition as a
prophet by all Israel (3:19-4:1).

As used in today's liturgy, the call of Samuel is presented as an archetype of all vocations to service.

Psalm: 39(40)

This continues the theme of the first reading by locating the community as willing to share in prayer the attitude of Samuel.

Second Reading: 1 Cor 6:13-15, 17-20

Here we are plunged right into the middle of one of Paul's letters without any introduction, rationale, or context; and are thus expected to make sense of this lection as a nugget of teaching. As such, it is well nigh impossible to do it justice or even to explain it in any adequate way.

1 Cor 5:1 to 6:20 is Paul's attempt to show his churches that becoming Christians is not a form of body-denying idealism or spiritualism. The body is important, and therefore how we live as bodily creatures, what we do with our bodies, and what we do to other bodies is important. God created our bodies, but what proof have we that our bodies are important to God? The proof lies in the fact that if God did not consider our bodily nature to be important, then he would not raise our bodies. The resurrection of the body of Jesus shows us the importance of the body. This key argument is now deployed in the snippet we are reading to show that we should therefore respect the sexuality of our own bodies and those of others. This is a way of approaching both our bodily nature and fornication that is very different from how many people perceive both Christian teaching and, indeed, Paul's teaching.

As with every mention of the body in Paul, and a running theme through 1 Cor, this teaching cannot be separated from Paul's ecclesiology (we are one body in Christ), his christology (the church is Christ's body), and his pneumatology (the body – whether it is the individual or the church – is the temple over and in which the Spirit of God dwells). We find this complex of ideas suffusing this reading.

First Reading > Gospel Links
Similarity of activity: in both readings there is a vocation to a life
of service to God, in both the men called answer the call and express their willingness to accept their vocations.

Gospel: Jn 1:35-42
This account of the call of Simon Peter and Andrew is a scene
found only in John's gospel, and is very different to the basic
synoptic story as found in Mk 1:16-20. Here the two are not presented as fishermen but as students/disciples of John the
Baptist, and their move in allegiance from John the Baptist to
Jesus is the symbolic that the ages of preparation have come to
an end, and the Chosen One of God – here identified using the
image of the Lamb of God – is now with his people. The two
have now 'found the Messiah', and so their history starts afresh
from that moment. For John, this movement by these two disciples (they are only identified in the second half of the passage) is
characteristic of the change that comes in the life of every disciple
on encountering the Christ. For John the Evangelist, the good
news is a new beginning in the life of everyone who hears it.

HOMILY NOTES

1. Today we set out on a journey of remembering. We do this
   by beginning to read a set of readings from the gospels that
   will take us from now until, roughly, the end of November.
   This journey will be in two parts: between today and the beginning of Lent, and then second part will begin after Easter
   and end with the Feast of Christ the King. It is a journey that
   is supposed to give us a sense of the mystery of Jesus being
   recalled among us each Sunday so that we as a community
   can get a better grasp of his message of forgiveness, of the
   love of the Father for us, and of how we can grow to be his
   disciples.

2. Today we open this journey by reminding ourselves that we
   are Christians because Jesus has called us to be his disciples –
   and we do this reminding by telling the story of the call of

just two of the disciples: the brothers Andrew and Peter.

3. However, for many of us this sense that we are called is not something that we feel. We are Christians, many of us think, simply as a matter of geography, a simple accident of birth. For many of us, we have never thought about any other religion or indeed that being a Christian was a definite act of choice: it just came to us as part of the fabric of life, like our language or our traditions of dress or our sense of nationality. We are, very often, cradle Christians. For us, the event of baptism was not so much a great moment of decision as a social event linked to a new baby when we got 'christened' – in the sense that we then formally were given our name.

4. But while we may have inherited our religion as a matter of geography – and that was true also of Jesus and Andrew and Peter – that is not the same as having a relationship with God. This relationship is always a matter of adult commitment. It is something that involves us mind and heart and soul.

5. This relationship is one of becoming disciples: followers and students of Jesus, people who share their lives with Jesus, people who wish to know where and how he lives.

6. This normally does not come about all of a sudden: like most of our relationships it is built up over time, it is a process of getting to know ourselves and getting to know him as the source of truth, the source of life, and as the way to the Father.

7. Today we hear the call to begin a process of discipleship: 'Come and see.' We are here, ready indeed to share the table of Jesus, but also in need to set out afresh in the commitment of discipleship.

    The invitation to 'come and see' is for some of us a call to begin an adult relationship of discipleship and then let it grow over the coming months through prayer, sharing, and Christian action.

    The invitation to 'come and see' is for others of us a call to revive an adult relationship of discipleship and then to revive

over the coming months a life of prayer, sharing, and
Christian action.

The invitation to 'come and see' is for other Christians a call
to renew an adult relationship of discipleship and then let it
grow deeper over the coming months by prayer, sharing,
and Christian action.

8. Each of us is called to be a disciple of the one Lord, and we
are all made one with him in baptism, but what that discipleship demands of each of us, our vocations, is something that
is specific and unique to each of us. That each of us has this
unique, non-transferable vocation is something that should
be a cause of our thanksgiving for us at this Eucharist; that
each of us still has other aspects of that unique vocation to
discover should be one of our petitions at this Eucharist.

Lectionary Unit II.I

This unit consists of twenty-one Sundays (Sundays 3 to 23 inclusive) whose overall theme is the Mystery of Jesus being progressively revealed. It is made up of three stages:

I.   Jesus with the Jewish crowds.
II. Jesus with his disciples.
III. Jesus's manifestation of himself.

The first stage runs from the third to the ninth Sunday. In these gospels we encounter Jesus around the Sea of Galilee, healing a leper and a paralytic, and answering questions about fasting and the Sabbath.

Third Sunday of Ordinary Time

Introduction to the Celebration

During this coming year we are going to read our way through the gospel preached by St Mark. And today we hear about Jesus's first actions in inaugurating the kingdom of God. He proclaimed the good news that we should repent and begin life afresh; and he gathered about him the first members of his new people.

Here, now, today, we are gathering as that new people, gathering around him and listening to him in the Liturgy of the Word; and then with him we are going to offer thanks to our heavenly Father in the Liturgy of the Eucharist.

Rite of Penance

Lord Jesus, you announce that the kingdom of God is close at hand. Lord have mercy.

Lord Jesus, you call us to repent and begin life again. Christ have mercy.

Lord Jesus, you invite us to believe in the good news. Lord have mercy.

Headings for Readings

First Reading

The prophet Jonah begins his teaching: people must change their ways, and if they do change their ways then God will show them mercy.

Second Reading

We Christians both belong to this world, and know that this world is passing. There is a tension in our relationship with material things: St Paul tries to capture this tension by saying that we must engage with the world but not be engrossed by it.

Gospel
Today we hear of the beginning of Jesus's work: he proclaims good news and he begins building a new community around him.

Prayer of the Faithful
President
As we recall the beginnings of the preaching of the Anointed One, let us join with him as his anointed people and put our needs and the needs of all humanity before our Father in heaven.
Reader (s)
1. For all our sisters and brothers, that they will hear the invitation of the Christ to repent and believe in the good news. Lord hear us.
2. For all who are already disciples, that we will renew our commitment to following the Way of the Lord. Lord hear us.
3. For all who are called to preach and teach the good news, that they will be given wisdom, courage, and strength. Lord hear us.
4. For this church gathered here, that we will be given the courage to leave all and follow the Christ. Lord hear us.
5. For the human family, that we will learn to use wisely the resources of God's creation, recalling that all these resources are God's gifts. Lord hear us.
6. Specific local needs and topics of the day.
7. For our sisters and brothers who have died, that they may rise in the fullness of the life offered us in Christ. Lord hear us.
President
Father, your Son announced to us the closeness of your kingdom. Be near to us now and hear the prayers we make in that same Son, Jesus Christ, our Lord. Amen.

Eucharistic Prayer
Eucharistic Prayer I lists the apostles and so picks up part of the list found in the gospel. There is no preface that is particularly appropriate.

Invitation to the Our Father
Jesus announced the closeness of the Father's kingdom, and so
we can now pray:

Sign of Peace
Having become followers of the Lord, all that can come between
us must be seen as secondary to the vocation he has given us. So
now he calls us to express our unity, and to declare our willingness to love each other as sisters and brothers in the kingdom.

Invitation to Communion
The Lord when he came among us gathered a community
around him at table; now he gathers us around this table and
transforms us into his Holy People. Lord I am not worthy ...

Communion Reflection
Here is a simple litany based on today's gospel. Rather than present it as 'The response is ...', the response can be simply added
by the reader, and the repetition itself focuses the minds of the
hearers

Lord Jesus, you came proclaiming the good news from God; and
now Lord you are among us here.
Lord Jesus, you came announcing the kingdom of God; and now
Lord you are among us here.
Lord Jesus, you came declaring the closeness of the kingdom;
and now Lord you are among us here.
Lord Jesus, you came calling us to repentance; and now Lord
you are among us here.
Lord Jesus, you came inviting us to a new way of life; and now
Lord you are among us here.
Lord Jesus, you came asking us to believe in the good news; and
now Lord you are among us here.
Lord Jesus, you came calling people to become disciples; and
now Lord you are among us here.
Lord Jesus, we recall your first coming among us; we celebrate

your coming among us here; and we looking forward to your
coming in glory. Amen.

Conclusion
Solemn Blessing 13: Ordinary Time IV (Missal, p 373).

Notes
Today there is the possibility of people hearing (1) the notion of
repent quickly in the first reading, (2) Paul's notion of an imminent *parousia* in the second, and (3) the closeness of the kingdom
in the gospel. This is almost inviting people of a more fundamentalist disposition to put two and two together and get five!
This is, therefore, a day when there is a good case for dropping
the second reading which is, anyway, a rather badly bounded
bit of text as it stands in the lectionary.

COMMENTARY

First Reading: Jon 3:1-5, 10
The Book of Jonah purports to belong to a very ancient time and
to a prophet that, unlike those sent to Israel, is sent by God to
pagan sailors and then to pagan Ninevites. In fact, the book has
no historical element whatsoever, rather it is a theological tale
whose date of composition cannot be fixed but it might be just
around the time it was included in collection of 'The Twelve
Minor Prophets' around 200 BC.

    This tale is an exploration of the theme of the links between
the divine justice and the divine mercy: the God we worship is
loving and forgiving and God is the source of justice in his universe. But how are these to be reconciled? This is the major
theme of the book and it is also the theme of this unit of text (3:1-
10) which is referred to as the 'Second Mission' to the Ninevites.
The solution is that God is going to exercise his just punishment
on all mankind (the people of Nineveh are explicitly pictured as
not belonging to the People of the Covenant because the author
wants his theology to be universally relevant), but before this he
will exercise his mercy by offering a last chance for repentance.

Then, if humanity does not respond to this last change, which is God's mercy, they have willingly accepted the consequences. However, as wise pagans they listen to the 'prophet' and take the necessary steps to repent, and God shows mercy.

Now a preaching note enters the book: if those pagans out there were that wise and thus benefited from God's mercy, should you not too be wise, repent, and obtain mercy.

Psalm: 24 (25)
This psalm is intended to pick up the theme from Jonah that those who walk in the ways of the Lord can count on God's mercy.

Second Reading: 1 Cor 7:29-31
These verses are all but unintelligible without reading the whole unit of text to which they belong (7:25-40) which deals with questions about sexuality in the Corinthian church. Even then, they have to be understood not absolutely, but in the light of Paul's belief at the time in an imminent *parousia*.

Care must taken today not to link this reading's notion of the imminent *parousia* with the notion of the closeness of the kingdom in the gospel. While there are many fundamentalists who link all such texts together, that combination is neither theologically nor liturgically legitimate.

First Reading > Gospel Links
The link is intended to be similarity in preaching: in both there is the preaching that God's action is close, then repentance, then mercy/good news. However, the actual vision of the writer of Jonah is so much at variance with what was distinctive about the preaching of Jesus, that it probably more obscures the gospel than throws light on it. Suffice to say that the combination gives a very particular slant to how the gospel is seen, and it is doubtful if that is the slant that Mark intended. It is an unhappy combination (to say the least).

Gospel: Mk 1:14-20

These two events (the first preaching; calling the first of 'The Twelve') mark the beginning of the ministry of Jesus which for Mark is set in train by arrest of John the Baptist.

The opening preaching (vv 14-5) contains two problems of interpretation:

First. What is the meaning of *metanoeite* that is usually translated as 'repent.' Does it mean being sorry after looking backwards or does it mean 'be converted' and look forward to a new way of life? Does repent mean have an attitude of repentance and sorrow, or does it mean do penance in the sense of seeking to make up for past damage? It probably means all these things and more still: the key note seems to be that whenever someone encounters the good news it brings about a moment of change in their lives which marks a transition from 'before' to 'after' – and such a change includes recognition and sorrow for past foolishness as well as the desire to start over.

Second. What does the closeness of the kingdom mean in Mark? In the preaching of John the Baptist (as in the scenario in Jonah) this closeness is that their time is running out: repent while you can or you will be caught in the great crunch! However, in Jesus's preaching the coming of the Day of the Lord is not the crunch, but the liberation from suffering and the banquet. So, here the closeness of the kingdom is that closeness of the availability of God's love and mercy to suffering humanity, not the closeness of doomsday.

HOMILY NOTES

1. There is a strange surprise in today's gospel if we just look at it for a moment. Right at the start we hear Jesus's great message: begin life afresh and believe in the good news that God loves us. This is exactly what we should expect: the story of a great prophet's teaching should begin with his core message. Then, immediately after that, we are not given any further explanation of this teaching, but we are told about how he recruited his first followers. We have all heard this so often that

we forget that this is really strange, but it is.

2. For most people today, whenever they hear talk about Jesus, their first reaction is to say that he is a great religious leader, a prophet, or a teacher who said many wise things about how people should lead their lives. This is nothing new: many at the time of Jesus looked on him in just this way – a figure to be compared with Moses or Elijah or one of the prophets. To many in the first years of Christianity as it spread around the ancient world, it seemed as if Jesus was simply a Jewish equivalent of a Greek philosopher: a wise man offering advice on how to live life well. Similarly today, many compare Jesus with the Buddha, Mahatma Gandhi, or some well-respected wise leader.

3. The basic idea in all these comparisons is that what we are seeking a wise teaching by which to live our lives. Alas, for people on this quest, very little of the gospel can be considered such 'teaching': indeed, this year, when we read Mark's gospel, we find that 37% is taken up with the account of the final days in Jerusalem. It is all about Jesus's life and death, not about how we should live our lives.

4. Anyone who looks on Jesus as just a wise teacher will be very surprised that what they think is a book of his teachings, a gospel, moves from his message directly to the comparatively ephemeral matter of his organisational arrangements.

5. But the fact that this way of looking at Jesus is in the air around us must prompt us to remind ourselves about a few matters that are often so taken for granted that they are forgotten.

6. Jesus is our teacher, but he also the One sent by the Father to build up the new community. This is why Mark moves immediately from the core teaching to the call of the first members of this new people.

7. Jesus not only teaches us the way to the Father, he unites us to himself within the church in order to present us to the Father.

8. To follow Jesus is to not only listen and agree with his mes-

sage, but to be willing to work with others he has called to build the kingdom.

9. Mark preached his gospel to help us know who we are as a people – those who have chosen to become one with Jesus in baptism; he did not imagine that he was writing down wise religious sayings.

10. For the people of the gospel, to hear the call of Jesus to start life afresh is also to hear the call to follow him as his community.

Fourth Sunday of Ordinary Time

Introduction to the Celebration

In today's gospel we hear of the reactions of people on encountering Jesus when they were gathered as a community: they encountered him as a brother, as a unique teacher, and as the Holy One of God. In our gathering today we are encountering him as our brother, our teacher, and the Holy One of God who is calling us together to share his supper.

Rite of Penance

Jesus of Nazareth, you are the Holy One of God. Lord have mercy.

Jesus of Nazareth, you are the Holy One of God. Christ have mercy.

Jesus of Nazareth, you are the Holy One of God. Lord have mercy.

Headings for Readings

First Reading

This is the classic account of the hope of Israel for a new prophet; a prophet who, as the New Moses, will speak in the name of the Lord. We believe that this new prophet is the Anointed One, Jesus, our Lord.

Second Reading

Paul is concerned that some people are speaking against marriage while others are speaking against non-marriage. His teaching is that people should be free from worry: both marriage and non-marriage have a place in the church.

Gospel

Jesus teaches with authority, even the spiritual powers obey him. We who follow him recognise him as the Holy One of God.

Prayer of the Faithful
President
Recalling the gospel we have just heard, there are many areas of
our lives we need to remember before the Father in prayer. So
now, made a people of priests through our encounter with Jesus,
let us pray.
Reader (s)
1. That hearing the words of Jesus today will make a deep impression on us. Lord hear us.
2. That the legacy of sin that makes us want to push Jesus away
from us, will disappear from our lives. Lord hear us.
3. That all who are afflicted will be liberated from what binds
them through encountering Jesus. Lord hear us.
4. That we as a church will proclaim the gospel and bring liberation and healing to all who are afflicted. Lord hear us.
5. That we will live in a way that does not abuse the environment that God has created around us. Lord hear us.
6. Specific local needs and topics of the day.
7. That all who have died will rise with Christ at the last day.
President
Father, we pray to you through the presence of the risen Jesus in
our midst, hear us and grant us what we ask in his name. Amen.

Eucharistic Prayer
Eucharistic Prayer IV, because it presents Jesus as the teacher
and liberator at the culmination of history, is suitable for today.

Invitation to the Our Father
Let us now pray in union with Jesus, the Holy One of God:

Sign of Peace
The Lord Jesus stands among us inviting us to become peacemakers and ministers of reconciliation. Let us now indicate to
one another our willingness to accept this ministry.

Invitation to Communion
He stood in the synagogue and beckoned people to establish new relationships with one another and with the Father. He calls now us to do likewise as we gather for his supper.

Communion Reflection
Silence, when we are all assembled, can be as eloquent as any set of words. So invite people to sit in silence, conscious of the presence of the community, and of the Holy One of God.

Conclusion
Solemn Blessing 14: Ordinary Time V (Missal p 373) is suitable.

Notes
The great danger in contemporary liturgy is that it becomes a matter of words or that it comes to be seen by analogy with a classroom event where the aim is to communicate information, to educate or to catechise. While all these things happen during the liturgy, liturgy is primarily celebration of praise – and it is certainly not an 'activity based catechetics'. One way of moving from a classroom environment is to celebrate the actual forms of the liturgy with solemnity. Today we recall that Jesus entered the synagogue and that synagogue liturgy is the origin of our Liturgy of the Word. So today heighten the ceremonial awareness of the Liturgy of the Word: more careful choreography of the coming and going of lectors from the ambo; use of a real book ceremonially opened (not bits of paper or print-outs), a procession with the Book of the Gospels, an escort of lights, and the sweet smell of incense. The Liturgy of the Word is supposed to be precious to us; it needs to be elaborated with the codes that indicate that it is something precious, a presence of the Lord (and not merely a 'Bible Reading' session).

First Reading: Deut 18:15-20

This is an extract from a section of Deut, which runs from 18:9 to 18:22, whose purpose is to set out guidelines (set in the mouth of Moses) for regulation of prophets within the community, and for distinguishing false from true prophets. As such, this section belongs to the desire of Second Temple Judaism for a more structured religion, and one that is less prone to fragmentation. The passage sets out the behaviour of false prophets (for example engaging in child sacrifice or occult divination), and the characteristic behaviour of true prophets: they speak in the Lord's name what the Lord wants them to speak. The true prophet becomes the man of God; but the false prophet (who says what God has not commanded him to say or who dabbles in foreign religions) is sentenced to death.

Enmeshed within this section lies the quite different theme of the promise of the ever-faithful God to raise up from among the people not just a prophet, but a New Moses (and it is the attempt to isolate this element in 18:9-22 that provides the rationale for the boundaries of today's lection). This promise, which has its classic 'original' formulation (in the sense that here it is based within the Law) here, played a very important role in many sections of Judaism in the first century, and it was a theme that was taken over by the followers of Jesus as a way of understanding him. So the use of this passage in the liturgy today is in complete accord with a tradition of Christian use of 'the scriptures' that goes back to the very beginning: when Mark preached his gospel – and in all the gospels the notion of Jesus as the New Moses is present in one way or another – this text from Deut was already being used to preach who Jesus is. However, the clearest evidence for how this text was used at the time of Jesus comes from Jn 1:21 when John the Baptist is presented as saying that he is not 'the prophet' (i.e. the future prophet promised in Deut) with the implication that Jesus is that prophet.

Psalm: 94 (95)
There seems to be no rationale for this choice. The psalm's content relates neither to the first reading nor the gospel.

Second Reading: 1 Cor 7:32-5
This is another snippet from the unit dealing with questions about sexuality in the Corinthian church (7:25-40). As it is extracted here, there are two consequences: (1) one cannot come to grips with the complexity of Paul's thought; (2) it looks like a praise of celibacy, for marriage and family are presented as a distraction. Moreover, by editing just as one finds it in the lectionary, we are presented with one of the classic proof texts on celibacy which established it as a 'higher' state which served the Lord, rather than the 'lesser' which served physical, this worldly, human ends. Whether or not such a position of celibacy was ever Paul's position (apart from his belief in the imminent Second Coming) is one question (and in all likelihood Paul was not in favour of celibacy). However, reading this text (especially when it is edited in this way) in the liturgy provokes three distinct questions:

Is it the case that there are higher and lower states of holiness which are functions of marital status? Until Vatican II this notion of a hierarchy of holiness based on celibacy was common teaching. Now it is far less explicit in public documents, and it is widely rejected by Catholics. Do you accept, however vaguely, the notion set out by Jerome: 'Virginity populates heaven, but marriage merely the earth'? If so, then this snippet will justify you position; but if you do not accept this notion, then reading this passage is a distraction.

Given that the vast majority of the congregation will be married and will have made special efforts to get to the celebration (far more onerous in most cases than those of full-time ministers), is it appropriate to suggest that they are less willing to serve the Lord than someone without commitments of love to other human beings?

This reading presupposes a relationship of subordination of

a woman to her husband, and is a stock example of the 'endemic patriarchy' of Christianity that is a by-product of its origins in a pre-modern male dominated society. Do you believe that this is the sort of relationship we should be promoting (it is a position taken by many American fundamentalists where it is called 'male headship')? If yes, then you will find this reading as promoting something valuable; if you do not accept the notion, then it is just annoying people who already find the fixing of roles in church by sex to be objectionable.

So, is there a case for simply omitting this passage from the lectionary (and so dropping it today) just as we do with so many other bits of this letter (see the table at the beginning of this book)? This is the real issue in pastoral exegesis for this Sunday.

First Reading > Gospel Links
This is an almost perfect example of the relationship of prophesy / fulfilment.

Gospel: Mk 1:21-8
In this passage Mark begins to show the spread of Jesus's message and fame, and does so by exploring the question of identity and authority. In the passage Jesus meets two groups: humans and demons (note that the 'unclean spirit' is a multitude of demons, see Mk 1:24: 'Have you come to destroy us?'). The first group hears and is amazed; but they do not really grasp the identity of Jesus – this will only come much later in the gospel. The other group, the demons, recognise immediately who he is: 'the Holy One of God'.

Mark is always anxious to present Jesus as a teacher, one who has a teaching, and who is the new teacher of the new teaching, and as such the New Moses (hence the choice of first reading today is perfect). And what is the hallmark of this new teacher? He teaches with a unique authority not only among the first group (the people) but also among the second group (the demons). He has only to utter a word and the new teacher can liberate the people from their enslavement to the powers of darkness.

HOMILY NOTES

1. Hearing the story about the possessed man brings a shiver to some of us, and a wry smile for others. For some, it is the tingly fringe of religion, an unsettling fear, and brings to mind films about possession or exorcism. This is where faith meets the eerie and the weird. For others, this is part of the historical dross that comes with Christianity having arisen before the modern psychiatry: it is just one more bit that needs to be dumped. For most people in an average congregation it will just be an item that does not seem important one way or the other: another bit of religion that just slips over us.

2. It is probably worthwhile acknowledging this range of reactions in the congregation. All too often people imagine that they, as individuals, are the only ones who have such reactions to the readings, and imagine that for the priest there are no such problems. This suspicion then breeds a form of alienation that makes people feel that they 'deep down' do not belong in the gathering.

3. So what can we learn from this passage despite our reactions to the exorcism? The whole passage is in the gospel to help a small group of Christians in the latter half of the first century to understand who Jesus is whom they are confessing to be 'The Holy One of God.' We can take 'Holy One of God,' the 'Anointed One,' and 'The Christ' to be just different forms of the same reality. Mark intended his preaching to be heard by the group when they gathered for the sacred meal which united them with one another and with the risen Christ, and so our hearing this gospel today is hearing it in a more formalised version of its original setting. So what aspect of faith in Jesus did Mark want to emphasise? Here lies the key to the passage: he wanted the gatherings to have an adequate appreciation of Jesus as the Christ.

4. Note that we are concerned with an adequate – adequate for us to realise that he is the Way – not a complete understanding: such might be possible in heaven, but never on earth. All the saints can testify that after a life-long pilgrimage of faith,

they are just scratching the surface in understanding the significance of the Christ.

5. Mark was concerned that people hearing about Jesus might just imagine him as another preacher – so he adds that the people who encountered him were struck by his uniqueness: he was a teacher like no other. But Mark, equally, did not want people to think of him just as the greatest teacher: Jesus having come among us does the Father's will, he liberates people from their demons, and he brings new life. But Mark, yet again, does not want Jesus just seen as a wonder-worker, a magician, so people must keep all these insights and try to understand them at the foot of the Cross. Only when we follow the teacher, the liberator, the one who suffered, and the one who rose from the dead do we start to imagine the mystery of the Holy One of God.

6. Getting some grasp of who we encounter in Jesus the Christ is the work of a lifetime. Sadly, many people think they know all about him. Our reflections here do not tell us who Jesus is; they merely attune us to being aware of the Holy One who encounters us in our loves, our trials, our fears, our talents, our demons, and right now in our gathering, our praying together, and in our sharing in his banquet.

Fifth Sunday of Ordinary Time

Introduction to the Celebration

Today we recall that Jesus 'went all through Galilee, preaching in the synagogues and casting out devils.' We gather at his table now because we acknowledge him to be the One who brings us healing, who has conquered evil, and who gives us life and hope.

Rite of Penance

Lord Jesus, you healed the sick, Lord have mercy.

Lord Jesus, you freed the enslaved, Christ have mercy.

Lord Jesus, you gave hope to the afflicted, Lord have mercy.

Headings for Readings

First Reading

Job – the model of the up-right human being who fears God – expresses the pain of our human condition in those times when life itself seems a burden too heavy to bear.

Second Reading

Paul tells us about his own vocation: he has been given the duty of preaching the gospel, and this is a task that has been given to him rather than one he has chosen for himself.

Gospel

Jesus is setting out on his ministry: he is bringing healing and deliverance to everyone he encounters and the powers of sickness and evil that can lay us low have no power over him.

Prayer of the Faithful

President

We stand here, sisters and brothers, as followers of Jesus and as a people in need of healing; and aware that our world needs healing. And standing here before the Father we pray:

Reader (s)

1. Let us pray for all Christians, that the Lord will transform us into a people bringing healing and hope to the world. Lord hear us.

2. Let us pray for ourselves and our local community, that we will be a community that cares for the sick, the lonely, those in need, and those who have lost hope. Lord hear us.

3. Let us pray for our neighbours, our friends and our relatives who are sick, that they may receive healing and wholeness, and grow in awareness of God's love. Lord hear us.

4. Let us pray for all those whose vocation involves caring for the sick, that God will give them strength and an awareness of the mystery of human suffering. Lord hear us.

5. Let us pray that the world's resources may be used for the benefit of all humanity and may be used in a sustainable way. Lord hear us.

6. Let us pray for all who are suffering through finding life a burden, for those who have lost hope, that the Spirit will give them new courage. Lord hear us.

President

Father, your Son brings healing and hope to our world. Hear us we pray and grant that we, and all humans, may share in those gifts of Jesus, the Christ. Amen.

Eucharistic Prayer

The Preface from the Rite of Anointing within Mass is ideal for today; use with Eucharistic Prayer II with the special inserted prayer for healing (Pastoral Care of the Sick, pp 114-5).

Invitation to the Our Father

The Father has sent us his Son to bring us healing and hope. Now with the Son we pray:

Sign of Peace
Healing and hope point us towards forgiveness, reconciliation and peace. Let us express this aspect of our being God's holy people.

Invitation to Communion
The Lord Jesus entered the houses of his brothers and sisters and brought them healing; he then invited them to eat at his table and gave them new hope; happy are we who are now called to his table.

Communion Reflection
The three prayers of thanksgiving (each beginning with 'Praise to you, God') from the Thanksgiving over the Oil (Pastoral Care of the Sick, p 108) express our thanks as a community for the healing and hope that come to us through the incarnation, and which can be our prayer now having being united with Christ through sharing his banquet.

Conclusion
Solemn Blessing B (Pastoral Care of the Sick, pp 117-8).

Notes
An ideal way to celebrate this Sunday's gospel is to replace the homily with an Anointing of the Sick within Mass (Pastoral Care of the Sick, pp 107-12) when the act of anointing itself will express the care for the sick that is part of the good news (and, incidentally, help to take away some of the superstitions that surround cultural memories of 'Extreme Unction'). However, some communities still find this just 'too much' and cannot yet cope with acknowledging that most of us are in need of healing in one way or another. But even a community that would find having an anointing as part of a Sunday Eucharist too taxing on their assumptions, must not imagine that the care of the sick is something that only belongs to ordained ministry: the whole community must be praying and working for the wholeness of

the whole community. This aspect can be brought out by making a special fuss today at sending ministers from the community's table to take Communion to the sick and the housebound in the community.

COMMENTARY

First Reading: Job 7:1-4, 6-7

It is very difficult to get a sense of where this reading is going for it comes from Job's response (6:1-7:21) to Eliphaz's first speech (4:1-5:27). Within the speech, this passage is a soliloquy and lament for the hardness of the human condition. Job is letting God know just how hard life is, and just how painful. The whole is expressed in generalised terms except for v 5 where Job describes the effects of this painful life on his own skin ('My flesh is clothed with worms and dirt; my skin hardens, then breaks out afresh') – hence this verse is omitted today.

Psalm: 146 (147)

Just as the first reading is the antitype to the gospel, so it has the same relationship to the choice of psalm: this psalm praises God's care, wisdom, and love.

Second Reading: 1 Cor 9:16-19, 22-23

Paul expresses his understanding of the source of his ministry: it is the duty laid on him and as such he must carry out this work come what may. He expresses this in order to defend himself against accusations that he was a financial beneficiary of the gospel or that he charged for his services. The text's boundaries in today's lection are none too neat, and the flow of the reading is not helped by the excision of two verses from the text.

First Reading > Gospel Links

The link is one of antitype and type: Job expresses the deep sadness and sickness of the human condition, and its essential loneliness; this is contrasted with the healing of the human condition that flows from the Christ, and the community that is formed around his table.

Gospel: Mk 1:29-39

In this passage we see the beginnings of the public itinerant ministry in Galilee. However, there are one or two points of interest. First, there is the combination of the public with the private. Jesus heals both in public, and in the private space of the house of Simon and Andrew. We hear of Jesus being in the public gaze of healing – 'after sunset' which we would express as 'doing overtime' – and then he is away in a private space in prayer and then back immediately to another public space to preach.

Second, it is interesting that the first private healing is of someone with fever – fever brought a dread to people in the ancient world that we cannot grasp (Luke in his version of this story links fever with demonic possession), and so being able to cure fever, and do it quickly, is a sign of heavenly power. The theme of the speed of the healing is expressed by the fact that Peter's wife's mother was ill with fever one moment, and the next was able to be up and about serving them.

At the outset of the ministry Mark wants to present Jesus as the one who brings healing and deliverance; now in this passage comes the additional task of preaching. But all the time, only the demons know his true identity, but he has such power over them that he can even keep them from speaking and spreading this news. Here we are getting our first glimpses of the Messianic Secret that is such a key theme in Mark's theology.

HOMILY NOTES

1. It is often the case that we perform actions in the liturgy while hardly ever thinking why we bother. Often when people are asked, for example, why we bring Communion to the sick, the only answer is that the priest wants it done, so because the minister likes to help out the priest, he or she does it. Even worse occurs, however, when people think up their own rationale for actions without recourse to the fundamental rationale of Christian liturgy. That process was, and still is, the great factor leading to deformities in the liturgy over time, such as the enormous deformities in the liturgy of the

Eucharist that were corrected after Vatican II. People often wonder why there was need for such a radical break with the 1950s: the answer is that the extent of the surgery was adapted to the extent of the cancer! But such confusions do not just happen in the past, but all the time. Ask your Eucharistic Ministers why they bring Communion to the housebound, and you might get some theological surprises! I did so and got this morsel of confusion: if the sick can get Communion on the days they cannot get to Mass, but ideally should, they build up less 'trouble' with God. Unpicking this, it was clear that this well-educated minister was not confusing 'not being able to get to Mass' with sin (or what old textbooks called 'material sin'), but did think that God was running a merit/demerit system as a basis of salvation. Coupled with this was a notion that celebrations of the Eucharist were really there as a way of producing Holy Communion: so if the sick person could get the result without watching the preparation, then all was well! This is reminiscent of the eighteenth-century casuists' question: why should bishops (presiding, not celebrating) be required by law to sit through long ceremonies when they had more important things to do, could they not just be given communion by their chaplains? Answer: Bishops and kings have to sit through the ceremonies on Sundays prior to receiving Communion as an act of penance! So the special minister I spoke to was the unwitting inheritor of a long tradition of teaching that we would all now rather forget.

2. Hence, it is a good idea to use the homily sometimes to reflect on just why we are doing what we are doing, and today's gospel with its links to Jesus entering houses, healing, and eating makes this a good day to reflect on the links between the celebration of the Eucharist and care of the sick in the community.

3 A simple explanation would include these elements:

• We gather each week to become one people as brothers and sisters with Christ.

- When we gather for the Eucharist we become the Body of Christ: Jesus is the head of this body, we are the trunk and arms and legs.
- We show we are one body by having shares of one loaf and drinking from one cup.
- The cup of blessing which we bless, is a participation in the blood of Christ.
- The loaf which we break, is a participation in the body of Christ.
- Because there is one loaf, we who are many are one body, for we all partake of the one loaf.
- But we recall that there are sisters and brothers in this community who cannot gather with us because they are sick or housebound.
- So we bring them a share of our one loaf, the portion carried to them by the Minister of the Eucharist.
- Then through that sharing, they become one with the rest of us and with Christ.
- The Ministers carrying portions of our loaf to the sick and housebound of the community are forming the links and sinews of the Christ's body.

Sixth Sunday of Ordinary Time

Introduction to the Celebration

We live in a world of suffering: suffering caused by diseases, suffering caused by the exclusion of people, suffering caused by greed and jealousy. But rather than just say that is 'the lot of humanity' we look towards Jesus as the one who brings healing, who welcomes people into his embrace, and who proclaims a new way of living. To belong to this community is to recognise the mystery of God's forgiveness and healing made visible to us in Christ Jesus, our Lord.

Rite of Penance

Lord Jesus, you touch each of us with your healing. Lord have mercy.

Lord Jesus, you touch each of us with your forgiveness, Christ have mercy.

Lord Jesus, you touch each of us with your welcome. Lord have mercy.

Headings for Readings

First Reading

This reading sets the scene for us for today's gospel. An ancient society had very strict rules to try to contain disease; and they saw illness as involving both the human and divine dimension of life.

Second Reading

To be a follower of Jesus is to imitate him; and do all for the glory of the Father.

Gospel

A leper breaks all the social conventions and approaches Jesus;

Jesus too breaks through human conventions and stretches out his hand and touches the sick man; and a new relationship between God and suffering humanity comes into view.

Prayer of the Faithful
President
Gathered in the Holy Spirit as the holy and priestly people of Jesus Christ who brings healing and reconciliation to the universe, let us pray for ourselves, our society, and the whole human family to our Father in heaven.
Reader (s)
1. For the holy church of God, that it may be healed of its infirmities, and that we may be a means of bringing healing and reconciliation to the world. Lord hear us.
2. For this church gathered here, that all our sick sisters and brothers may receive healing and strength, and we may foster among ourselves a spirit that brings joy to our society. Lord hear us.
3. For all who care for the sick in our society, that the Lord may bless their work with those who are ill in mind or body, and give them an awareness of the sacred dimension of their work. Lord hear us.
4. For people who are sick who have asked our prayers. *Pause.* Lord hear us.
5. For all human beings, that just as we have grown in technical skills in using the creation, that we might grow in wisdom in using what God has given us. Lord hear us.
6. For those who have died, our sisters and brothers who have gone before us marked with the sign of faith, that they may come, fully reconciled with the Father in Christ, to the fullness of life. Lord hear us.
President
Father, we gather here, your family in need of healing, in need of forgiveness, and in need of your loving mercy. Hear our needs and grant them in Christ Jesus, our Lord. Amen.

Eucharistic Prayer
The Eucharistic Prayer for Masses of Reconciliation I is suitable.

Invitation to the Our Father
Gathered around as a people reconciled to the Father, let us express our commitment to forgive and reconcile as we have been forgiven, as we pray:

Sign of Peace
Jesus brought healing and forgiveness to each person he encountered. May we now imitate him in greeting one another.

Invitation to Communion
Behold the Lamb of God, behold him who brings us healing and is our reconciliation with the Father. Happy are we who share in his supper.

Communion Reflection
God of power and might,
We praise you through your Son, Jesus Christ,
Who has come to us in your name.
He is the Word that brings salvation.
He is the hand you stretch out to sinners.
He is the way that leads to your peace.
Amen.
(Adapted from Eucharistic Prayer II for Reconciliation)

Conclusion
That anyone who is suffering and who meets one of us during the coming week may encounter the Father's care. Amen.
That anyone who is sick and who meets one of us during the coming week may encounter the Son's healing. Amen.
That anyone who is marginalised and who meets one of us during the coming week may encounter the Spirit's reconciliation. Amen.

Notes

In our society healing has been technologised, such that we think of health services as a product, while those who work in healthcare are seen in terms of their technical abilities. However, healthcare always involves us as individuals, and human beings are more than biological organisms. The human beings that are the subjects of healthcare are also beings open to the mystery of the divine, and care must embrace all the dimensions of our humanity. Because we believe that humans are God's creatures, we Christians have a 'holistic' vision of health that is far more embedded within our vision of life than most, yet this is an almost forgotten aspect of Christianity. On this Sunday when we recall a healing by Jesus, it is a day when some way should be found of visibly involving in the liturgy those in the community who are involved in healthcare. The aim of this involvement should be to show the aware ness that healing and liturgy are intimately linked. This could take the form of inviting them to read the intercessions at the Prayer of the Faithful or presenting the gifts at the Preparation of the Gifts. Trying to forge links between our vision of humanity as created in God's image with the vision of humanity that underlies much modern medicine is not an easy process, but the attempt has to be made.

COMMENTARY

First Reading: Lev 13:1-2, 45-6

In most ancient religions the functions of priest (one concerned with the cult) and that of the medic (one concerned with health and disease) were closely related: the realm of the divine and the realm of unseen forces of plague, contagion and hygiene (itself a concept that was medical, ethical, and social) were seen as closely interwoven. It is, therefore, not in the least surprising that in the midst of the book of the priests' roles and duties (e.g. on the Day of Atonement in Lev 16) we should have a long section on medical problems relating to the skin (Lev 13:1-14:57). We see the scope of the tasks of the Levites in that section is interspersed with sections on clean and unclean animals (11:1-47), regarding childbirth (12:1-8), and sexual uncleanness (Lev 15:1-33).

Today's reading introduces the problem of skin diseases (13:1-2) and the social sentence that the priest is expected to pass as a result of his diagnosis (13:45-6) omitting the graphic details on boils, rashes, and sores. However, there is an ancient problem in the text that makes the reading of it with meaning almost impossible. It is this: the Hebrew word *sara'at* means a skin complaint and would cover such matters as rashes, eczema, and other problems that were seen as transitory in nature (hence the need for a healing process). This word was translated into Latin by the word *lepra* which eventually came to mean a disease that was virtually incurable – and gave us the name 'leprosy' and then 'leper' for a most severe medical condition and a sufferer from that disease. So in its original meaning this passage of the law would have affected most people in the society at some time or another in their lives. The prescriptions of social exclusion were based on the belief that every skin complaint was contagious and therefore needed isolation until it went away or was cured. The torn garments, the long hair, the covered moustache are all visible signs of someone in quarantine and the duty of that person to make sure that they stay away from the rest of the group and that others do not touch them lest they spread the disease. So there is a strong case for getting rid of this word 'leprosy' – now a term, like 'manger', virtually confined to biblical translations and which leads its hearers off to the wrong conclusions. The reading becomes more clear, and throws more light on the gospel, if 'leprosy' is replaced by 'skin complaint'.

Knowing this background, what is surprising about the man in the gospel is not that he believes Jesus can cure him, but that he breaks the law by approaching someone to speak to him/her, and then, in turn, Jesus is prepared to break the law and not only reply to this man, but is prepared to touch him. Both actions are the equivalent of going into an isolation ward in a hospital without authorisation and then wandering off to the cafeteria and serving food without washing hands and gowns and what not. You can imagine the furore that would result from such a lapse in bio-security.

Psalm: 31 (32)

The implication of the choice of this psalm is that healing is equivalent to forgiveness of sins. It is a rather unhappy choice as it can easily support the notion that sickness is a divine punishment resulting from sin, or that if someone repents of their sins, then that could be causative of healing. This is a day when the psalm could be replaced by a hymn.

Second Reading: 1 Cor 10:31-11:1

This is part of a section of the letter (10:23-11:1) where Paul is concerned that the 'strong' Christians should not flaunt their behaviour in a way that scandalises 'weak' Christians or non-Christians. For Paul this is more than 'not frightening the horses' – behaving in a sensitive manner is how his hearers can become more like Christ.

First Reading > Gospel Links

The relationship is that the first reading provided the content and background for the gospel. Jesus assumes that the leper knows the prescriptions of the Mosaic Law. The first reading sets them out so that we can appreciate the reference to them in the gospel.

Gospel: Mk 1:40-45

This story is found in its fullest form here in Mark (it is edited by both Matthew (8:1-4) and, to a lesser extent, by Luke (5:12-16)). The man with the skin complaint expects that his condition is curable and, therefore, when cured by Jesus it is reasonable that he should go and make the offering prescribed in the law for someone who is healed for all healing is understood as ultimately God's gift. What we are to be surprised by, from Mark's perspective, is that the reputation of Jesus as a healer is already going before him to such an extent that someone with a skin complaint is prepared to break the law and approach him directly and ask for healing. Equally, Jesus is so prepared to be moved by mercy for a suffering brother, that he too will break the law and reach out to touch and heal.

This story conveys two aspects of Mark's message: first, Jesus operates both within the Law and at the same time is greater than it; and, second, he is the great healer who brings the Father's mercy to those who ask. So he is, at once, both becoming famous as a healer and yet telling those healed that they are to say nothing about it. This enigma of the great healer continues throughout Mark's gospel.

HOMILY NOTES

1. There is always a strange tension when we gather as God's people. On the one hand, we become conscious of our unity in the Christ: people who are sisters and brothers in baptism. The way we speak at the liturgy reminds us of this. On the other hand, we recall in prayer the brokenness of humanity: people who are sick, people who are warring with one another, people who are suffering because of the actions of fellow humans. Today we remind ourselves that Jesus entered into this suffering world bringing healing and peace, and that he has called us to carry on this work of reconciling people to one another and to the Father.

2. Put bluntly, if we want to gather here as sisters and brothers – and that is the condition of taking part in the Eucharist – then we have to be individuals who bring healing and forgiveness to those we encounter.

3. Jesus encountered the man with the skin complaint, touched him and brought healing. We encounter others and touch their lives; that encounter should be one that promotes peace and trust between people.

4. We often get carried away by the wow-factor when we hear of Jesus's miracles. Then instead of concentrating on what they show us about the world God wants, we ask questions about how it could happen. Miracles show us another world. The question is not 'how did that happen?' but 'how can we make this glimpse of another world a plan for our action in this world?'

5. Likewise, we often get carried away by high-sounding ideas:

the world would be a better place if only ... and if only ... and if only; but then nothing happens. In the gospel we hear of Jesus the healer of humanity when he meets one sick person; and something happens. We meet as his people who have a vision of a transformed society, and which is built up whenever any one of us makes a difference to someone who is ill, or excluded, or marginalised.

6. The odds are that each of us gathered here will encounter one fellow creature during the coming week who is our equivalent of the socially isolated sick person: someone on the margins of society, reviled, suspected, suffering. When that person encounters us will she or he encounter more of the same or will it be more like encountering the Christ? The greatest miracle of change may be in how we react in that encounter.

'Celebrants' or 'Presidents'?

Our throwaway everyday language can be most revealing. How we refer to someone or something in our general references can often show us what we actually think far more than if we were asked to make a careful study of an issue. Likewise, the way we refer to things in our everyday speech can actually mould our attitudes and the way we act without our being aware of it. This is a phenomenon that can be particularly important when it comes to religious matters because language is related directly to our imagination, and it is in our imagination that we see the universe that envelops the physical universe that we touch and see with the senses.

Consider how each of these statements captures a different image, has a different feel, and, indeed, rests on a different theological vision:

A 'The priest said the Mass at 10, and there was a large congregation of about 100 people.'

B 'The Parish Priest celebrated the Mass with a congregation of about 100 present.'

C 'The assembly celebrated the Eucharist with the Parish Priest presiding.'

D 'The Eucharist is the action of the whole people of God hierarchically assembled.'

E 'I like to say my Mass on the side altar.'

F 'We are celebrating this Eucharist today ... '

All these statement refer to the same activity, but they reflect very different attitudes and understandings. One of the confusions that the Second Vatican Council set out to correct was the notion that the Eucharist was the private act of the priest at which people were present, and in its stead to return to the original understanding that it was the activity of the whole People of God – acknowledging that in some unusual circumstances this might just be the president and one other person. It is the whole community that is the celebrant, because it is the whole community that offers thanks to the Father in Jesus Christ. The role of the presbyter lies within the community and his presence orders it and he presides within the community as the figure of the Christ.

The language of statements A and B reveals people who are implicitly and silently thinking of the Eucharist as 'something the priest does' either for the people or with the people in attendance at his action. But the assembly is not at someone else's Eucharist, the assembly is not a bunch of spectators, rather the assembly is a unity, it – all the individuals acting as one because they are made one by that Spirit – celebrates the Eucharist, and it has one of its members as president. Within the body of Christ there is one who presides over this unity which is the work of the Spirit, and this body, including every single member, offers a sacrifice of thanksgiving to the Father. To think of the priest as acting 'on behalf of' the group is to draw one's theology from the Book of Numbers without recognising that Jesus has split the temple curtain (Mk 15:38; Mt 27:51; Lk 23:45), and so we are all able to enter the Holy of Holies in him. It is as a priestly people we celebrate alongside a fellow member of the baptised who has been ordained to preside at the Eucharist.

Can we improve our language? Yes, is the simple answer; and improving our language so that we more accurately convey the good news should be the task of everyone charged with preaching the gospel and celebrating the liturgy.

A simple starting point is to use the verb 'to celebrate' always of the whole assembly, and avoid references to celebrant when one means the presbyter or bishop who presides in the place of Christ.

Then, where we normally use the words 'priest' or 'celebrant' (in relation to the Eucharist) to use the word 'presider' or 'president'.

This might seem a lot of bother, but just how much confusion would we have been saved if the word *missa* / 'Mass' (from the dismissal: *Ite! missa est* – literally: 'Go! It is now over') had not been allowed to gain prominence.

Finally, theological improvements in our language do happen: hopefully no priest today would utter statement E, yet just a few decades ago it would not have raised an eyebrow.

Seventh Sunday of Ordinary Time

Introduction to the Celebration

We gather here as a people who have been forgiven our sins by Jesus, the Christ. We have recognised him as the one who brings us the Father's mercy. We have heard his preaching of the kingdom, and we have sought to become part of his holy people. Gathered in his name and forgiven our sins, we are a people who now share in his banquet as the people to whom he has imparted his new life. Here today, we are the people of the resurrection who recall his mercy, healing, and forgiveness, and with him we offer thanks to the Father.

To bring this great mystery home to us, we are today recalling the healing of the paralysed man who was lowered through the roof so that Jesus could heal him. Jesus forgave him his sins, enabling him to walk away and begin a new life. Let us recall that we are a people who have been forgiven and who have been called to live the new life of faith.

Rite of Penance

Lord Jesus, Son of God and Son of Man, you have come to us announcing the kingdom. Lord have mercy.

Lord Jesus, Son of God and Son of Man, you have come to us as our healer. Christ have mercy.

Lord Jesus, Son of God and Son of Man, you have come to us with authority on earth to forgive sins. Lord have mercy.

Headings for Readings

First Reading

The prophet reminds us that our hope is based on our vision of God whose love for us grants us the gift of forgiveness, renewal, and a fresh start.

76

Second Reading

Later on at this gathering, at the end of the Eucharistic Prayer, we will answer 'Amen' to the prayer 'through him, with him, and in him'. Here Paul uses this expression to remind the church in Corinth and us that it is in union with Christ, 'through him', that we offer our praise to the Father.

Gospel

This is the story of an encounter between Jesus and someone in need of healing and forgiveness; it can be a story that expresses much of what we mean when we say that Jesus is our healer, our saviour, our redeemer, our reconciliation, our high priest, the one who brings us back to the Father, and the one who forgives our sins.

Prayer of the Faithful
President

Recalling that Jesus has brought us healing, has reconciled us with the Father, and made us a priestly people able to stand before the Father and intercede for our needs and the needs of all humanity, we now pray:

Reader (s)

1. For healing and reconciliation among ourselves as members of this community, we pray to the Lord. Lord in your mercy, hear our prayer.

2. For healing and reconciliation among all Christians, that we may all be one, we pray to the Lord. Lord in your mercy, hear our prayer.

3. For healing and reconciliation among states, nations, and peoples, we pray to the Lord. Lord in your mercy, hear our prayer.

4. For healing and reconciliation among divided families, we pray to the Lord. Lord in your mercy, hear our prayer.

5. For healing and reconciliation at the end of time, that we may rise again with Jesus, we pray to the Lord. Lord in your mercy, hear our prayer.

President
Father, your Son is our health and reconciliation. Hear the
prayers we make to you and grant them for we ask in union
with Christ Jesus, our Lord. Amen.

Eucharistic Prayer
Given the central words of Jesus in today's gospel there can be
no better choice today than the Eucharistic Prayer for Masses of
Reconciliation I. The fact that it also fitted well for last week
points to the similarity of the gospel pericopes for these Sundays
and, in any case, these prayer texts are not so well known that
repetition is not beneficial in itself in making their phrases part
of our memory.

Invitation to the Our Father
We rejoice that the Father has sent the Christ to offer us forgiveness of our trespasses, declaring our willingness to forgive those
who have trespassed against us. Let us now pray:

Sign of Peace
Christ Jesus has brought us peace through his healing and reconciliation; now we must declare our willingness to heal divisions in this community, and to offer reconciliation to our sisters
and brothers in this community.

Invitation to Communion
Behold the Lamb of God,
Behold him who offers us healing and reconciliation,
Happy are we who are called to share his supper.

Communion Reflection
Lord Jesus, the people pressed about to enter your presence,
The sick man was lowered into your presence through the roof,
In your presence the sick found healing; those in sorrow, joy;
and sinners peace.
You told the sick man that his sins were forgiven;

You told him that he could stand up and walk;
You told him that he could go home and begin life anew: healed,
restored, and reconciled

Lord, we now press about your table in your presence.
Hungry for reconciliation with the Father and one another, you
have united us with yourself and with one another in our sharing of our common loaf at your holy table.
Thirsty for new life you have shared your life's blood with us in
our drinking of the common cup at your holy table.
Through you we have become the adopted daughters and sons
of the Father, and with you have offered him thanks and praise.
Lord, now send us away reconciled, healed, and strengthened,
empowered to bring your healing and reconciliation
to all creation.
Amen.

Conclusion
The Solemn Blessing from the Rite of Reconciliation of Several
Penitents is suitable for today's Eucharist.

Notes
1. Reconciliation within recent western Christian traditions has
been invariably thought of in individualist terms: the individual
being forgiven his/her sins by God. This has fitted with the emphasis on 'justification' within many churches whose origins lie
in the Reformation, and in the practice of Confession as the para-
digm for reconciliation within the Catholic Church. This individualist emphasis has also led to an understanding of sin in private
terms, and often led to an attitude of unconcern with the impact
of sin on victims or on a community. Indeed, the notion has become commonplace that once one is reconciled with God – and
so one's place in heaven assured – then the other aspects of reconciliation are but matters of no consequence. However, (1) reconciliation with God cannot be separated from reconciliation
with the community; (2) reconciliation between communities,
nations, states, is as much a matter of Christian interest in recon-

ciliation as that of the individual sinner; and (3) one cannot think of reconciliation without thinking of the peace of the whole creation: one cannot practice reconciliation between people while being oblivious to the destruction of the planet's ecosystem.

However, thinking in these ways is still very far from the common body of thought in most communities. For many Catholics the notion of a reconciliation service with 'general absolution' is just a way of avoiding the embarrassment of the confession box; and in places where such common services do not take place, given the general abandonment of 'going to confession', what has happened is that reconciliation as a ritual process has just disappeared from consciousness. Moreover, far from moving away from the individualist notion of sin/reconciliation, that notion has remained unchallenged and is now compounded by a dismissal of the whole notion of a process of reconciliation due to guilt-feelings over having given up on Confession. This is a major crisis in Catholic pastoral life, and beyond the scope of any one community. However, a day like this Sunday should provide an opportunity for liturgy groups to discuss this problem. The task is to find a ritual that enables members of the community to see their individual reconciliation as part of a process that involves the whole community; that this work of the church must embrace the quest for peace among humanity; and also embrace a care for the whole of the creation. After all, in the formula of absolution we declare that the Father, in the Paschal Mystery, 'has reconciled the world to himself' – this use of *mundus* refers to the whole universe, not a collection of individual humans.

2. The first three readings today (Isaiah, the Psalm, and Paul) are the sort of selection that gets the lectionary a bad name: the first reading is a muddle, the psalm is open to the interpretation that it presents sickness as a punishment for sin, and the little snippet from Paul is so clipped from its context that it has to be treated as just a few true propositions. It is no use on such an occasion trying to hide the fact that the readings are not exactly a piece of fluent communication, but, equally, it is important to remember

that it is the gospel reading, that is the core of the Liturgy of the Word, and all the other readings are really only 'supporting cast'. This is one of those days when trying to mitigate the 'noise' factor is important: so there is a strong case for altering the first reading, replacing the psalm with some other item such as a hymn (for instance, the first verse of 'Praise my soul the king of heaven' fits with both first reading (vv 18-21) and the gospel), and then omitting the second reading.

COMMENTARY

First Reading: Isa 43:18-19; 21-22; 24-25
If this reading does not seem to hang together, or, indeed, seems as if its first and second halves contradict one another, then you have recognised that today we have a noticeably incompetent piece of editing. Two of the major units of Deutero-Isaiah meet in the midst of this reading: the first is a unit that runs from 42:14 to 43:21, and the other begins at 43:22 and runs to 44:23. This maladroit editing is then compounded in that verse 20 is omitted from the first section, which is the part of the reading that is intended to set the scene for the gospel. As the reading stands in the lectionary, it cannot be said to have any meaning whatsoever.

However, if the reading is confined to 43:18-21, which forms a neat little unit, then the meaning is that the restoration that will come from the Lord is such that it will be a wholly new beginning – and it is this theme that is picked up in the gospel. So, given that the text as printed does not have any coherence that allows for comprehension, what does one do? The simple answer is to read verse 18 to 21, without omission, and then stop. You will then have a good starting point for the gospel.

Psalm: 40 (41)
The choice of this psalm seems to depend on the second stanza: a man on a bed of pain (parallel with the paralytic) cried for mercy in the form of forgiveness of sins. It does not really act as a meditation on the first reading, nor does it prepare for the

gospel because its focus is upon the penitence in the form of pain that the sinner is undergoing. In the gospel, the man asks for healing and then this is presented as being equivalent to forgiveness.

It should be noted that there is a problem of perspective in this psalm also: it makes an explicit link between illness and sin, which is a link that many fundamentalists like to make within their 'gospel of prosperity' – namely, if you are suffering you deserve it as punishment for sins. Not a message that coheres with today's gospel.

Second Reading: 2 Cor 1:18-22

Paul's aim is to clarify for the Corinthians the identity of Jesus in terms of their relationship to him as his followers. Jesus is the Anointed One, the Christ, and the Son of God, who has brought about now, in the world of time in which they live, all that has been promised. In Jesus, they have access to God, for he is the Anointed (i.e. the Christ) and through him they are anointed (i.e. made christs).

First Reading > Gospel Links

The first lection is edited in such a confused way that no link can be seen. However, if the first reading is confined to 43:18-21, then it perfectly coheres with the gospel as a portrait of the totality of divine forgiveness: the Lord's salvation is a wholly new creation (first reading). In this way Jesus presents the forgiveness to the paralytic. Moreover, there is a prophetic promise that the time of salvation will be a completely new beginning, and Jesus presents the arrival of salvation to the paralytic as just such a fresh start.

Gospel: Mk 2:1-12

In contrast to the healing of the leper that Mark has already preached (1:40-45), there is a new element in this story: conflict. It is the first of a series of conflicts between Jesus and other groups such as the scribes and the followers of John the Baptist –

and while 'the scribes' (a very indistinct group) are the named group with which he is in conflict here, the actual content of the teaching is probably aimed principally at challenging John's disciples' views of how God relates to sinners. This transfer of the focus of the conflict from John's followers to 'the scribes' may reflect Mark's time when many of those followers were being absorbed within among the followers of Jesus, and who very often did not appreciate the differences between the way John preached about the coming kingdom (a great divine act of cleansing/punishing justice) and the way Jesus presented the new kingdom of the Father's forgiveness.

We are to imagine a scene based in Peter's house in Capernaum – Mark assumes that this was the base for Jesus' ministry in the area – and we are to assume that the house is crowded with people: this is not only necessary for the dramatic way the paralytic is introduced to the scene through the roof, but it also probably resembles the actual situation in which Mark was preaching – a house, perhaps a tenement in Rome, crowded with people anxious to learn about Jesus. In this scene Jesus addresses the sick man, and one whom we will soon find out is in need of forgiveness, as 'my child', which is a form of address early Christian liturgy used of the relationship of Jesus to the Father. By using this term of address, the sick man is shown to be in intimate relationship with Jesus, and so with God, even at this time when he is sick and in need of forgiveness. Then come the words and deed of healing and forgiveness, with the implication that the man can now go on his way healed, restored, and forgiven. The past has been put behind in an absolute way, and a wholly fresh start has been initiated. This notion of an absolute break with the past can be found in several forgiveness stories – most famously that of the woman caught in adultery (Jn 8) – and clearly this notion provoked conflict at the time (be that the time of Jesus or the time of the early church) just as it has proven awkward for preachers of repentance down the centuries. An absolute break with the past, and therefore the gift of a new start without strings attached, seems to be 'going soft

on sin' and to be too much of an affront to human feelings of
people having to pay for their past: the insistence on penance –
John's position – can simply transfer to the divine realm the
notion of vengeance.

As the story develops there are three questions intermingled
in the conflict. The first is the question of whether or not there is
forgiveness of sins; and this is compounded by the second question: if there is forgiveness, then is it a generous act of divine
love, which is parallel with a divine healing? The answer to both
of these questions, which are central to the whole ministry and
preaching of Jesus, is yes. God will forgive, and will do so gener-
ously so that the man is forgiven in the same way that he is
healed: he can go off to his home. These two questions can easily
be ignored under the shadow of the third question: is Jesus the
one who can forgive sins? This is the apologetic question that
most modern readers jump to directly, but that would not be
how the first community heard it: they have assembled as a
church to hear the evangelist precisely because they have already accepted that Jesus is Lord and Son of God, and so is the
one who brings the Father's forgiveness. The key question they
heard answered in this conflict was that there is continuing forgiveness for the children of God and this is God's loving freely
given gift. It is this focus that accounts for why Mark has combined the issue of healing with the forgiveness of sins.

Following from such a reading of the story, the focus of
interpretation is upon how the community of Jesus imagined
the nature of the divine forgiveness as Jesus, uniquely, preached it.

HOMILY NOTES

1. The desire to be able to start afresh, to be able to put the past
   behind one, to be free of the legacy of foolishness, or the
   awareness of the guilt that can flood back into our present, is
   deeply rooted in each of us as human beings. If we are honest
   with ourselves, then the legacy of our moral failures, or
   greed, or our ingratitude stalks every one of us and can

weigh us down like a paralysis. Joy would be a new start, a moving beyond the shadows of the past.

2. When this legacy of past failures confronts us, the default setting in most of us is denial: deny the fact of the failure, deny responsibility for the failure, deny the implications of the failure, and then seek forgetfulness and hope that forgetfulness will blank out the past, wipe the slate of guilt, and enable life to start afresh. Alas, denial merely compounds the problem and buries us ever deeper in a world of self-delusion; but we all try it and hope that it might bring us freedom from our past and from ourselves.

3. The tradition of the People of the Covenant, reaching right back to the time of the prophets, is startlingly different: admit failure, admit responsibility, and then seek to become reconciled with the community and with God. Seeking this reconciliation was the work of the high priest and his annual rituals on the Day of Atonement. The people publicly announced that their behaviour had set them at odds with God, and they sought restoration within his sight, and that restoration would allow the whole people to begin afresh.

4. It was in the light of that covenant that we seek to understand the new covenant with God into which Jesus has admitted us. Jesus forgives us, reconciles us, and offers us the strength we need to rebuild relations with one another and to seek to mitigate the damage our sins have caused. Hence the many titles we give him: Jesus is healer, saviour, redeemer, our reconciliation, our high priest, the one who brings us back to the Father, and the one who forgives our sins.

5. But how can we capture all these aspects of our created nature and our faith in a memory? Can we glimpse this mystery in a little nugget of memory? This little story of the sick man being lowered through the roof, being healed, being forgiven, and then told to pick up his bed and go away captures all our beliefs about Jesus in a moment. In it we can see Jesus as healer, as saviour, as redeemer, as our reconciliation, as our high

priest, as the one who brings us back to the Father, and as the one who forgives our sins.

6. However, is this how you imagine the encounter of yourself as a sinner – in need of healing and reconciliation – with God?

7. Many people who may call themselves Christians think of this encounter more in terms of being dragged to a police station than of pressing forward to be close to Jesus. Many of us think of it more like a painful visit to the dentist than the calm words of Jesus telling the man he could get up and walk. Indeed, many people who preach in the name of Jesus are happier to announce a vindictive God who punishes any sinner that is encountered, rather than to think of Jesus forgiving this man and telling him to go off home.

8. Hearing this story challenges us to convert our own imaginations on how we see ourselves and how we see Jesus.

Trinity Sunday

Introduction to the Celebration

By giving today the name 'Trinity Sunday' we mark it off from the rest of the calendar when we celebrate mysteries, such as the incarnation at Christmas, events such as the Last Supper on Holy Thursday or the dedication of a building on its anniversary, or people such as the feast day of a saint; for 'trinity' is a concept used by theologians as a short-hand for the whole set of basic beliefs that mark us out as Christians. So if today has a focus it is not some distinct aspect of our Christian identity, but an invitation to explore some of our most important insights as followers of Jesus the Christ. We believe that the universe we know is 'somehow' enveloped in a great mystery. That mystery we cannot understand, comprehend, nor describe, but we label it 'god' and believe that it is unique, personal and seeks to have a relationship with us. That relationship is established in tradition and within that came Jesus. In recognising him, we recognise that he gives us access to that mystery in his own person, speaks to us of the Father who loves us, and promises us the presence of God the Holy Spirit. Today is a call to reflect on these relationships which began for each of us in baptism.

Rite of Penance

Lord Jesus, you have shown us the way to the Father. Lord have mercy.

Lord Jesus, you are Son of God and Son of Mary. Christ have mercy.

Lord Jesus, you have sent the Spirit among us for the forgiveness of sins. Lord have mercy.

Headings for Readings
First Reading

The mystery of God is greater than all we know and we believe that mystery has revealed itself in human history. We know of its nature through our reflection as a people on what God has done for us and on the need to live a life of doing what is right.

Second Reading

It is the Spirit of God that enables us to call on the Father. And it is the Spirit that makes us children of God through Jesus, the Son of God.

Gospel

We have an identity as a people: that is we are all baptised. We see this as plunging our lives into the mystery of God, whom we acknowledge to be Father, Son, and Spirit. The God that is revealed to us by Jesus is not some distant static power, but a community of persons swirling together in love, and gathering us up in that love.

Prayer of the Faithful
President

Gathered in Christ, given life as the church by the Spirit, let us petition the Father.

Reader (s)

1. That we may seek the way to the Father. Lord in your mercy, hear our prayer.
2. That we may bear witness to his Son, Jesus Christ, in our lives. Lord in your mercy, hear our prayer.
3. That we may rejoice in the strength of the Holy Spirit. Lord in your mercy, hear our prayer.
4. That all who seek the truth will find it. Lord in your mercy, hear our prayer.
5. That all who seek justice shall be satisfied. Lord in your mercy, hear our prayer.

6. That we may learn to respect the creation and all the earth's resources as the Father's gift, made through the Son and hovered over by the Spirit. Lord in your mercy, hear our prayer.

7. That all the dead may find joy in the Father's house. Lord in your mercy, hear our prayer.

President

Father, hear your people's prayers for we ask them in the power of your Holy Spirit, and in the name of Christ Jesus, our Lord. Amen.

Eucharistic Prayer

Preface of the Holy Trinity (P43) (Missal, p 446); Eucharistic Prayer II is ideal for today as it presents the trinitarian pattern of all prayer in two opening sentences which taken together are among the most elegant, and concise, statements of trinitarian faith in the whole of the Latin liturgy: 'Lord you are holy indeed, the fountain of all holiness. Let your Spirit come upon these gifts … that they may become for us the body and blood of our Lord, Jesus Christ.'

Invitation to the Our Father

In the power of the Spirit and the words of the Son, let us pray to the Father.

Sign of Peace

We have been baptised into the life of the Father, Son and Spirit, where strife and ill-will have no place. Let us express our desire to become more God-like in our lives by exchanging a sign of peace with one another.

Invitation to Communion

Through sharing in this meal we have a share in the divine life. Blessed are we who are called to this supper.

Communion Reflection
Our God is the God of all humans.
The God of heaven and earth.
The God of the sea and the rivers.
The God of the sun and moon.
The God of all the heavenly bodies.
The God of the lofty mountains.
The God of the lowly valleys.
God is above the heavens;
and he is in the heavens;
and he is beneath the heavens.
Heaven and earth and sea,
and everything that is in them,
such he has as his abode.
He inspires all things,
he gives life to all things,
he stands above all things,
and he stands beneath all things.
He enlightens the light of the sun,
he strengthens the light of the night and the stars,
he makes wells in the arid land and dry islands in the sea,
and he places the stars in the service of the greater lights.
He has a Son who is co-eternal with himself,
and similar in all respects to himself;
and neither is the Son younger than the Father,
nor is the Father older than the Son;
and the Holy Spirit breathes in them.
And the Father and the Son and Holy Spirit are inseparable.
Amen.
Bishop Tírechán, c 700

Dismissal
Every good gift comes from the Father of light,
May he fill you with his blessings. Amen.
The Redeemer has given you lasting freeedom,
May you inherit his everlasting life. Amen.

The Spirit inspired different tongues to proclaim one faith,
May he strengthen you in faith, hope and love. Amen.
May almighty God bless you ...

COMMENTARY

First Reading: Deut 4:32-34, 39-40

The Deuteronomist is concerned with law and with a precise formulation of belief lest Jews confuse their beliefs with the religious systems that they were in contact with constantly. Here we see both interests: God is the creator beyond the heavens – he is not a cosmic power (i.e. a power in the universe) – and he has made his interest in humanity known. The response is that the people must acknowledge their creator and keep his covenant.

Second Reading: Rom 8:14-17

The language we hear in this reading of the 'Spirit' moving us and making us sons, of calling out to 'Father', of being 'heirs with Christ' is typical of the personal intimacy that Christians have always felt as the gift of Christ, that he revealed to us that the mystery of God is the mystery of divine relationships into which we are drawn. It was this kind of language that was later systematised to produce the explicit theology of the divine nature, and within that system the term 'trinity' is the shorthand for the nature of God whom we hear mentioned as Father, Son, and Spirit.

First Reading > Gospel Links

The two readings are without any intrinsic connection as readings. They are linked within a larger theological framework where they are assumed to be wholly consistent.

Gospel: Mt 28:16-20

This text reminds us that liturgy, in this case the liturgy of baptism, is more intimate to the life and history of Christianity than the texts that are referred to collectively as 'the gospels' or 'The Bible'. Here Mt uses the church's liturgy for the beginning of the

Christian life as a fitting note on which to end his account of the group's founder. For us it reminds us that the early church not only saw baptism as an initiation into the group (which it did) – a ritual which defined the group's boundaries, but saw that entry as simultaneously entering into the life of God.

HOMILY NOTES

1. A mystery is something which embraces us, not a mathematical conundrum. Alas, for most people to say 'I believe in the Trinity' is to declare an interest in a sort of divine arithmetic that does not 'add up'. Whatever else you do today, avoid the language of 'one in three and three in one' as if the All Holy could be counted and boxed. Equally, avoid saying things like 'we believe in the Trinity' when what we mean is that Christian belief is trinitarian. That is we believe that we are caught up into the life of the Being upon whom we depend, but who does not depend on the universe. And that we are caught up in that through our relationship with the Son, who gives us access to the Father, and sends us the Spirit.

2. There are two basic ways of thinking about the divine. The first way – by far the most common throughout history and still the most common today – is to ask 'how many gods are there?' The answer is simple: one or more than one or less than one. The atheist says there are none, the deist says that there is just one, the polytheist opts for several, while most agnostics do not want to commit themselves but think there might just be one but that it's all rather guesswork. What unites these groups is that they all know exactly what a god is, and therefore they can be sure there is one, or that there is no such being, or that they have found many of them. They are happy with their own understanding of what a god is or should be, and this proves the basis of their religious quest. In the strict sense, they have made their image of 'god' the object of their religious life, and so have worshipped or rejected an idol.

3. The great monotheisms reject the very question of 'how

many' as impudent and blasphemous: their aim is to have some appreciation of what God is and the desire is not a number (0, 1, 1+), but a glimpse of 'the face of God' (cf Ps 24:6). This glimpse is not a curious question about 'is there anything beyond?' but a conviction that the universe is good because it is the handiwork of a greater Being beyond our imagination. It is the conviction that this mystery reveals itself as loving and interested in us, and that in committing ourselves to this Being we somehow 'touch' our source and bliss.

4. For Christians, this mystery has touched our humanity most closely in Jesus, and through him we hear of his 'Father' who become 'our Father in heaven'. From him also we hear that he sends his Spirit. When we relate to Christ's invitation we have the conviction of this great mystery not as some distant beyond-knowing, but something more intimate, a great dance in the heart of the mystery of the Father loving the Son, the Son returning that love, and the relationship being the Spirit. We hear of this great dance, but we cannot appreciate it nor describe it, but confess that through Jesus we can be given a share in it. To be baptised is at once to join a people with a precious memory, but it is also to declare our desire to be caught up in the life of the mystery beyond.

5. The trinitarian aspect of our believing is brought out more effectively today by replacing the recited creed with a renewal of baptismal promises as on Easter Day (Missal, p 220).

The Body and Blood of Christ (Corpus Christi)

Introduction to the Celebration

When Vatican II sought to restore focus to our approach to the Eucharist so that it would be the 'centre and summit' of the Christian life, there was a correcting shift away from the Eucharist as an object ('the Blessed Sacrament') which might be received ('Holy Communion') to it being the action of gathering, thanking, and eating/drinking. The Eucharist is the activity of the church united in Christ, not something that exists alongside the church which they have access to. Gathering for the Eucharist constitutes us, and we in gathering celebrate the Eucharist.

Rite of Penance

Option C vi (Missal, p 394).

Headings for Readings

First Reading

The relationship of the people with God – the covenant – was, in accord with ancient near eastern practice, sealed with blood smeared on an altar; when Jesus died on the cross, the first Christians, knowing that he had shown them a new way to re-late to God, saw his bloodshed as being like that earlier sacrifice: it sealed a relationship, and we share in that relationship when we drink from his cup at the Eucharist.

Second Reading

The images of the blood used in the temple rituals is strange, even repulsive, to our ears; yet it was within the drama of the temple that our first Christian sisters and brothers made sense of what they believed Jesus had done for them. Just as the High Priest in the Jerusalem temple used blood – the token of God's gift of life – to restore the life of the people and heal them; so Christ is the one who restores our lives and gives us healing.

Sequence

The *Lauda Zion* (optional) is rich in the number of ways it speaks of the Eucharist as food and our encounter with Christ. However, a sequence is a hymn with a very definite drum-beat and was ideal for processions. If it is simply read, then it becomes a set of obscure words pointing to the Pointer to the presence of the Lord in the assembly's meal – and becomes a distraction. However, as a part of the richness of our tradition it should not be simply 'drop it as it's optional', but it should be a challenge to find music and movement so that it can be an adornment of today's gathering.

Gospel

This meal of Jesus with his disciples – note it is not just 'the twelve' as we imagine it from pictures like Leonardo's Last Supper – is that which gives them new life as the Passover, and it establishes a new relationship – '... the blood of the covenant ...' – between each one of us, by making us into one people, and with God through eating from the one loaf and drinking from the one cup.

Prayer of the Faithful

President

We have gathered for the Lord's banquet. Now as his priestly people let us present our needs to the Father.

Reader (s)

1. For ourselves gathered at this holy meal. Lord hear us.
2. For friends absent from this meal. Lord hear us.
3. For all Christians, may we be united around the Lord's table. Lord hear us.
4. For all who are hungry. Lord hear us.
5. For all who are excluded from the world's riches. Lord hear us.
6. For the world's leaders, may they respect the creation. Lord hear us.

7. For the dead, that they may share the banquet whose foretaste we now celebrate. Lord hear us.

President

Father, as we eat the Lord's body and drink his blood, fill us with your grace, and grant our needs through that same Christ, our Lord. Amen.

Eucharistic Prayer

Preface of the Holy Eucharist II (P48) has a narrative quality that makes it more accessible than P47; moreover, the emphasis of P48 is more on the actual celebration than P47 and therefore is more suitable for today.

The Our Father

Gathered as the body of Christ around this table, let us pray to our common Father, Our Father ...

Sign of Peace

In Christ we are united into his body around this table; disharmony and strife have no place here. Let us show this now to one another.

Invitation to Communion

We are his people when we recognise him in the breaking of the loaf, happy are we who are called to this supper.

Communion Reflection

They knew it was the Lord, Alleluia;
In the breaking up of the loaf, Alleluia.
The loaf we break is the body of Jesus Christ, our Lord, Alleluia;
The cup we bless is the blood of Jesus Christ, our Lord, Alleluia;
For the remission of sins, Alleluia.
Lord, let your mercy rest upon us, Alleluia;
Who put all our confidence in you, Alleluia.
They knew it was the Lord, Alleluia;
In the breaking of the loaf, Alleluia.

O Lord, we believe that in this breaking of your body and pouring out of your blood we become your redeemed people.
We confess that in taking the gifts of this pledge here, we lay hold in hope of enjoying its true fruits in the heavenly places.
(From an early medieval hymn for use during the fraction found in an eighth-century Mass book from Ireland)

Conclusion
Prayer over the People 18 (Missal, p 382) is suitable.

COMMENTARY

First and Second Readings: Ex 24:3-8 and Heb 9:11-15
These are the classic texts of the theology of 'atonement' (note that this word describes a ritual: the smearing of blood by a priest – think of toner for a photocopier – and then that action, as interpreted by Hebrews, has been the source of all the theologies of atonement, and all the bitter strife between Christians since the sixteenth century. In the context of this day in the liturgy we should note:

(1) The theology of atonement which is the focus of these readings is not the liturgical focus. The liturgy's theme is the larger set of imagery relating to Christ's blood as redemptive which linked with both the theology of the Eucharist and the church as the community of the new covenant. Indeed, the normal way the liturgy uses this imagery is in connection with the imagery of the Sacred Heart, see Preface 45 (Missal, p 448). And if we want to see its exact relevance within today's liturgy look at today's Preface (n 47): 'As we drink his blood which was poured out for us, we are washed clean.'

This means that any formal exegesis of these as snippets from two larger texts (e.g. examining how the early church adapted temple rituals to explain its faith in Jesus) misses their contextual liturgical meaning.

(2) The language of blood sacrifice and of blood smeared on sacrificial altars is debased currency. Since its use to explain the senseless slaughter of World War I, it has been rendered too

bloody to be part of our imagination of divine love. In our experience only a brute wants to see innocent blood; and when
humans bring all their genius to bear to make others suffer, we
do not have the imagination to read such rituals as poetic evoc-
ations of a desire to receive life from God. So it is probably wiser
to steer clear of the topic in preaching; if, however, someone
wants an explanation of why Christians ever bothered with such
language, then the best user-friendly introduction I know in
English is Margaret Barker, *On Earth as it is in Heaven: Temple
Symbolism in the New Testament* (T & T Clark, Edinburgh 1995).

First Reading > Gospel Links

The first two readings form a theological 'standpoint' from
which to view the actuality of the Eucharist in the church (as the
new sacrifice), whose 'origin' is then related in today's gospel.
This is a relationship of theological ideas, not a relationship of
events related in texts nor a relationship between the texts themselves.

Gospel: Mk 14:12-16, 22-26

This is the earliest detailed gospel reference to the eucharistic
liturgy (the *Didache* and 1 Cor are earlier), and it points out for us
a key aspect of gospel-formation directly relevant to today's
liturgy. We have a bad habit of thinking that the Eucharist is
'based' in scripture (due to later Western theological controversies), whereas, in fact, exactly the opposite is the case: the
gospels are based in the liturgy. Before ever the message of Jesus
was written down in anything like our gospels, Christians were
gathering weekly for 'the breaking of the loaf' and it was the
need of these gatherings to have conveniently available to them
the 'memories' (*apomnémoneumata* – Justin's term) of Jesus that
was a major prompt to produce gospels which are episodic, yet
with a narrative structure.

By Mark's time, in many communities (e.g. Paul's Corinth),
the weekly gathering for the breaking of the loaf and the sharing
of the common cup were being interpreted in terms of a Paschal

event, and Jesus was being presented in terms of the paschal lamb whose blood makes intercession for his people (cf 1 Cor 5:7): this was probably the most important development in the history of Eucharistic theology. Thus a specifically Christian weekly celebration-meal was being interpreted in terms of an annual Jewish celebration-meal which was then seen as its anticipation. And this was being further interpreted in two ways: first, that a specific event in the life of Jesus – 'the last supper' – was being seen as its archetype which was being entered into in memory at each eucharistic meal; and second, this was being seen as a sacrificial meal through which the Christians entered into the new blood covenant.

This poses us a task. The basic Christian demand is that we join in the Eucharistic meal by taking a share in the loaf and then drink from a common cup – this ritual, this doing, underlies all the different theologies of the Eucharist, be they the various ones in the New Testament or later. Given that, we must try to appreciate just how highly the churches valued this meal and the key to this is to note the central theological significance they gave it.

HOMILY NOTES

1. There is a curious anomaly in most teaching about the Eucharist. The doctrine has pride of place, then the celebration is seen as a matter of practical details. However, the *lex orandi* comes before the *lex credendi*: the Eucharist comes with a command to *do*, then in the process of explaning what is *done* there emerge various frameworks pointing out the significance of our actions. One should not start with a set of doctrines to be inculcated, explained or defended, one should start with an attempt to carry out the basic ritual as appropriately as possible, and then draw lessons from what has occurred (this insight has been vestigially preserved in the West in the Catholic insistence on the *opus operatum*). So it is better to see if you can specially adapt your practice today, rather than use time on abstract thought about the meal; in short, have a better meal rather than describe what one should be like.

2. In Jesus's choice of a meal as his central event with his disciples – these meals were a part of his whole ministry – we should not think of just one great 'Last Supper' event – and were probably weekly – he committed himself to a certain 'grammar of meals'. Every shared meal, even in a fast food outlet, has ritual aspects about sharing and hospitality and belonging, and these apply also to the Eucharist.

3. There are three key elements to this grammar as it applies to the Eucharist.

A. Welcome at a table. To be excluded from a table is one of the most hurtful things that can happen (cf Lk 14:7-11). There is something inherently welcoming in being placed round a table and being called a friend. The arrangement of people at the Eucharist should reflect this. We are at a table, so avoid the theological reflection – the word 'altar' – upon what that table stands for in Christian imagination. Therefore, the table must speak to us of 'tableness' in shape and decor. Moreover, it must speak of welcome which means, de facto, a certain informality – see Lk 14:13.

B. Characteristic of a shared meal is shared food: we share a single loaf, we each have a part, a share in a loaf, and so we participate each in one another and in a unity greater than us: Christ. The part we receive is not a separate whole, indeed it is visibly only a bit – the totality is only glimpsed at the beginning and known at the end in so far as each has committed themselves by eating the common loaf. Pre-cut roundels make nonsense of this basic element of Christian ritual.

C. While it is culturally acceptable to share food on some occasions (e.g. in a restaurant: 'Do you want to taste some of mine?'), and necessary on others: one has to have a piece of the birthday or wedding cake; sharing a common cup is not – and never was, (cf ancient Passover regulations) – culturally acceptable. We might buy a common bottle of wine but, emergencies excepted, we each have our own wine glass! Therefore, the use of a common cup is a radical innovation that must go back to Jesus's own practice with his group. It is indeed so unusual that it led to the withdrawal of the chalice from the people; and even in those churches where that was rejected, many found the 'one cup' just *de trop* – hence the little thimbles of wine used in some Reformed congregations which is a practice as unwitting of basic Eucharistic grammar as pre-cut bread roundels. The intimacy of one cup speaks of the intimacy that must exist in the members of the body of Christ, and it is a most challenging symbol, as shocking today in some congregations as it was in Jesus's time.

4. Table, loaf, a common cup are powerful symbols – so daring in fact that many shy away from them into a haze of pious words. But if done, they speak forth the basis of a theology of the Eucharist more effectively than any sermon.

Eighth Sunday of Ordinary Time

Introduction to the Celebration

Every Sunday is a day of rejoicing for Christians because it is the Lord's Day: we recall that he is with us. Risen and victorious over sin and death, he stands among us. Now, with Jesus, we gather for his holy meal. Through Jesus, we give thanks to the Father for creating us, for making us his people, and for sending us his Son.

The Lord is with us, let us rejoice.

Rite of Penance

Option c. ii (Missal, p 392) is appropriate.

Headings for Readings

First Reading

This reading presents the Lord's concern for us and his desire to be with us using the imagery of a bridegroom seeking out a bride whom he loves continuously with tenderness.

Second Reading

Paul wants the Corinthians to know that the proof of his authority as an apostle is to be found in the effect that his ministry has had on them through the Spirit of the living God having enlightened their minds and hearts.

Gospel

In this gospel we hear Jesus say that while the main guest is at the party, the whole party celebrates; but the mystery of the Eucharist is such that right now we are celebrating with only thoughts of joy and rejoicing, because the risen Lord is among us. It is Jesus, victorious over death, who has gathered us to his table for this feast.

Prayer of the Faithful

President

Standing before our Father in heaven, in union with Jesus who has gathered us here and made us children of God, we now make our petitions.

Reader (s)

1. That the Spirit will open our minds and hearts to recognise the Bridegroom present among us at this feast. Lord hear us.

2. That the Spirit who grants wisdom and unity to the church may unite all Christians everywhere. Lord hear us.

3. That the Spirit who is the giver of joy may help all Christian communities who gather today to have a renewed appreciation of Christ's presence in the eucharistic meal. Lord hear us.

4. That the Spirit, who guides all of us into the truth, may enlighten the minds of all who exercise authority in the world. Lord hear us.

5. That the Spirit who hovers over the creation may give all humanity a respect for the earth and its resources as a precious gift. Lord hear us.

6. Specific local needs and topics of the day.

7. That the Spirit who has gathered us at this feast may gather all the departed to the wedding-banquet of the Lamb. Lord hear us.

President

Father, we rejoice that the Lord is with us. Hear us and grant what we ask in union with him, Jesus Christ, our Lord. Amen.

Eucharistic Prayer

Preface of Sundays in Ordinary Time VI (P34), with Eucharistic Prayer I.

Invitation to the Our Father

Gathered with the Bridegroom at his feast, in joy let us pray to the Father:

Sign of Peace
Coming among us the Lord has granted joy, unity and peace.
Let us celebrate that gift.

Invitation to Communion
The Lord is with us; with joy we have gathered at this feast;
happy are we who have been made his people and called to
share in this supper.

Communion Reflection
Silence is a rare commodity: everywhere we have background
noise to distract part of our attention. Yet silence is a key to reflection, and these few moments may be the only time this week
when for most people there is silence. Moreover, we tend to
have an attitude to the liturgy somewhat akin to the policy of
radio stations: more than a few seconds silence will make people
think there is something gone wrong, so keep every second
filled with words. However, silence that is not structured is apt
to be considered just 'waiting time' and people shuffle and
cough waiting for the 'next thing.' But here it is the silence that is
the thing! So structure it like this: announce, 'We will now spend
two minutes in silence reflecting on what we as a community
have just celebrated'; then measure the two minutes with your
watch; then conclude the silence with, 'Let us pray.'

Conclusion
Solemn Blessing of Ordinary Time IV (Missal, p 373).

Notes
1. This is one of those occasions when we recognise clearly the
Liturgy of the Word is not simply the liturgy of words read from
ancient texts, but an invitation to encounter the mystery of the
Word, the Logos, present in our midst. As the *General Instruction
on the Lectionary* expressed it: 'That Word constantly proclaimed
in the liturgy is always the living, active Word (see Hebrews 4:2)
through the power of the Holy Spirit. It expresses the Father's
love that never fails in its effectiveness towards us' (n 4).

When we read about the time when the Lord will be with his people, we recognise that this is the actual time of the liturgy: we are in the presence of the Lord gathered here at the Eucharist, and so should behave accordingly. And the appropriate way of behaving while the Master is with us is to engage in joyful feasting: fasting belongs to another time.

2. However, if we look at our actual style of celebrating the Eucharist, we might be forgiven for not recognising that it is a time of joyful feasting. We may say 'happy are those who are called to this supper' but it looks neither like a supper nor a group of happy people! This failure to actually celebrate in the style we claim we should celebrate has a long history. Ancient canon law forbade fasting on Sundays lest we fail to honour the presence of the risen Christ and so Sundays were not counted in the Lenten fast, but that did not stop the invention of yet another fast that did bind on Sundays – the fast before communion. This fast meant that it was either a foodless sacred Supper (the conundrum of how one participates in a sacred meal without eating was quietly sidestepped until the 1950s) or else one worried more about what was not to be eaten than about the Lord's meal. To sort out this liturgical confusion, the Eucharistic fast was shortened to the present token amount and that it was not abandoned entirely was due to committee structures where there were members who did not understand that it was wholly inappropriate.

Likewise, ancient canon law forbade kneeling on Sundays – kneeling is a sign of sorrow and penitence, not one of rejoicing. We stand in the presence of the Lord because 'he has stood up anew' (*resurrexit*) and has given us new life and made us able to stand around his table. Gradually, in the Latin churches this prohibition on kneeling on Sundays as inappropriate became blurred and was finally forgotten. However, the earlier tradition, still adhered to among the Greeks who find our kneeling an insult to the goodness of God, is still preserved in the Roman Canon: *Memento, Domine, famulorum famularumque tuarum et omnium circumstantium* (Remember, Lord, your servants, male and female, indeed everyone who stands around here) – but the confusion was so ingrained that it was missed by the Missal's translators: 'Remember all of us gathered here before you.' So the question is this: can one be a joyful gathering when people kneel in rows rather than gather around the Lord's table as one does at a joyful feast? We do not fast; nor do we kneel when the Lord is with us.

3. So if the celebration style is to reflect what we read in today's gospel, we have to address certain practical issues:

First, this is a day to encourage people to stand throughout the entire Liturgy of the Eucharist – standing as a joyful, priestly people.

Second, an exposition style elevation and bells draw undue attention to the elevation and recall deep bows and genuflections which stem from a time when it was imagined that the Eucharist could be participated in by adoration. So, for today at least, drop all the bells – they are not needed in the vernacular in any case – and simple show the loaf and cup after the institution narrative.

Third, have communion under both kinds.

Fourth, consider gathering the assembly around the table.

Fifth, have a loaf that can be broken for at least a good number of the assembly.

COMMENTARY

First Reading: Hos 2:16-17, 21-22

Hosea presents, as his central theme, the relationship of Israel to the Lord in terms of a marriage. The Lord is faithful; Israel is the unfaithful wife who must return to the Lord for reconciliation and forgiveness. In the first two verses of this reading we have the final lines of the prophet's complaint against the faithless wife, and in the latter two verses part of the assurance that there will be reconciliation if Israel returns to the Lord. As edited here, it is a stark statement that the relationship of the Lord, the Christ, to the people of God, the disciples, can be thought of using nuptial imagery as that is used in the bridegroom image in the gospel. Of course, we should remember that the primary focus of that imagery in the gospel is not the mystery of Christ and the church, but that of the day of greatest happiness (when it would be inappropriate for disciples to fast) which is the day the Lord is with the disciples (i.e. when we gather to celebrate his resurrection – Sunday).

Psalm: 102 (103)
While the first reading expresses the attitude of God towards his people in terms of marriage, this psalm expresses that love in terms of merciful forgiveness.

Second Reading: 2 Cor 3:1-6
Here we have a snippet of Paul's concern to prove to the Corinthians – after there has been a disruption between them and Paul – that he is an authentic apostle. This is a theme that runs from 2 Cor 2:14 to 6:10. Paul's basic attitude is to say that they are in no position to put him through some tests: it is the Spirit of the living God that is his identity document.

First Reading > Gospel Links
Jesus uses the imagery of the wedding feast to refer to his being with the disciples. This is then taken as a cue to the nuptial imagery of the mystery of Christ and the Church (Eph 5:32; and see also the imagery of the marriage feast of the Lamb in Apoc 19) which has as its Old Testament background the marriage imagery of Hosea (and today's first reading is just one example of Hosea's use of that imagery).

Gospel: Mk 2:18-22
This is the third of five conflict stories in Mark: we read the first last week, and the second (Mk 2:13-17) has not been used in the Sunday lectionary. In all these stories the basic question concerns with whom Jesus, and so by extension Mark's listeners in the early church, is in conflict. In the first story it is ostensibly 'the scribes,' in the second it is 'the scribes of the Pharisees,' and

now it is presented as 'the Pharisees'. But the interesting thing is that here the Pharisees – an establishment group – are concerned that Jesus is not like John the Baptist! And it is with this mention of 'the disciples of John' that the real target of all the conflict stories comes into view: the disciples of John who have become disciples of Jesus but do not like many things they find in among Jesus's disciples and who are apparently unwilling to make a clear break with John's approach nor able to see how different is the approach of Jesus. Mark is troubled by these followers of the Baptist, but clearly does not want to antagonise them – so the responsibility for the awkward question and the odium for being in conflict with Jesus is given to the Pharisees – but also wants to make it clear that they are the group whose approach he wants to challenge.

Fasting is a complex subject in the early church because most forms of Judaism not only practised it as a ritual discipline that marked them as a group, but it was similarly taken over as a group exercise by many communities of Jesus's disciples. For Mark, either the whole practice of fasting has no place in Jesus's teaching or else the penitential fasting of John's disciples has no place. His reasoning turns on the basic act of faith: Jesus, crucified, is risen and with his people. This reading of Mark is further supported by a first-century tradition about James (preserved only in Latin by Jerome) that he fasted from the time of the Last Supper until he joined Jesus in a eucharistic meal after Easter Sunday morning: for that tradition, like Mark, the time the master was not with the disciples was in the period of the tomb, and then there was fasting!

The imagery of the bridegroom on the wedding day is a commonplace: within Jewish thought of the time there was considered to be no better image for happiness than that of a man on his wedding day. It is that level of happiness that the church should have when it gathers with the risen Christ.

The final verses (21-22) re-iterate the notion that Jesus is a radical break with John: Jesus is new, his approach is new, he is not to be made into a copy of someone else – and for those who had been John's disciples, he is not even to be seen in terms of their former master and his teachings.

HOMILY NOTES

1. When this gospel is proclaimed in the assembly gathered for the Eucharist – pre-eminently on Sunday when the liturgy imagines a whole community, a local church, assembled – it has but one meaning: the Bridegroom, risen victorious from death, is with us.

2. This gospel does not point to a physical time after the Ascension (i.e. Jesus is with the disciples at the moment he makes the statement, and then there will be another time – later on – when he will not be with them), but to the basis of our faith, the Lord is risen, he is with us now, he is among us.

3. Therefore, we do not fast (note that in the days before the renewal of the liturgy the Sundays of Lent were not fast days) or do penance, nor originally did we kneel down (it is very hard to be joyful at the Lord's presence on one's knees!). Every Sunday is a day of rejoicing: the Lord is among his people.

4. This is one message that we have to communicate today: we are a new creation, an Easter people; the Lord has gathered us around him to celebrate at his feast.

Ninth Sunday of Ordinary Time

Introduction to the Celebration

We are all fragile creatures, we live a fragile existence and, for the most part, we do not see clearly the ways that lead to happiness. Into this fragile darkness comes the light of Christ. Jesus is the light shining in the darkness, he radiates to us the Father's love, and we encounter the glory of Father in him. It is this conviction, that Jesus Christ is the light and hope of the world, which has gathered us here. Let us recall that in him we glimpse the glory of our heavenly Father.

Rite of Penance

Lord Jesus Christ, you are the light shining in the darkness.
Lord have mercy.
Lord Jesus Christ, you are the light shining in our minds.
Christ have mercy.
Lord Jesus Christ, you are the radiance of the Father's glory.
Lord have mercy.

Headings for Readings

First Reading

The seventh day of the week, the Sabbath, was God's gift to his people as a day of rest, it was a day when they recalled that the all creation was God's gift. We rest on the first day of the week, Sunday, because we not only recall the gift of creation and life, but the gift of being a renewed creation who have been promised risen life.

Second Reading

In Jesus we see the reflection of the radiance of the Father.

Gospel

Jesus reminds us that the duty to do good can be more urgent than the duty to observe even the important patterns of ritual that give shape to our existence as a community of believers.

Prayer of the Faithful
President
We are gathered here by the Father's love: he has enlightened our minds to see the glory in the face of Christ. Therefore, as the People of God, let us pray to the Father.
Reader (s)
1. For the holy church of God throughout the world: that we will rejoice in the glory on the face of Christ. Lord hear us.
2. For all the churches: that in every gathering of the disciples this treasure of faith will be held intact. Lord hear us.
3. For all people of good will: that they may grow in the awareness of the mystery of God's love for all creatures. Lord hear us.
4. For all humanity: that we may listen to the groans of the creation and respond as individuals and communities in the way we live. Lord hear us.
5. Specific local needs and topics of the day.
6. For the dead: that they may rise into the fullness of the light of heaven. Lord hear us.
President
Father, through your gift of light we come to know you in Jesus. Hear us who follow him and grant our needs, through that same Christ, our Lord. Amen.

Eucharistic Prayer
The Preface of Christmas I (P3) uses Paul's theme from 2 Cor of light enlightening the eyes of faith to recognise the vision of glory that is the Christ as its basis; it is therefore the perfect preface for use with today's second reading. Moreover, while it is a Christmas preface it is the least 'seasonal' of the Christmas Prefaces and so tends not to be used at Christmas; and, in any case, there is little chance that many in the assembly on hearing it today will be disturbed that this was written for use on 25 December.

No Eucharistic Prayer is particularly appropriate.

Invitation to the Our Father
Gathered in the presence of the Christ in whose face we see the radiance of the Father's glory, we now pray:

Sign of Peace
Made sisters and brothers by Jesus, let us now offer forgiveness to one another.

Invitation to Communion
Behold the Lamb of God, behold him in whom we see the radiance of the Father's glory. Happy are we to be in his presence and his guests around this table.

Communion Reflection
We are here 'giving thanks to the Father, who has qualified us to share in the inheritance of the saints in light.'
We recall that 'once we were darkness, but now we are light in the Lord' and called to 'walk as children of light'.
'We are a chosen race, a royal priesthood, a holy nation, God's own people, that we may declare the wonderful deeds of him who called us out of darkness into his marvellous light.'
We remember what Jesus told us: 'I am the light of the world; he who follows me will not walk in darkness, but will have the light of life.'
'I have come as light into the world, that whoever believes in me may not remain in darkness.'
We recall that 'the Lord has commanded us, saying, "I have set you to be a light for the Gentiles, that you may bring salvation to the uttermost parts of the earth".'
'For it is the God who said, "Let light shine out of darkness," who has shone in our hearts to give the light of the knowledge of the glory of God in the face of Christ.'
'If we walk in the light, as he is in the light, we have fellowship with one another, and the blood of Jesus his Son cleanses us from all sin.' Amen.

Conclusion
Prayer over the People 7 (Missal, p 381).

Notes
1. While the greatness of the lectionary is its continuous reading of a single gospel each year in Ordinary Time, there is one drawback. Often when one of the evangelists pursues a theme at length (e.g. a sequence of healings or a sequence of parables), we can get three or four Sundays where it is very difficult not to appear to repeat the same homily. This is true today when, for a third Sunday in a sequence, we hear a conflict story. On the other hand, it is very often the case that the epistle reading is so short and devoid of context that it is very difficult to use it as the basis of the homily. Happily, today is not one of those days. So in the notes given here, there is a concentration on the second reading and its image of Jesus as the one in whom we see, through the gift of light, the Father's glory.

2. Today's gospel is made up of two conflict stories (2:23-8 and 3:1-6) and the second can be omitted by choosing the shorter form of the gospel (2:23-8). Since already one of the conflict stories has been omitted from the lectionary (see the notes for last Sunday), omitting the final story does not disrupt any continuity that might be remembered over the three Sundays. Therefore, there is good reason, if your focus is upon the second reading, for using today the shorter form of the gospel given in the lectionary.

3. The communion reflection is a mosaic of passages from the New Testament which are linked by references to 'light'. Their sources are (in the following order): Col 1:12; Eph 5:8; 1 Pet 2:9; Jn 8:12 and 12:46; Acts 13:47; 2 Cor 4:6; and 1 Jn 1:7.

COMMENTARY

First Reading: Deut 5:12-5
This reading is taken from one of the statements of the Decalogue that is found in the Pentateuch. In Deuteronomy, the Decalogue runs from 5:6-21 and the longest single command is

this section relating to the Sabbath. What is notable is that here the rationale for God's gift of the Sabbath is that it is a day of rest. The Sabbath responds to the human need to have time that is free from labour, and as such can be seen as a sign of God's care for those of the people who are oppressed with the burdens of hard physical labour in a subsistence economy. By contrast, the rationale for the Sabbath in Ex 20:8-11 is very different: 'because in six days the Lord made heaven and earth, the sea, and all that is in them, and rested the seventh day; therefore the Lord blessed the Sabbath day and hallowed it.'

In both cases the basic quality of the Sabbath is rest from labour. But while in Exodus this rest is essentially ritual remembrance of the priestly creation narrative and indeed an imitation of God's own rest, in Deuteronomy it is the rest itself that is the sole focus of attention. In these two perspectives we have two differing attitudes to the Sabbath that were eventually to be transferred by some Christians to Sunday and which produce the, often conflicting, positions of the Lord's Day as 'the day of no labour because God ordered rest' and the Lord's Day as 'the day of rejoicing because God ordered that attention be paid to remembering the creation'.

Psalm: 80 (81)
This picks up the theme of the Sabbath as the day of celebration when God has given freedom from slavery and the burdens of work.

Second Reading: 2 Cor 4:6-11
Most commentators see the first verse of this lection as belonging to a different part of Paul's argument to what follows; but as it is laid out in the lectionary vv 7-11 form a commentary on v 6: on the description of the manifestation of the Christ. Confronted with the glory of God in Jesus, Paul dwells on the fragility of human beings and the situation of constant difficulties in which we find ourselves. This situation is then contrasted with the death and new life of Jesus. In effect, Paul can understand his

own life (and so, by extension, his hearers can understand their lives) by seeking to understand the death, and the life, of Jesus.

First Reading > Gospel Links

The first reading supplies the necessary legal background to understand what is at issue in the gospel. Then when read together it heightens the perception of Jesus as even greater than Moses and the law, because 'the Son of Man is master even of the Sabbath.' In this reading we have the hermeneutic – found as early as the time of the Letter to the Hebrews – of the law being the shadow pointing forward to a time of actual presence of the law's source.

Gospel: Mk 2:23-3:6 (shorter version: 2:23-8)

Here we have the fourth (2:23-8) and final (3:1-6) conflict incidents that belong to this section of Mark's gospel (2:1-3:6). Both stories have to be read at two levels. First, there is the intention of Mark to show that there was a growing gulf between the way Jesus preached and acted, and the approach of many of those in religious authority. Reading it at this level, this is the theme of conflict between the law as embodied in Jesus and the law as inherited that reached its climax in the desire of those authorities to put Jesus to death. The second level at which we have to read these stories is the message that Mark wants to convey to his audience where there were many who were very familiar with, and indeed zealous for, the practices of the law; whereas many other Christians had a much freer attitude to the Sabbath and were, in fact, refocusing their interest in the community meal on Sunday. In this situation, that of his audience, Mark is (as in the other conflict stories) emphasising the distinctiveness of the practice of Jesus with that of those who emphasised the need to continue with Jewish practices.

The second conflict story is a neat combination of a miracle and a debate which presents the Son of Man as not only greater than Moses, but as one mighty in deed and word (cf Lk 24:19).

HOMILY NOTES

1. There is a popular credal statement that runs: 'What we
    Christians know about God is what we see in Jesus.' Like all
    one-liners it misleads as much as it enlightens, but it does re-
    mind us of an important truth that is all too often forgotten.
    We Christians do not know *what* God is, we simply know
    that God *is*, and that this mystery is a mystery of love, and
    that we are given access to this mystery through our union
    with Jesus, the Son of the Father, and our master.

2. This holy agnosticism about God is in marked contrast to the
    attitudes of most people in the developed world today.
    Christian saints and mystics have sought to know God and
    have asked the question 'what is God?', not because they
    would 'have an answer', but because the mere searching
    would lead them towards the light. By contrast, most people
    today do not ask 'what is God?', but actually ask the question
    'how many gods are there?' To this they give one of the three
    possible answers: one, less than one (i.e. there is no 'god'), or
    more than one (i.e. many gods). But in asking this question,
    how many gods, they are assuming that they know what
    God is. They know more about God than any of the saints,
    and know so much that they know there is no such being!
    The basis of this conundrum is that they make up an image of
    what a god could be, and then declare whether or not they
    think that such a being or beings is/are likely.

3. The most usual projection is that of a motor for the universe,
    a figure of mighty power, and often one who would treat
    humanity as puppets. But Christians claim to no such de-
    tailed knowledge of the mystery that is greater than all, be-
    yond words and beyond being. We simply claim to have seen
    his glory by reflection. We see that in a dim reflection in the
    order of the cosmos, we glimpse it in the moral ordering to-
    wards the good in human nature, we see it in the lives of the
    people of God from the time of Abraham our father in faith,
    and we see it in the face of the Christ.

4. To look upon Jesus is to see the Father's radiance reflected in

our world and we can only see the glory of that radiance through the Father's own gift of light. In Jesus 'we see our God made visible and so are caught up in the love of the God we cannot see.'

5. Paul expressed this as 'God has shone in our minds to radiate the light of the knowledge of God's glory, the glory on the face of Christ', or we could say 'what we know about God is what we see in Jesus.' Amen.

Lectionary Unit II.II

The second stage of this unit, which is concerned with the Mystery of Jesus being progressively revealed, focuses on Jesus with his disciples.

This stage runs from the tenth to the fourteenth Sunday. In these gospels we encounter Jesus facing serious criticism, preaching parables of the kingdom, calming the storm, healing, and being rejected at Nazareth.

Tenth Sunday of Ordinary Time

Introduction to the Celebration

During his life Jesus faced serious criticism, misunderstanding, abuse, rejection, and finally death at the hands of those who believed that he was wicked. In today's gospel we hear of all these attitudes coming not only from his religious opponents, but from his relatives and even his immediate family. Faced with this rejection, he asks who are his mother and brother? The answer Jesus gives is: those who do the will of God. It is as his family, those who are trying to do the will of God, that we have gathered here.

But although we call ourselves sisters and brothers of the Lord, we are also conscious that our discipleship is flawed and that we fail to carry out the will of God in the way we live.

Rite of Penance

Option C iii (Missal, pp 392-3) is appropriate.

Headings for Readings

First Reading

The scene of our first reading is the Garden of Eden, and the story of Adam and Eve. This is one of the stories that the People of God have used down the ages to point out that we are people who have freedom, and therefore people who must act responsibility. We are not just puppets of some higher power nor creatures of no importance: God loves us so much that he has trusted us with freedom, and therefore he takes us, and our actions, seriously.

Second Reading

Paul writes to encourage a community: our sufferings are passing, and we share in the new risen life of Jesus.

Gospel

The scene of today's gospel is outside the family home of Jesus in Nazareth. Speaking there Jesus reveals that the Day of the Lord has come: Satan is being conquered; the time of forgiveness is at hand; and anyone who does not acknowledge this is offending the Holy Spirit by denying that he acts through Jesus.

Profession of Faith

Because of the references to Satan and the works of Satan in today's gospel, this is an appropriate day to replace the declarative creed with a Renewal of Baptismal Promises from the Easter Sunday morning liturgy which includes an affirmation of the rejection of Satan, his works and his empty promises. See Missal, pp 220-1.

Prayer of the Faithful

President

When we stand to offer these petitions, we declare that we are disciples of Jesus the High Priest who are willing to share in his mediation with the Father, but we should remember that this means we are also willing to accept the insults we receive as his followers.

Reader (s)

1. For all our sisters and brothers in all the churches scattered throughout the world, that we might have the courage to be disciples. Lord hear us.

2. For all who are finding discipleship a heavy burden, that they may receive comfort. Lord hear us.

3. For all who are being persecuted for bearing the name of Christ, that they might be delivered from their sufferings. Lord hear us.

4. For all those who mock us, deride us, or persecute us, that their eyes may be enlightened, their minds opened, and their hearts changed. Lord hear us.

5. Specific local needs and topics of the day.

6. For all humanity, that just as we have grown in technical skills in using the creation, that we might grow in wisdom in using what God has given us. Lord hear us.

President

Father, your Son has shown us your love and given us access to you so that we can stand in your midst and pray for ourselves, all our sisters and brothers in every church, and all humanity. Hear us, we ask you, and grant us what we ask in union with Christ Jesus, our Lord. Amen.

Eucharistic Prayer

Preface of Sundays in Ordinary Time I (P29) is appropriate, with Eucharistic Prayer II.

Invitation to the Our Father

Let us pray that we will do the will of God as brothers and sisters of the Lord, as we say:

Sign of Peace

If we are seeking to do the will of the Father, then we are committed to building the kingdom of peace. Let us offer each other an assurance that building the kingdom of peace is part of our plan for living.

Invitation to Communion

The Lord Jesus gathered as his family all who sought to do the Father's will; he now gathers us as his sisters and brothers and calls us to share in his banquet.

Communion Reflection

The danger at every celebration of the Eucharist is that it becomes so over laden with words that we forget that 'thanksgiving' is an activity that takes place through sharing the Lord's meal with sisters and brothers. So spend the time after communion visibly sending out a part of the common food of the group to those who cannot be physically there.

Conclusion
Solemn Blessing 14 (Ordinary Time V), Missal, p 373, is appropriate.

Notes
Today's gospel presents anyone who has to comment upon it with difficulties between what it states clearly and the long-standing traditional presentation of the family of Jesus by Christians. These difficulties can be viewed under three headings:

1. *References to Satan, and to possession by the devil.* The early church had little problem with accepting that there was a malevolent spirit who presided over evil, inspired people to commit wicked deeds, took possession of them so that they became his instruments, and caused madness. Much rather simplistic theology has been produced on this over the last century and a half, and has resulted in confusion. This has taken forms such as 'possession' is just a primitive name for schizophrenia (or some other psychiatric problem), therefore 'possession' does not exist! Another approach has been to suggest that any discussion of 'the devil' is simply a projection of our fears – a taboo or a bogeyman writ large – or the remnant of a dualism: a perpetual struggle between good and bad. But while such dismissals may meet with approval in many quarters, to dismiss the notion that there is some spiritual force which promotes evil – whatever its origins in the universe – and which can only be countered with divine assistance, runs directly counter to the tradition of wisdom found in all the monotheistic religions. Moreover, it does not match the darker side of our experience: after a century of the most brutal horrors ever known, it seems curiously inadequate to imagine that such suffering is explicable simply because individuals were deranged or uneducated. There is a curious fascinating attraction for human beings in destruction and processes of destruction. It defies our rationality and our best wishes, but it must be taken seriously as a factor within our existence. Such irrational attractions cannot be adequately ex-

plained, and in such a situation it is perhaps more appropriate that we pray for help rather than baldly dismissing 'Satan and all his works' as a figment of a less-enlightened time.

Today's references to Beelzebul, Satan, and the kingdom of Satan, while there is no need to draw attention to them, must be accepted as part of our wisdom reminding us that the suffering, wickedness, and evil that is part of our condition is somehow greater than us and can only be assaulted in union with the Christ who is the conqueror of all sin.

2. *References to the mother and brothers of Jesus.* Since the fourth century it has been taken for granted within preaching that Jesus was an only child and, therefore, his mother was 'ever virgin' – and this has been presented as a 'fact'. This fact, however, flies in the face of a wide variety of early Christian documents. In the gospels it is openly noted that Jesus had four brothers (James, Joses, Simon, Judas) and, at least, two sisters (see Mk 6:3; and compare Mt 13:55); while elsewhere it is assumed that people know his brothers and their children. This conflict between the growing memory of Mary as the dedicated virgin and the canonical texts which were growing in authority has produced some of the funniest exegesis of the patristic period where scholars, e.g. Jerome, sought to prove that brothers and sisters actually meant cousins even if there is no linguistic basis for this, or were Joseph's children by an earlier marriage, or even (one senses desperation) that Mary had a blood sister who was also called Mary and on-lookers got confused between the children of the two sisters both named Mary! The actual problem is based on the fact that the cult of Mary as a virgin (*in partu et post partum*) is a much later growth in the history of Christianity, but by the time it appeared the four gospels which we hold as canonical were already established as fundamental authorities and as such could not be altered on this point.

Until recently, since most Catholics never heard these texts outside a controlled classroom environment, there was little problem with references to the family of Jesus such as we have in today's gospel. Moreover, the fact that Protestant biblical scholarship has accepted since the late nineteenth century that fourth-fifth century 'exegesis' was irrelevant to the question and, therefore, presented Jesus as one of a family of seven was seen a simply proof of their rejection of the role of Mary! However, the problem just will not go away. Today we have a major problem in presenting the whole question of Jesus's family: we often refer in the liturgy to Mary as 'ever virgin', while any scholarly work on the life of Jesus – be it by a Catholic or a non-Catholic – now acknowledges that Jesus had real brothers and sisters. While it would be simply raising unnecessary doubts to draw attention to this aspect of today's gospel, we must have an answer for questioners that is neither patronising ('Oh! It's a very complex matter of scholarship') nor obfuscatory ('Oh! It's a mystery' or 'You would need to ask an expert!'). The simplest answer is this: Matthew presents Mary as a virgin at the time of the conception of Jesus (Mt 1:23), but does not imply that she remained a virgin for the rest of her life (cf Mt 13:55); and this is all that we acknowledge in the creed: 'born of the virgin Mary'. At a later date there was such an excessive regard for virginity as a religious state in itself that some people could not bear to think of Mary as a normal married woman and so imagined that the references to brothers and sisters must be wrong. This was an excess and we should bear in mind that in every age the community of Christians remembers some forgotten aspects of discipleship and forgets other – in this process of remembering and forgetting there is always the risk of excesses of one sort or another.

3. *The first reading as the 'proto-evangelium.'* Part of today's first reading has been known for centuries by Catholics as the 'proto-evangelium': the first announcement of the divine promise that just as Satan had entered the human domain and brought suffering and pain, so eventually one would come who would contend with Satan and crush him. However, that text in Genesis has attained a secondary, derived, meaning in Mariology whereby it became 'she shall crush your heel'. As such, the proto-evangelium did not look forward directly to the Christ, but to Mary and through her to her Son. It is this reading of the

text of Genesis that inspired many of the marian themes, such as co-redemptrix, that had such a prominence until a few decades ago and which still surface in various ways today. Such a marian reading of this text was always a departure from the main-stream of the Christian reading of it, and care must be taken that this marian 'interpretation' is not used today as its juxtaposition with today's gospel indicated that it is to be read as a prophecy of the Christ, and the age of the Christ, rather that the coming of the mother of the One who is the Christ.

COMMENTARY

First Reading: Gen 3:9-15

This is a passage that is edited from the larger story of the first sin with today's gospel in mind. Rather than try to comment on what it may have originally meant either as a distinct story or as component within the Book of Genesis, it is more important to note the reactions that reading this story causes today.

First, the creation accounts in the Book of Genesis have be-come over the past two centuries a touchstone in the cultural life of Western Europeans on the place of religious knowledge in modern society. Put bluntly, for most people including most in an average congregation, notions about the analogical nature of truth and of distinctive modes of historicity relative to different aspects of human investigation are simply 'bunkum'. The story is either 'true' or 'false' and if it is true then Darwin (= modern science) is wrong, and if science is right this is just primitive superstition. We may rightly reject this as naïve or simplistic, but that is how the biblical creation stories appear within our culture; and in this simplistic view of religious truth there is agreement between militant 'scientific' atheists (e.g. Richard Dawkins) and biblical fundamentalists (e.g. 'Creationists'). Hearing the story, many people in the average congregation feel uneasy as they imagine themselves on the horns of a dilemma if they engage with the story: either they must reject it and accept the atheist position (which they do not want to do) or accept the story as explaining humanity's condition and then become fundamentalists (which, likewise, they do not wish to become).

Second, most Christians link this story, where it originally was the account of the first sin (and as such an etiology of each evil act), with the theology of Original Sin which is its most famous interpretation. As Original Sin it is not an explanation of how sins occur, but the account of the cause of the condition of humans as sinful (i.e. guilty before God and so meriting punishment) irrespective of any sinful act of the individual. This notion is probably the most problematic within the whole of Christian theology, and still today many people – not simply fundamentalists – look back to this story as a statement that there must have been some ancient cataclysm which put an enmity between humanity and God. This, in turn, then has theology dictating history and the whole problem of the historicity of Genesis recurs not under the question of literal truth of the text, but in a pseudo-scientific form such as the 'monogenism'/'polygenism' disputes that raged within Catholicism prior to the Second Vatican Council. It is worth remembering that the notion of 'Original Sin' is a *theologoumenon*: namely something that we speak of as a fact when we are thinking of a way of having a causal explanation of what are fundamental mysteries of faith. In this case, on the one hand, we engage with it as a way of describing the existential condition of humanity: we are in a God-created world, God is loving and caring, yet things are still awry. On the other hand, Jesus has been sent to us by God as healer and reconciler, but why is that needed? Ah, 'original sin' – linked to this story – would offer a 'reason' for both real facts, i.e. human alienation and the advent of the Christ. However, once the story becomes problematic, this piece of theological 'back engineering' also becomes problematic. Alas, the notion of 'Original Sin' is so all-pervasive that it constantly distracts us from the real issues of faith: one has only to think of the number of luxury (or fattening) products that are marketed using the imagery of the garden story or with a tag-line: 'eating this is the original sin – go on, enjoy yourself.'

Third, this story is linked in the eyes of many people with the religious demonisation of women: the woman is the agent brings sinfulness to the man (and one has only to read 1 Tim 2:14 to see this). For this reason many in the congregation will be uneasy that this view of women is being handed on to another generation.

Lastly, it is being used today in the liturgy not because of any original meaning it might have had, but simply to read the notion that it will be a seed of the woman that will confront Satan (i.e. the famous patristic interpretation of this passage as the 'protoevangelium'), whereas in text of Genesis this phrase simply implies that humans (i.e. the descendent of the woman) would have a hatred of snakes.

This text brings to our attention, in a nutshell, many of the basic difficulties both of using ancient texts and of apologetics today. These are not issues that are appropriate for the liturgical homily nor can they be addressed in that context. These are the sort of issues that are thrown up within our culture and then highlighted when a text like this is read at the liturgy: these are issues that can only be handled in the proper discursive context of adult education

Psalm: 129 (130)

This is read in the light of reading the first reading as the protoevangelium: a people looking for the redeemer cry out from the depths of the condition into which they have been cast for the divine mercy which is the sending of the saviour. This soteriology-driven christology, which in many ways sounds Calvinistic through the juxtaposition of this psalm with this first reading, is then softened by the response: the Lord is full of mercy. It is this response that prepares the way for the gospel today, with the rest of the psalm merely being an occasion to make the statement of good news: God is brimfull of mercy. Today requires the skill of the musicians so that the gathering shouts out the response while the psalm itself slips into the background.

Second Reading: 2 Cor 4:13-5:1

The very opening words of this reading shows that this lection is badly edited as it does not form a unit when read on its own. Anyone hearing 'As we have the same spirit' realised that this is the sequel to a piece of thinking, not the beginning of a chain of thought! Indeed, unless one has read from 4:7, one cannot make sense of 4:13, and then this throws one off the note for the rest of the reading.

Paul's letter can be broken into two units which overlap in today's reading: 4:7-15 forms a unit dealing with the manifestation of Jesus in the life of the churches; then 4:16-5:10 forms another unit dealing with the life of the Christian in the face of the certainty of our death. As we have it in the lectionary we get bits of both, and the more attentive the listener, the more confused this reading will seem!

There is a simple solution: start at 4:7, reading again a few verses that were read last week, and stop at 4:15. Then next week begin the second reading at 4:16 and stop where that lection stops at 5:10. If you take this course then the community recalls that in its life and suffering it is carrying on the work of the Christ, manifesting his resurrection, through bringing new life into the creation.

First Reading > Gospel Links

This is almost a perfect example of the relationship of promise (in the time of the Old Covenant) and fulfilment (in the Christ-event).

Gospel: Mk 3:20-35

What we read today is a single episode of Mark's story. It is, however, complex for Mark has brought several pieces of teaching together in a single incident (the unit is framed by references at the beginning (3:21) and end (3:31-5) of the story to where it occurred: outside his family home in Nazareth) with a single purpose: to show how Jesus contended with opposition from those who denied that in him the age of the Christ had come,

that he was possessed by the devil, or that he was simply deranged; and in the course of this he makes a point directly aimed
at his audience: it is discipleship not a family-link with Jesus that
is of significance within the church.

The scene set (3:19-21), the occasion for the teaching of Jesus
is initiated by scribes who accuse him of being possessed (3:23),
and this calls forth two distinct refutations aimed at distinct crit-
icisms of the person and ministry of Jesus. The first is that he is
an agent of Satan; and this is refuted by the parable of the house
divided against itself. The second is to state that Jesus – while
perhaps acknowledging him as a wise teacher or great healer –
is not the one who inaugurated the new age of reconciliation. To
say such a thing is to be guilty of being in 'the wrong age' and
thus to deny the work of the Holy Spirit. In Mark's narrative
these two elements are connected in that the age of the Spirit's
reconciliation is also the age of the defeat of the power of Satan.

Lastly, we know that whatever the opposition of the family
of Jesus – his mother and siblings – to his work at an early moment in his ministry, later on the family figured prominently in
the life of the early church (although it is only the role of Mary
that has been widely remembered for most of our history). The
best example of the role played by his brothers is that James was
leader of the Jerusalem church (e.g. Gal 1:19). The likelihood is
that some brethren were claiming that authority in the churches
was linked to being connected to the family of Jesus – this is a
theme that can still be heard in Eusebius – rather than discipleship. In that context, Mark – repeated by Matthew and Luke –
has a clear answer from Jesus: to be a relative of the Christ,
whether close or distant, is to be one who does the will of God.

There is a tendency – at least 1700 years old – to dismiss Mark
as little more than a summary (the older view) or a dry-run (the
modern view) for Matthew/Luke, and to assume that if we read
Matthew or Luke we get all that is in Mark 'thrown in' for good
measure. It is obvious that this attitude limits our view both of
Jesus and the early church for it ignores another perspective, yet
this attitude also prevents us seeing what a subtle theologian
Mark is in his own right. The elegant way Mark interweaves so

many strands of his good news into this little incident should remind us to read him and value him for his own distinctive
preaching.

Technical Note: In the lectionary you find that Jesus refers to
'Beelzebul' (pronounced: be – ell – zeb – bull) and in so doing the
JB (along with the RSV and NRSV) is following the best Greek
manuscripts (and the best critical edition) which read:
Beelzeboul. However, older translations usually follow the
Vulgate form 'Beelzebub' and, indeed, this form is often used in
modern studies. This slight shift in sound seems to worry some
people whenever this gospel is read. The correct form is
'Beelzebul' when reading the gospel; but it is equally clear that
both names were in use among Jews at the time of Jesus as alternative derogatory names for Satan.

HOMILY NOTES

1. We do not expect to hear of Jesus being thought of as mad –
    at least in the gospels. We expect to hear of Jesus performing
    healings, preaching the Father's love, or offering wisdom to
    humanity. Yet today we hear that those closest to him, those
    who knew him from childhood, thought that he was out of
    his mind, silly, and in need of some serious help.

2. Moreover, down the centuries this has been one of those little
    bits of the gospel that Christians have found most embarrass-
    ing: and they have ignored it, they have wondered if it is a
    mistake, or they have tried to explain it away. Indeed, it is the
    only reference in the gospels to the mother of Jesus that has
    not figured in the cult of Mary within the church. But the
    question is this: should we really be so surprised at it?

3. Just look at the number of people who think that being a
    Christian, someone dedicated to following the way of the
    Lord Jesus, is silly, and who think that the approach of
    Christians is a mad way to think about the world. If people
    around us think that we are stupid or mad to believe in a lov-
    ing, forgiving and caring God, then why are we surprised
    that people thought Jesus was mad?

4. To be a disciple involves far more than following the tenets of religious practice or a particular moral code. Being a disciple is having a radically different view of why the universe exists, what human life is all about, and where it is all going.

5. In the face of a world that proclaims that the universe is purposeless, we proclaim that it is the handiwork of a loving Creator which has been entrusted to us to interact with responsibly.

6. In the face of a world that proclaims that life is fearful, that it is about economic security and restrictive control of resources, and that happiness equals accumulation of stuff, we Christians are expected to live lives of generosity, thanking God for his goodness.

7. In the face of a world that proclaims that individual enjoyment is the highest good, we proclaim that the purpose of life is to spread goodness and happiness and that life only reaches its purpose in the presence of God.

8. Two questions: first, to the person giving the homily: does this gospel embarrass you? Does its implications make you fearful?

   Second, for the assembly: if you suggested that, at the next meal your family has together, the group should offer thanks for God's gift of the food, would you be afraid of being thought mad?

Eleventh Sunday of Ordinary Time

Introduction to the Celebration
An Alternative Approach

Every Sunday we introduce the celebration by saying how people are welcome to the Lord's banquet, made one in Christ, made brothers and sisters in baptism, and members of the church and of the family of God. This is all true as a set of abstract statements about what we believe about ourselves. However, that is not how it feels and in every celebration the first interaction is at the level of feeling: if we do not feel welcome, then no matter what happens, we feel rejected and that sense of rejection is a fact of human living. If we are to talk about banquets and welcome, then perhaps the first thing is for people to welcome one another, shake hands, and introduce themselves.

This notion of introducing oneself is so important psychologically that at meetings where everyone really already knows one another, it is often a good thing to go around and for each to give her/his name, say a word of self-introduction, and tell others why they are there. The Eucharist is intended to be intimate in two ways: first, it is a meal of sisters and brothers with the Lord (and family meals are, by definition, intimate); and second, it is to be the centre of our religious lives for the week, and anything that is at the centre of our spirituality is also, by definition, intimate.

So rather than give an introduction, say something like this:

We are gathered here at the Lord's banquet as his sisters and brothers, so it is appropriate that we should introduce ourselves to each other. Let's do that now.

Rite of Penance

Lord Jesus, you came to establish the kingdom of God. Lord have mercy.

Lord Jesus, you come now to gather us as the kingdom of God. Christ have mercy.

Lord Jesus, you will come again to the present the kingdom to the Father. Lord have mercy.

Headings for Readings
First Reading

The effect of the work of God among us is compared to the way a great tree begins life as a tiny shoot.

Second Reading

Today Paul is reminding the church in Corinth of that aspect of our faith that we express each Sunday in the creed: Jesus 'will come again in glory to judge the living and the dead, and his kingdom will have no end.'

Gospel

The kingdom of God is the mystery that enfolds all of us: we cannot simply understand it in the way that we might find out about a club or a movement. We only learn what it means to be a member of the kingdom by following Jesus slowly and patiently.

Prayer of the Faithful

Use Sample Formula 10 (Ordinary Time II), Missal, pp 1002-3.

Eucharistic Prayer

Since 'the kingdom' and what it means is a focus today, the Preface of Christ the King (P51) is appropriate; it works well with Eucharistic Prayer III.

Invitation to the Our Father

As a people who are seeking to build the kingdom, let us now pray for its coming:

Sign of Peace
Let us express the bonds of peace that should unite us as sisters and brothers within the kingdom of God.

Invitation to Communion
The Lord calls us to share in the banquet of the kingdom, and now he invites us to share in this meal as the pledge of his love.

Communion Reflection
When he was with people walking along the roads of Galilee long ago, the Lord Jesus spoke to people in parables.
Parables that gave them pointers, hints, glimpses of what the kingdom was like.
They are like shadows, images, and reflections.

'With what can we compare the kingdom of God, or what parable shall we use for it?
It is like a grain of mustard seed, which, when sown upon the ground, is the smallest of all the seeds on earth;
yet when it is sown it grows up and becomes the greatest of all shrubs, and puts forth large branches, so that the birds of the air can make nests in its shade.

Then he would only speak in parables.

Now he is among us in this gathering;
He is among us in sharing this meal together;
He is among us in the loaf we have broken and shared;
He is among us in the common cup we have drunk from.

This too is a pointer, a hint, a glimpse of the heavenly banquet.
These gifts and this sharing are but a reflection of what is to come.

Now we stand here and thank the Father for his goodness;
One day we shall praise him face to face.

Conclusion

May the Father of all consolation bless you in all your work during the coming week; and may your constant prayer be: Thy kingdom come! Amen.

May the Son, our Lord, give you his strength to build the kingdom in all you do and say; and may you act in union with him in your work. Amen.

May the Spirit empower you with hope in all the challenges of discipleship; and may his presence enable you to see the signs of the kingdom throughout the creation. Amen.

Notes

Avoid letting catechists (or teachers with classes at the Eucharist) or those who hold the parallel Liturgy of the Word for children embark on the 'parables are Jesus's stories for children' narrative. Anyone reading today's gospel, and particularly Mark's comment at the end about the use of parables by Jesus, should be able to see just how confusing is the notion that 'the parable are simple teaching'.

COMMENTARY

First Reading: Ezek 17:22-24

As this passage stands in the lectionary – a blunt oracular statement – all that we can say about it is that it is an affirmation that the Lord is lord of all life.

It comes from a unit of text (17:1-24) which is 'allegory of the eagles'; and which in turn is but one item among many that go to make up that section of Ezekiel labelled 'allegories of judgement' (15:1-19:14). However, the passage has a completely different significance when read in context – one would have to read 17:1-24 to appreciate the imagery – from any possible meaning that it has when just these verses are read in the liturgy. Therefore, a study of this passage in its scriptural context is irrelevant here.

Psalm: 91 (92)

The choice is based on this using the image of the cedar tree also used in the first reading (itself chosen for using an image found in the gospel). What are we to make of it since it is three different types of growth that are indicated using tree imagery in first reading, psalm, and gospel? It is probably best to see it as a meditation on the notion that with God there is always growth (however, the psalmist sees this in almost mechanical terms: 'Be just, then you grow' – a notion that our experience tells us needs to be teased out very carefully!).

Second Reading: 2 Cor 5:6-10

As this reading stands in the lectionary it is very hard to draw a useful exegesis from it: we have just a bit of a larger argument in Paul. The unit of text within this fragmented letter runs form 4:16 to 5:10 (see the notes for last week), so the best thing is to read this whole section which is Paul's answer to those who reflect on life and then fear death. To such fear Paul offers the contrast between 'what really matters' and the passing things of life. Placed in a scales, the important matters outweigh the transitory: the unseen are what really matter, the seen are gone in a moment. Hence living by faith and not by sight, the community move toward the point when the Christ will judge those who have lived in accord with what 'really matters'.

If reading the whole unit of text seems too much, then read 5:1-10: such a lection can, at least, be heard as a passage that makes sense.

First Reading > Gospel Links

The link is at the level of imagery: the first reading is the image of the Lord planting a shoot that grows into a great tree, a similar image is used in the gospel's second parable. What are we to make of this linking: that there was a long continuity in trying to use natural metaphors for the mysterious work of God. Anyone who approaches these readings with consumerist questions: 'what have these to tell us or teach us?' or 'what [piece of information] do they reveal to us?' will be sorely disappointed.

Gospel: Mk 4:26-34

We have today a classic example of the way parables were used by the evangelists – and most notably Mark – in their preaching. We can see three items of tradition combined here by Mark using the image of seeds. First, we have the parable of the seed growing secretly (vv 26-9) which is only found in Mark; second, we have the parable of the mustard seed (30-32) which is found in all three synoptics; and then a comment in the voice of the evangelist on Jesus's use of parables (33-4) which is also found, but with a completely different theological slant, in Mt 14:34-5.

The text poses us problems at two levels: first, at the level of our common perceptions of what parables are; and, second, what these particular parables might mean. Despite the work of two centuries of scholarship on the nature of parables, most people believe that the parables are the easy parts of the gospels to understand, that Jesus told them as simple stories – indeed as children's stories, and that they are very suitable for teaching! This misconception is grounded on using a text that is not a parable but a forensic allegory (a 'what if …'): the story of the Good Samaritan. The up-shot of this misconception is that when the average congregation hears today's gospel, they expect that it should be simple, and then they are either disappointed or they simplify it to the point of nonsense! So the first task of anyone addressing this text today is to try to dispel the notion that parables as nice simple stories. Even Mark (and certainly Matthew and Luke) were troubled by the fact that Jesus used these stories and that they were so opaque. Mark links this style of Jesus with his notion of the 'messianic secret' – that Jesus did not want to be taken as a hero-saviour, and that only those who were willing to see him on the cross could enter into the fullness of his teaching. Mark was not an adherent of the 'keep it simple' school of theology that has dominated most views of preaching since the 1970s.

Then we have the second problem: what might Jesus have been trying to get his audience to grasp with these two seed parables? A probable explanation is that his hearers were not to see the kingdom as some great, obvious 'new age' when all would be changed and the power of God would be visible before everyone. God does not force his way into human affairs to impose his order from outside: rather, the kingdom starts small and is only seen by those who can accept the contingencies of history. A history that saw one divine 'seed' (Jesus who was just one individual whose ministry apparently ended in the crucifixion) die; yet, and this is Mark's hope, that seed lives and grows: otherwise there would not be the gathering to which Mark was preaching (or indeed the gathering to which you will preach).

HOMILY NOTES

1. 'Think global, act local' is the wise motto of the ecological movement: have the big picture, but actually make a difference, no matter how small, in the right direction. However, the approach is one that is far older than the ecological movement: it is the basic notion we find in Jesus's teaching about the kingdom. And we see it laid out in today's gospel: the kingdom is not like the spread of a great empire, it is like tiny seeds scattered here and there. Where does one find it: in vast systems and worldwide schemes? No, rather it is discovered in little things. It is more like a tiny plant than some mighty building. But if it is given time, then the kingdom grows and spreads.

2. But 'thinking global, acting local' is far harder to put into effect than we like to think. It always seems easier to lay the blame far away in some vast system and it seems very easy to decry our little efforts – in recycling for instance – as not really making a difference. In the same way, thinking in terms of God's vast plan but then loving one's neighbour is far harder than it appears. One can give up because the plan does appears to be off-track, or because the little acts of forgiveness and love seem to make no difference to the world. Indeed, there is always a body of people who see such little actions as really no more than a delusion to distract us from 'real' action.

3. In the face of these difficulties and objections, we have to remind ourselves of three aspects of the activity of building the kingdom.

First, the building of the kingdom is nothing less than bringing God's love closer to creation. It is not the equivalent of recruiting converts or seeking out adherents to our way of doing things. The kingdom happens when it happens: whenever someone looks at the world afresh, has new joy, rejoices in beauty, or is encouraged to seek the good. This intimate scale of the kingdom is proportionate to the scale of the deeds we are called to perform every day. If we cannot communicate love in little things, then we will not succeed in bigger things.

Second, each of us is called to carry out the activities of building the kingdom as part of a community, this community, this church. We are not just a bundle of individuals who happen to share a view of the universe; we are one people bonded together as the body of Christ. We engage in all these little things knowing that all of those we can call brothers and sisters can work in the same way, we can encourage one another, support one another, and comfort one another along an often arduous path.

Third, we are people who are called to live by faith, act with love, and walk with hope. Hope is living with the 'not yet,' the apparent incompleteness of what we do, the energy to get up again after we have confronted frustration.

4. 'Think global, act local' (or as we might rephrase it into more religious terms: 'Think God, love neighbour') also fits into the basic plan of salvation. We seek to build the kingdom of the Father – and we pray for its coming. We do this in union with the Son – we act as the body of Christ. We press on in hope which is an effect of the Holy Spirit living within us – and the Spirit enlightens and enlivens us.

5. 'Think global, act local' has become one of the valuable slogans for many groups. We Christians must also make this slogan our own: it can help us link the values of the kingdom to the practical actions our human situations demand, and it can give concrete expression to one of the pressing urgencies of discipleship.

Twelfth Sunday of Ordinary Time

Introduction to the Celebration

Each Sunday we gather together as the church for many reasons. One of the basic reasons is to give thanks to God for the wonder of the creation. We live in a creation that is the Father's gift; it has come into existence through his Son, Jesus our Lord, for it is through him all things were made, and over the creation hovers the Holy Spirit, the giver of life, imparting life to it. And, in today's gospel we shall hear a story that reminds us that Jesus, the Word made flesh, is Lord of all creation. So today we have to be thankful.

But we often act as if the creation is not God's gift but is 'just there' for us to use as we like; we often think that how we behave in the creation is not important to God; we often forget that wonder and praise is needed if we are to understand the universe. So today, remembering that the Christ is the Lord of all creation, we have also to be sorry for our carelessness.

Rite of Penance

Lord Jesus, you are the Lord of all creation. Lord have mercy.

Lord Jesus, you are the Word through whom all things were made. Christ have mercy.

Lord Jesus, you are the Wisdom praised by all creation. Lord have mercy.

Headings for Readings
First Reading

Nature that we see around is not something 'just there': it is a creation, the work of God.

Second Reading

How can we grasp all that the Christ should mean to us? Here Paul asks us to reflect that we who have become united with Christ have become a new creation.

Gospel
This gospel is an invitation to praise Jesus as the Lord of Creation: he is Word through whom all things were made.

Profession of Faith
This is not a day to use the Apostles' Creed. The Nicene formula has a far more developed theology of creation: creation is through the *Logos*, and it is the *Logos* who has become flesh for our salvation.

Prayer of the Faithful
President
Fellow creatures, we gather here as a people called to be stewards of the creation, and we stand here as the priestly people of Jesus Christ, so let us place our petitions before our Father in heaven.
Reader (s)
1. That we grow in our appreciation of the creation as having come into being through the Son through whom all things were made. Lord hear us.
2. That we grow in our appreciation that we are part of God's creation. Lord hear us.
3. That we grow in our appreciation that we are to be the stewards of creation and called to praise its creator day by day for his marvels of wisdom and power. Lord hear us.
4. That we grow in our appreciation that we must respect the creation, care for our environment, and seek to waste nothing that has been given to us. Lord hear us.
5. That we grow in our appreciation that we must commit ourselves to protecting life and all creation, be it water, earth, or air, and know the limits set by wisdom. Lord hear us.
6. That we grow in our appreciation that the fullness of the creation is life in God's presence, and we pray that all who have died may come to the fullness of life. Lord hear us.
President
Father, we see your loving goodness in your creation, which has

come into being through your Word, now made flesh. Hear us, your stewards, for we make our prayers through that same Word made flesh, Jesus, our Lord. Amen.

Eucharistic Prayer
Preface of Ordinary Time V (P33) is a succinct expression of the theology of creation that accords with Job 38. It works well with Eucharistic Prayer III which has the notion of the praise of God ascending from the rising of the sun to its setting. This is better expressed if the phrase 'so that from east to west a perfect sacrifice ...' is read as 'so that from the rising of the sun to its setting a perfect sacrifice ... ' (*ut a solis ortu usque ad occasum oblatio ... offeratur ...*)

Invitation to the Our Father
Let us pray that the Father's will be done on earth as it is in heaven:

Sign of Peace
With a word Jesus brought peace to the stormy waters: let us celebrate the peace he can bring into our hearts.

Invitation to Communion
The Lord has called us to share his table and with him to offer thanks to the Father. Happy are we who are gathered for his supper.

Communion Reflection
The time after communion is intended to be a time of quietness and personal reflection on who we have become through our eating and drinking. We have engaged in an act of communion: we have been transformed by this eating and drinking, we are now the body of Christ – united with one another and with Jesus. However, for many people reflection is difficult – this may be the only structured moment of reflection in their week – and for others the silence can only be interpreted using the notion of a thanksgiving prayer 'for what they have received' or a mo-

ment of petitionary prayer to Jesus 'inside them'. The reflection is, however, the church's reflection as part of the church's liturgy and, therefore, should focus on who we have become (private individual prayer is a matter for afterwards). But such reflection usually needs to be given focus and be led.

Today, one simple way is to re-read the gospel – just the text, no greeting or conclusion or ceremony – in a meditative way as an account of the Lord being with his people and encouraging them. This re-reading should be done in a low, calm voice, and so as to give the sense of it being an aid to reflection has to be done from 'off stage' (i.e. read by someone who is not seen reading, but simply heard). This means it cannot be done by the presider, nor by anyone at the ambo. Since there is a preponderance of male voices in the liturgy from the gospel onwards, this reflective reading is, preferably, done by a woman sitting among the community.

Conclusion

We rejoice that God is our creator and ruler; may he renew us and keep us in his love. Amen.

We rejoice that God has called us to be stewards of creation; may we live responsibly and wisely in the coming week. Amen.

We rejoice that God has shown us his generosity; may we continue our thankfulness right through this week. Amen.

Notes

1. Our liturgy must express our ecological concerns both as creatures – 'citizens of the planet' – and as Christians – people who profess that 'through him all things were made'. But trying to combine this with the Sunday liturgy is often something that is difficult: the liturgical cycles are more geared to celebrating the history of salvation rather than our place within the creation. However, this is one Sunday when a link between the liturgy and the theology of creation is neither forced nor arbitrary. Therefore, this is the day to celebrate those groups within the community who are involved in promoting sustainability, care of the environment, recycling, and 'the green church.'

2. There is a coincidental link between today's gospel where Jesus is presented as the Lord of creation and the second reading where we hear 'in Christ, there is a new creation.' This coincidence makes it tempting to announce that there is a common theme to all three readings; but this temptation should be avoided as it only reinforces the erroneous notion that this is always the case with the readings in Ordinary Time.

COMMENTARY

First Reading: Job 38:1, 8-11

Job 38 stands within the book as a treatise apart: it is a complex cosmology based on a belief in a creator who is wholly transcendent of the universe and, so, is on the one hand 'always greater' (note the old shorthand: *Deus semper maior*) and on the other, a creator who depends on nothing apart from himself (expressed, if not often correctly understood, in the shorthand: *creatio ex nihilo*). The God of the people of Israel cannot be reduced to being one more actor in a cosmological process, nor imagined as if there was 'god' and a primeval chaos which this supreme principle gives order to. Rather the whole of creation stands in an absolute dependence on him, and so his words, which brought it into being in the beginning, can now control it. This section of Job has been chopped up to get the little bit that seems to parallel the gospel. Perhaps if the environment was a larger concern in the late 1960s when the lectionary was compiled, they would have proposed reading verses 1 to 11 as today's first reading.

Psalm: 106 (107)

This is the classic 'sea' psalm: the power of God as Lord of creation is seen in the mighty waters of the sea: he controls the might of the sea with a word from his mouth.

Second Reading: 2 Cor 5:14-7

This reading only makes sense in terms of the larger framework of this part of the letter (5:11-6:10), where Paul wants to set out the purpose of his ministry. As it stands we have to read it as a series of 'sound bites': e.g. 'The love of Christ overwhelms us' (JB version)/'The love of Christ urges us on' (a more accurate translation, as well as the motto of many religious orders); or 'In Christ there is a new creation.' Such sound bites do little to convey any sense of the riches of Paul's theology or that reading his letters can help us today as disciples.

First Reading > Gospel Links
The link can be seen at two levels: on a simple level we have the common factor that in three readings (first, psalm, and gospel) God can control the might of the creation, seen in the power of the sea, with his voice.

However, at a more profound level the combination of readings conveys the continuity between the two covenants, whereby the Anointed One brings the first covenant to its completion. The first reading reminds us that God is the Lord of creation in that the sea obeys his laws; in the gospel the lord of creation speaks with his human voice – and the sea obeys him – for he has entered the creation as the Word made flesh. This combination of readings draws on a wealth of our christology which indeed may be far more embracing than anything Mark preached.

Gospel: Mk 4:35-41
This story is taken up by both Matthew (8:23-7) and Luke (8:22-5), but is preserved in its most perfect form in Mark, and only in Mark does Jesus utter words – Be at peace! Be still! – which effect his will within the creation. Those who heard Mark and came from a Jewish background would have recalled the manner in which the divine power was expressed in passages like Job 38, and seen in this a witness to Jesus's divine identity. Those who came from a Mediterranean background would have remembered that kings claimed to be such divine figures that even the powers of the sea were in awe of them. It is this sort of hyperbole that is ridiculed in 2 Macc 9:8: 'Thus [King Antiochus] who only a little while before had thought in his superhuman arrogance that he could command the waves of the sea, and had imagined

that he could weigh the high mountains in a balance, was brought down to earth and carried in a litter, making the power of God manifest to all.' It is worth remembering that 2 Macc comes from the same milieu that many of the early Christians came from; therefore, this is a theme that would have resonated deeply for them.

Unlike even Moses, Jesus does not pray to God to calm the sea but simply commands it and it recognises its Lord (implication: if the sea can know who Jesus is, you too should be able); unlike the greatest earthly kings who can only boast falsely of their power over the sea, Jesus can actually order it about (implication: you should recognise that here truly is 'the great king').

HOMILY NOTES

1. The miracle of Jesus stilling the sea has been an embarrassment to many western Christians since the late-eighteenth century. All miracles became simply frauds for the simple, but while (1) 'healing miracles' could be tolerated as somehow linked to religion as personal, or psychological, phenomena, and (2) 'feeding miracles' could be passed over as having a moral to teach us – they could be reduced to Jesus preaching famine relief and seeking to develop social awareness among his followers, that third group, the 'nature miracles' (and this was seen as the worst example of the type) were seen as wholly the product of a naïve, superstitious and gullible age. Miracles like that in today's gospel were, for liberals, to be quietly forgotten as belonging to the silly end of religion. At the other extreme were the fundamentalists, where proving the occurrence of an actual event two thousand years ago became the focus of attention: truth was simply 'did it happen?'

2. The truth of the gospel lies in that it can lead us towards God, a mysterious leading that involves a fuller understanding of God's universe, a fuller engagement as human beings within the universe, and towards a fuller life in union with God. So does this story help us? Hearing this story should help us to

reflect in three distinct ways on our identity and way of life as the community of Jesus.

3. First, we have a tendency to be so busy working in the creation that we forget its creator. Moreover, we hear so often that Jesus is a 'moral leader' that we forget that while non-Christians might see him as just one more teacher, for us, his people, he is the Son of God living among us, he is the Word through whom 'all things were made'. We not only greet him as a teacher and guide, but we greet him as the Lord of all creation. It is because Jesus is the Word made flesh, and, as we profess in the creed, it is in him that all things came into being, that we Christians cannot be indifferent to any abuses or destruction of the environment.

4. Second, we move through life as Christians, not just a bunch of individuals, but as a community that is cared for by the Lord. The disciples in the boat calling on the Lord remind us that we are a community who call upon the Lord to help us in our distress. When we call out Lord have mercy, Christ have mercy, Lord have mercy, we are engaging in the same activity as the disciples in the boat who called on him when they were frightened.

5. Third, because we are disciples of the Christ, the Lord of the creation, we are called to acknowledge our human duty to be stewards of creation. We are supposed to be the people who have a very clear and precise appreciation of the value and beauty of the creation. This means that today we should be in the forefront of reminding people of the importance of caring for the earth.

6. When we hear this gospel as if it were a 'news item', we ask questions about whether we think something happened long ago on a little lake in Palestine; when we as a community of disciples hear this with our hearts and our minds, we recall:

- who we are as a people;
- what we profess about Jesus;
- what we must do as inhabitants of the planet.

Thirteenth Sunday of Ordinary Time

Introduction to the Celebration

Every Sunday is a little 'Easter Sunday': because Jesus rose on Sunday, triumphant over death, we gather on Sundays. We gather to rejoice and celebrate his meal: he died, yet he lives; he has departed from us, yet also he is here among us.

To celebrate that Jesus rose from the dead is to celebrate that in him is our victory over suffering, pain, and death itself.

In proclaiming that the Father raised Jesus from the dead, we are stating our conviction that all those parts of life that strike us as absurd and destructive are not part of the Father's will for us: death is not of God's doing, and the Father has sent among us a healer who restores us to the fullness of life.

Jesus is risen, Jesus is amongst us, let us rejoice.

Note: The alternative form of the Opening Prayer ('Father in heaven ... ') is more appropriate today.

Rite of Penance

Lord Jesus, you healed the woman suffering from the haemorrhage; may we all know your healing. Lord have mercy.

Lord Jesus, you forgave all who came to you with faith; may we hear your words: 'Go in peace and be free of your complaint.' Christ have mercy.

Lord Jesus, you restored life to the daughter of Jairus; may we too all receive your gift of new life. Lord have mercy.

Headings for Readings

First Reading

In the face of human misery, the sufferings of illness, and death itself, we proclaim our basic faith in the loving goodness of God who has made us in his own image.

Second Reading

Paul reminds the Christians who made up the church of Corinth that they have a duty as followers of Jesus to use their wealth to help those in need. Paul was organising a collection of money in the churches around the Mediterranean to help out Christians in Jerusalem who were in need due to a famine. Paul thought that the Corinthians were not pulling their weight in this collection and this reading is his plea to them to be more generous.

Gospel

The Lord is with us in all our moments of suffering, frustration and fear: from the Lord comes healing and new life.

Prayer of the Faithful

President

Standing together as the members of this church, in union with the Christ, let us pray to the Father for our needs, the needs of those who suffer, and the needs of all humanity.

Reader (s)

1. Let us pray for ourselves, and all Christians, that we will bring healing and new life to all the situations in which we live. Lord hear us.

2. Let us pray for all the member of this church who are suffering, who are housebound, who are fearful or worried, that they may experience the closeness of the Christ. Lord hear us.

3. Let us pray for all who are suffering, for all who are in need of healing, that our hearts, and those of our brothers and sisters may be opened to helping them. Lord hear us.

4. Let us pray for who care for the sick, those who belong to the caring professions, those who care for loved ones, those who care for others in the community, that God will give them strength and that they may see the face of Christ in those they serve. Lord hear us.

5. Specific local needs and topics of the day.

6. Let us pray for all who have passed from this life, that they may have the fullness of healing and life in God's presence. Lord hear us.

President
Father, we look to you for all we need. Hear us, and grant us
healing and new life in Christ Jesus, our Lord. Amen.

Eucharistic Prayer
The Preface from the liturgy for an Anointing within Mass
(*Pastoral Care of the Sick*, pp 114-5) is ideal for today; then
Eucharistic Prayer II with the special addition (*Pastoral Care of
the Sick*, p 115).

Invitation to the Our Father
Let us pray that we shall be delivered from evil, suffering, and
death, as we say:

Sign of Peace
Christ's coming among us announces the reign of reconciliation
and healing: let us celebrate this with one another.

Invitation to Communion
The Lord Jesus stands among us with healing, strength, and new
life; happy are we who share his supper.

Communion Reflection
In some communities it is the standard practice to have ministers who bring communion from the community's Eucharist to
the sick and housebound members of the community. And in
some places this is done with some ceremony both to highlight
the importance of this ministry, and to express the interconnec-
tion between 'communion' in the sense of sharing in the
Eucharist and 'communion' in the sense of the communion of
the church. Moreover, this practice can be traced back to, at
least, the mid-second century, and stands as the remote prede-
cessor of the whole notion of the 'Blessed Sacrament'. So on a
day when we confront Jesus being called to the house where
there is one who is sick, it would be inappropriate if we were not
(1) carrying on the practice of linking sick people into the church

through being brought a share in our banquet, (2) seen to bring the care of Jesus to those too sick or infirm to join us, and (3) doing this with due acknowledgement in some sort of sending forth ritual which shows the concern we as a community have for the sick.

If there is not already a ritual for sending ministers to the housebound, to those who are known to be sick, or to local care-homes and hospitals, then you could use something like this:

1. When everyone has returned to their seats after communion, have the purifications of chalices, ciboria and the like done by a minister privately, away from the Eucharistic table. Leave one ciborium in front of the place where the presider stands at the table.

2. The ministers who are going to bring communion should then come and stand immediately to the right and left of the presider. This should show they are taking communion from this, our table, to the house of the sick: they are not being given a sacred commodity from the tabernacle.

3. The presider then can address them:

Brothers and sisters, this church charges us to take a share of our holy meal to those other sisters and brothers who cannot be with us here today. Bring them our love and prayer. Help them to share our joy in Jesus Christ who brings healing and life. Link them to us and to the Lord through this holy communion.

4. Then each minister in turn takes particles from the ciborium and puts them in their pyx or corporal.

5. When each have done this, the presider requests they depart with 'Go in peace.'

6. The ministers then set off walking through the assembly.

7. The presider moves to his chair for the post communion prayer, while another minister takes the ciborium to the tabernacle.

Conclusion

Solemn Blessing 13 (Ordinary Time IV), Missal, p 373, is suitable.

Notes

The longer form of the gospel

Today's gospel looks like, at first sight, a story with an interruption in it: there is the opening of the story of Jairus's daughter, then an intrusion with another little episode, and then we get back to where we left off. Clearly, this sort of thinking influenced some of the compilers of the lectionary and they put brackets around the incident of the woman with 'the flow of blood' and so created a 'shorter form' of today's gospel. However, in offering this opportunity to shorten the liturgy by approximately 90 seconds, they have created the possibility that the creative tension of Mark's preaching is lost, and an important aspect of his christology ignored (see commentary on the gospel).

So, why should you opt for the longer form?

1. Part of the fundamental rationale of our Sunday lectionary is that we hear the distinctive voices of each of the evangelists: in today's gospel we hear the very distinctive voice of Mark (whose voice is the most hidden as we imagine that all he had to say has been absorbed by Matthew) and so cutting that distinctiveness by using 'the shorter form' subverts the very purpose of having a three-year cycle.

2. The story of the woman, as Mark tells it (this would not be true of either Matthew's or Luke's re-use of the story) is most accessible to people listening in the assembly. We can hear her desperation, her frustration, her fear, and even how marginalised she feels. When it is a widely held popular notion that the gospels no longer speak to our situation in life, this story has immense value. Here is a little incident that speaks to most human beings either for themselves or those they love.

3. Stories of women do not figure in the tradition in proportion to their presence in the community of the faithful: indeed, many hold that the memory of ordinary women is continually sidelined within Christianity. Given that people have access to books/booklets that show both long and short variants, if one omits this story, what silent message does this decision send out?

4. The whole Markan unit (vv 21-43) – and it is a unit in Mark – was chopped about in both Matthew and Luke, so today we have these stories in their most complete, and comprehensible form.

5. If the decision does come down to the importance of saving 90 seconds, then drop 90 seconds from the homily (Mark is still better value as a preacher than most of us).

COMMENTARY

First Reading: Wisdom 1:13-5; 2:23-4

This book, the Wisdom of Solomon, was written in Alexandria very shortly before the time of Jesus. Part of its objective was to create a credible theodicy for a monotheism (i.e. God is absolutely unique, and upon him the universe depends), such as we profess, in distinction from a henotheism (there is one divine being in the universe). If God is absolute goodness, and the absolute source of being, then how does one account for evil, suffering, and death?

This is made all the more problematic if one believes in the goodness of the creation as coming from God and that human beings can be brought into relationship with God because they are made in God's image and likeness (Wisdom echoing and interpreting Gen 1).

The solution adopted is to see God's original plan as having been perverted by the envy of the enemy with death and suffering being the result of this intruder's work (here Wisdom involves a re-reading of Gen 3 as the classic temptation followed by the fall story). This theodicy then provides a background for a more general theology of sin/death which lies behind much early Christian theology: Jesus is the one who contends with the devil and conquers evil; Jesus is also the one who refashions humanity and destroys death. As read here with the gospel, Jesus is presented as the one who restores humanity to the original divine plan.

The JB translation presented in most copies of the lectionary is especially incompetent: use the NRSV and omit the word 'for' at the beginning of 2:23 so that it reads as a single passage.

Psalm: 29 (30)

This psalm stresses our need for God's gift of healing and new life, and that in our need we cry to him for help. But we should note that while calling on God for help it is not just a cry for help, it is also a prayer of praise for God's goodness.

Second Reading: 2 Cor 8:7, 9, 13-5

As it is edited in the lectionary this reading is a mix of pious sound bites and a call for Christians to realise that part of being a Christian is the need to open one's purse! The background is that this part of 2 Cor is a collage of short letters which seek to persuade, encourage, and embarrass the church in Corinth to be as generous as the Macedonians have been (the logical unit of text is 8:1-15) in the collection Paul is making for the poor Christians in Jerusalem. His underlying theology is that Jesus has been generous with us; we should be generous with our possessions; now the Macedonians have understood this, so why not you?

First Reading > Gospel Links

The relationship of the God of love to suffering humanity is set out as formal teaching in the first reading; it is then exemplified in the gospel when Jesus restores health and life. Taken together, these readings express the unity of the two Covenants.

Gospel: Mk 5:21-43

This story, found in its most complete form in Mark, is a unity and a masterpiece of narrative: the tension mounts in both the story of Jairus's daughter and in the woman with the flow of blood, so that is it only in the second 'half' of each story we see the Christ show his mercy. Yet at the end of the story, Mark's messianic secret comes back yet again: the Lord has come among us with healing and new life, but we shall only understand the Lord's life and ministry if we hold off speaking about him until we know his end on the cross.

HOMILY NOTES

1. The simple didactic homily has been the bed-rock of preaching down the centuries. In the last few decades it has fallen into an unmerited obscurity partly because the meditation / reflection sermon has gained a new prominence, partly because the 'challenge of discipleship' style has been seen as a way of showing up the radical nature of the gospel, and partly as we have moved to more exegetical style homilies. Today, we have a very structured unit of Mark's preaching and it was formulated by him with close attention to how fear acts on us as human beings. Because it grasps attention so well, it can be followed with a little bit of didache such as this:

2. This story makes visible for us three of our basic beliefs as disciples of Jesus.

First, that the Son of God, the Lord is one with us, he knows 'from the inside our fears' and anxieties, our needs, our nature. God, for us Christians, is not thought of as some far-off energy or power, he has come close to us in a human individual: Jesus.

We can paraphrase the creed like this:

* For us human beings and our health and well-being
* he has come down from heaven,
* and by the power of the holy Spirit has become a man
* who was named Jesus.

Second, we look to Jesus as the source of healing, of forgiveness, of reconciliation, and of hope.

Jairus and that woman – both making requests of Jesus because of their desperate situation – are typical of all of us who call upon him in our need.

We believe that Jesus is with us and one with us, we call on him for mercy and healing and forgiveness.

We acknowledge Jesus as

* the one who brings us healing: we call him 'the divine physician'
* the one who brings us forgiveness: we call him 'our redeemer'
* the one who brings us peace: we call him 'the prince of peace.'

That is why we who are his disciples get involved with:

- helping and caring for the sick
- promoting understanding and reconciliation
- working as peace makers.

Third, Jesus is the one who has risen from the dead and shares his resurrection with us.

Jesus has conquered sin and death:

- that is why we are the people of the resurrection
- that is why we gather on Sunday to celebrate
- that is why we are the people of the good news.

Fourteenth Sunday of Ordinary Time

Introduction to the Celebration

When we assemble each week on Sunday, we are continuing an earlier tradition of God's people who met on Saturday – the Sabbath. For the Jews, the Sabbath was, and is, the day to rejoice in the goodness of God in creating the universe, and our human family. The first Christians moved the celebration to Sunday as this day was seen as the day of resurrection: God's great act of restoring and renewing the creation in Jesus.

But whether it is celebrating the creation of all by God, or the renewal of all in Christ, the celebrations have some common elements: the people are to recall God's love in a meal and in reading the scriptures. For the Jews, the meal takes place in their homes on Friday evenings and they gather on Saturday to hear the Law and pray. We listen to the scriptures first, what we call the New Law, and then have our meal together here.

Today we recall that Jesus entered the assembly on the Sabbath in his home town; we believe that he is here among us in this assembly today. Let us recall his presence, and pray that he may find us a community of faith.

Rite of Penance

Lord Jesus, you are our teacher. Lord have mercy.
Lord Jesus, you are our prophet. Christ have mercy.
Lord Jesus, you are our healer. Lord have mercy.

Headings for Readings
First Reading

The prophet is the one charged by God to go to his people and show them the way that leads to life.

Second Reading

We are often told to look at our problems 'philosophically'. Paul will have none of that idea. Rather, when he looks at his own weakness and his chronic illness (we do not know what sort of illness it was) he is glad because it shows that it is the power of Christ – not his own skills – that brings people to the good news.

Gospel
The people were baffled for they encountered one they knew as the guy next door, but also heard the wisdom of God made present among them.

Prayer of the Faithful
President
Jesus is amongst us in this assembly. With him we now pray to the Father for our needs, the needs of the whole Christian people, the needs of the world, and for those with special needs today.

Reader (s)
1. For our local church which assembles here each Sunday, that we shall be a faithful community of disciples. Lord hear us.
2. For the whole church gathering today in some many places around the globe, that we will all hear the Lord teaching us the way to the Father. Lord hear us.
3. For those who hold authority and responsibility in the world, that they may act with wisdom and justice towards humanity, the animal kingdom, and the environment. Lord hear us.
4. For those who are in need of healing, of comfort, and of new hope, that the Lord's healing and wisdom may enter their lives. Lord hear us.
5. Specific local needs and topics of the day.
6. For all who are poor, who are victims of injustice, or who are suffering for their beliefs, that the Lord will help them, and move our hearts to help them. Lord hear us.

President
Father, your Son is among us in this assembly as once he was present in an assembly in his home town, so hear us in him as you heard him then, and grant us wisdom, help, healing, and peace. Amen.

Eucharistic Prayer
No preface or Eucharistic Prayer is particularly suitable. However, Eucharistic Prayer IV has a summary of the work of Jesus that is somewhat analogous to the summary in today's gospel. There is now a formal permission to use this prayer on Sundays, and since it is not widely known, this is a good day to use it.

The one Eucharistic Prayer that should not be used today is Eucharistic Prayer I with its reference to Mary being 'the ever-virgin mother' of Jesus, for to use it today is just to create dissonance in the minds of those who hear it.

Invitation to the Our Father
It is the Spirit dwelling within us that empowers us to call on the Father, as we say:

Sign of Peace
Through our relationship with Jesus, each of us here has become part of a family of brothers and sisters. Conscious of this new set of relationships, let us greet one another and offer peace to one another.

Invitation to Communion
Behold, the Lord has called us into his own house and made us members of his family. Happy are we who are called to his supper.

Communion Reflection
Have a structured silence. Introduce it with something like this: When Jesus entered the synagogue on the Sabbath he caused astonishment to those who heard him in that assembly. Let us reflect in silence for just one minute that we are in his presence now in this assembly.

Then measure off a minute on the clock, rise and conclude the silence with the 'Let us pray' of the concluding prayer.

Conclusion

The Lord Jesus came among us teaching us the way to the Father. May his wisdom enlighten you today. Amen.

The Lord Jesus came among us as a prophet bearing witness to the Father's love. May you be his witnesses in these days. Amen.

The Lord Jesus came among us curing the sick. May he lay his hands through you on all whom you will meet that are in need of healing, comfort, or help during this week. Amen.

Notes

1. The names of Jesus's brothers

In the JB version found in many lectionaries the names given for Jesus's brothers is James, Joset, Jude, and Simon. This reading 'Joset' is, among English translations, peculiar to this version and has much to recommend it as a rendering of *Ióséthos*. However, the generally accepted form of the name in English is 'Joses' (cf Mk 6:3 in the NRSV: 'Is not this the carpenter, the son of Mary and brother of James and Joses and Judas and Simon, and are not his sisters here with us?'). It is probably best to use 'Joses'. There is already enough confusion over the names of Jesus's brothers (compare Mk 6:3 which reads 'the son of Mary and brother of James and Joses and Judas and Simon, and are not his sisters here with us?', with Mt 13:55 which reads: 'Is not his mother called Mary? And are not his brothers James and Joseph and Simon and Judas?').

2. The question of Mary's perpetual virginity

It is the established position of the Roman Catholic and Orthodox churches – and of individuals in other churches – that Mary was not only a virgin at the time she conceived Jesus (which is all that is affirmed in Lk 1:27 and the creeds), this is the *virginitas ante partum* ('virginity before parturition'), but also that her virginity was not destroyed in the act of Jesus passing through her body from the womb – this is what is referred to as the *virginitas in partu* ('virginity during the act of parturition'). This was necessary as virginity was defined in pre-modern medicine not simply as not having had sex with a man, but never having any object within the vagina; therefore, this virginity was seen as a second miraculous intervention by God: the first was the virgin conceiving, and the second was the birth of a child without the physical state of virginity being destroyed. But there was also a third virginity: the *virginitas post partum* ('virginity after parturition'): that Mary never had sexual intercourse after the birth of Jesus, and thus she could be described as *aeiparthenos, Maria semper virgo*, Mary 'ever virgin'. That being taken as a fact, what was one to do with the many references in the gospels and elsewhere to the fact that Jesus was understood to belong to a family and his mother to have been the mother of at least seven children: Jesus, four brothers, and several (therefore, at least, two) sisters?

Since the notion that the gospel writers could be mistaken was not entertained, some way had to be found to explain away the references and the most usual set of explanations for the Western churches were those generated by Jerome in the late-fourth and early-fifth centuries. However, there never was any single explanation, for Jerome tacitly admitted that he was grasping at straws to explain away the obvious: this admission was made in that he found new explanations as he got older and abandoned earlier ones. In the face of this discrepancy between beliefs about Mary – ever more deeply embedded in her cult – and the gospel texts, discretion seemed the best course and these gospel readings never appeared in the liturgy and were further hidden, in that the gospel texts were in Latin and increasingly beyond access except to those who had already been given one or other of Jerome's explanations as an exegetical fact. Therefore, the problem only became visible for Catholics in the 1970s.

There is no simple answer: even conservative biblical scholars accept that Mary was the mother of many children and that Jesus grew up in a sizable family, yet the liturgy still greets Mary as 'ever virgin'. There is no substitute for an honest answer.

In the world of late antiquity, there was a deep-seated notion that virginity was a sacral state in its own right. The Greco-Roman religious world believed that virgins had mystical religious power to have their prayers and sacrifice answered by God. Jerome himself refers to the Greek legend of Iphigenia as indicative that even the pagan Greeks had an inchoate awareness of God's preference for virgins. The Homeric legend is that Agamemnon needed a fair wind to sail his fleet to Troy. The seer told him that only if he sacrificed a virgin could the gods be induced to help him. The only woman of whose virginity he was certain was that of his own daughter, Iphigenia. She was murdered and as her body was beginning to burn, they noticed a slight wind carrying the smoke sideways, so off they ran to the ships, and the rest is history!

In point of fact, Jerome is merely taking his own culture's obsession with the notion of virginity as intrinsically sacred and projecting it into Christian cult. In other words, it was so abhorrent to his cultural values as a late Roman citizen, embedded in the classical legends even if this part of his culture shocked him, that he could not imagine Mary being a holy servant of God and also engaging in sexual intercourse with her husband. Once this idea had gained currency, it spread like wildfire, but now today we recognise it as just one way that the gospel can become so embedded in our social culture that it is mutated by it. So the muddle should teach us three lessons:

(1) the gospel must become culture, not culture become the gospel;

(2) the church is always forgetting and always remembering its past; and

(3) we will only understand all truth at the eschaton.

On the other hand, no one in the community may raise this problem with you – but this may not be a good thing: it could be that no one is listening carefully to the gospel nor thinking about it.

COMMENTARY

First Reading: Ezek 2:2-5
This is part of the opening section (which extends from 1:28 to 3:11) of the book that deals with the call of the prophet and the nature of the prophet's task. The prophet must convey the

Lord's message, his judgement and deliverance, to the people whether they want to listen or not. The prophet must expect rejection, and the reason for this is that the people who need his message have hardened hearts which are the product of their disobedience.

The prophet is addressed as 'son of man' (a title used for the recipient of the Lord's message throughout the book) and this title emphasises that contrast between God (who speaks) and the prophet: the prophet is not giving his own message or judgement, but conveying that which is told him.

Psalm: 122 (123)

The rationale for this choice of psalm seems to be found in the third verse: it is the prayer for mercy from those whose hearts are hardened, filled with contempt, scorn and disdain. That is the group who have failed to listen to the prophet or who cannot see Jesus as anything more than the boy 'from up the street.'

So the psalm has to be used in the manner of a confession of guilt and plea for mercy; if someone sees herself/himself in the role of defiant/obstinate before God (on hearing the first reading), then this is the prayer for mercy of such a person.

Second Reading: 2 Cor 12:7-10

The first ten verses of chap 12 concern Paul's visions and revelations – and these are an important means by which he makes sense of his life and vocation (as can be seen in the way a revelation is used in the middle of this lection). The 'thorn' appears to be some sort of physical or psychological ailment; while his 'weakness' appears to be a way of showing that his power is God's working in him rather than his own prowess.

First Reading > Gospel Links

The relationship is based on the persistence of patterns in human reactions to God's initiatives. The prophet Ezekiel is warned that his words will be rejected; the prophet Jesus is rejected by those who hear him preach.

Gospel: Mk 6:1-6

In this short unit of text, Mark summarises several themes that he has already preached in his gospel: the question of discipleship and faith; Jesus as teacher; Jesus as miracle worker/healer; and Jesus as the prophet. Now his gospel reaches a climactic moment. At the end of all his teaching and miracles in Galilee we have a snapshot of reaction to him: his home town, Nazareth, rejects him. This rejection by his own people, his own people in the sense of those he grew up with, those who knew him and his family, presages the greater rejection that comes at the crucifixion.

Underlying the whole scene is the question of what is it to know Jesus and accept him, and this question is framed in terms of faith. They cannot accept this individual as a prophet even if they are amazed at him, and their rejection is seen as unbelief.

HOMILY NOTES

1. Who are we following when we say we are 'Christians'?
The question seems so obvious that most of us think it a silly question even to ask: it's obviously 'Jesus', isn't it? But the question is not silly, nor is the answer obvious, because who Jesus is and what he means to us is far from obvious. Indeed, it is because it is anything but obvious that there have been so many disputes down the centuries among Christians, and there is a whole branch of Christian theology called 'christology'.

2. Let us begin by noting that most people like 'to keep it simple' – and that means they imagine there should be a simple answer to the question 'who is Jesus?' – but the reality is that life is complex, and the more any issue involves human beings, the more complex life becomes. Everyone knows that her/his human relationships are complex – how many of us can say 'I know myself!' – so why think that understanding Jesus is easy?

3. The situation recorded in today's gospel shows a reaction that must have been widespread: the local people have Jesus in one box in their imaginations: he is the guy from down the road – they know him, his brothers and sisters, and his background. For anyone who comes from their town they have a box for what

they expect for and from that person: fine to get him to do a job for you, fine to go to the well with his sisters, fine to engage with them socially. That's all there is to them: another family, just like us, and they should not think of themselves as anything special. So if Jesus stands up and presents himself as a leader, that is just not on!

On the other hand, they have heard him in the synagogue: he comes across as one filled with wisdom, he is a teacher like they have heard, he speaks in a way they have always imagined a prophet would speak. They have another box marked 'prophet' and he seems to fit there too! But that box comes with a label: prophets are very distant from everyday life, they are exceptional in every way, they are 'not like us'.

So when these people find that Jesus ticking both the box marked 'prophet' and ticking the box marked 'ordinary bloke'/ 'regular guy'/'one of our own,' they cannot cope with this complexity. So, since they are more sure that he is the guy down the road, they reject him as a prophet.

4. Faith is the ability to imagine that God's goodness is greater and closer than the bits-and-pieces around us and the ups-and-downs of life. In this case, faith was the ability to imagine that God was so close that Jesus was both the guy from down the road and the great prophet and the wise teacher and more besides. But the group could not make that leap of imagination – and Jesus was amazed at their lack of faith.

5. Would we have been among that group that could not imagine that God's goodness was that close?

6. Surely not! After all, we are Christians, who publicly declare our faith in Jesus each week in the creed.

7. But we have problems of our own in imagining the goodness of God coming close to us in Jesus.

8. For many people, it is fine to think of Jesus as a wise teacher – a proclaimer of great religious or moral truths – and as such one who should inspire us to high ideals. This is all true, but is there a label on that box which says: 'Not needed on a day-to-day basis in life'?

Jesus is a wise teacher, but he also calls us to become united with him for it is through him we come into the presence of the Father. We do not just listen to Jesus, we relate to him in prayer and living, and with him we are brought to the fullness of life which is larger/greater/beyond the whole universe we see around us.

9. For many people is it fine to think of Jesus as a central part of religion, he is the named focus of devotion, his image is everywhere, and when we see crosses and the like they remind us of the religious dimension of life and the 'great certainty' of death and the importance of religion. But the box marked 'religion' often comes with labels like: 'Religion is useful to make me feel better' or 'Religion is useful for society.' In other words, Jesus is just part of the *status quo*! This is all true: religion does make people happier and it is a stabilising factor in society, but Jesus is also the prophet who comes proclaiming the closeness of the kingdom of God and this is disruptive. Jesus is disruptive because his is the kingdom of truth (as opposed to illusion which is so often used to control people), justice (as opposed to a culture of greed), and peace (as opposed to rule of fear and might). Jesus the prophet does not fit any cosy box for those who want a quiet life for themselves or others.

10. The people who heard Jesus in his home town found it hard to cope with all he is – and for many it was too hard. It is not easy for us either: to follow Jesus is to be always trying to delve deeper into the mystery of who he is.

Lectionary Unit II.III

This stage of the second unit (whose overall theme is the Mystery of Jesus being progressively revealed) focuses on Jesus's manifestation of himself.

This stage is unusual in the lectionary for Ordinary Time in that it is made up of sections from John as well as Mark. It begins with two Sundays (15-16) where Jesus gives The Twelve their mission and then manifests compassion on the crowds. This mention of crowds around Jesus is then the cue for a five-Sunday selection from Jn 6 on the Eucharist (see the note, below, on 'John's Gospel in Mark's Year located between Sunday 16 and Sunday 17'). The stage then concludes with two more pericopes from Mark on Sundays 22 and 23.

Fifteenth Sunday of Ordinary Time

Introduction to the Celebration

We assemble as a people who have been called to be bearers of God's love to all humanity. Each of us is called to be a witness to God's presence in the world in some unique way in some unique part of the creation. Each of us has been sent out by the Christ to proclaim good news, announce forgiveness, and to build the kingdom of peace. This is the reality of vocation. And thinking about and celebrating our individual vocations is something we are going to do today.

Rite of Penance

Lord Jesus, you have called us to be your witnesses. For those times when we have failed to proclaim the good news, Lord have mercy.

Lord Jesus, you have called us to announce forgiveness. For those times when we have failed to practise repentance and reconciliation, Christ have mercy.

Lord Jesus, you have called us to be peacemakers. For those times when we have failed to bring healing and peace to our world, Lord have mercy.

Headings for Readings

First Reading

Amos was not part of the official religious leadership, he was not a professional prophet, indeed he was agricultural labourer looking after sheep and gathering food for cattle. Yet, he was called by God to preach his message to his people.

See the note below about the need to make this reading clearer.

Second Reading

Today we read one of the earliest Christian hymns that have come down to us. It is a hymn of praise of God the Father, and to appreciate it we need to start out with this question in our minds: for what aspect of his goodness to us does this hymn bless God the Father?

Gospel

Up to this point in St Mark's gospel, Jesus has been proclaiming the good news and bringing healing and forgiveness. Now he shared his vocation with the Twelve and sends them out. They are the first group he sent out, and in that first mission we can glimpse the call and task Jesus gives each of us.

Prayer of the Faithful
President

Friends, we have gathered here, different individuals with separate and unique vocations, as the priestly people of Jesus. Now, in union with the Lord, let us intercede for ourselves, the people we encounter, the universal church, and all humanity.

Reader (s)

1. For this church gathered for this Eucharist, that each and every one of us grows in awareness of our unique vocation within God's people. Lord hear us.

2. For all the people whom members of this church meet in their daily lives, that they may encounter good news, healing and peace of the Christ through us. Lord hear us.

3. For the whole church, that every Christian may be given a new insight into his or her vocation given in baptism and the strength to carry out his or her mission. Lord hear us.

4. For Christians everywhere, that we appreciate the unique sets of gifts each person has received from the Holy Spirit. Lord hear us.

President

Father, your Spirit empowers us to be the body of your Son. As his people we call on you: hear our prayers and help us to follow our vocations in Christ Jesus, our Lord. Amen.

Eucharistic Prayer
Preface of Sundays in Ordinary Time I (P29) emphasises our
calling to be a priestly people who everywhere proclaim God's
mighty works. Eucharistic Prayer II works well with P29.

Invitation to the Our Father
The Lord Jesus has called each of us to become a daughter or son
of the Father, and so we can now pray together:

Sign of Peace
We are each called to be bringers of peace into the lives of those
we meet. Let us now strengthen the network of peace among us
here.

Invitation to Communion
The Lord has called each of us to a special vocation within the
kingdom. Now he calls all of us to his table to share in the banquet of the kingdom.

Communion Reflection
The 'Ephesian Hymn' – today's second reading – is a perfect reflection on us as the church having offered in union with Christ
the thanksgiving sacrifice to the Father. So read the hymn again
now – repetition helps us all to deepen our appreciation of these
texts.
   It is best read by one reader, slowly, and introduced as 'We
shall now use the ancient hymn of praise that we read in the second reading as our expression of praise and thanksgiving.'
   There are several musical settings for this hymn, but if it is to
function as a reflection it is best if it is sung as a solo piece.

Conclusion
You have been called by Jesus to proclaim his good news. May
you have the courage to fulfill your vocation during this week.
Amen.
You have been called by Jesus to be ministers of reconciliation.

May you have wisdom to fulfill your vocation during this week. Amen.

You have been called by Jesus to build the kingdom of peace and love. May you have the strength to fulfill your vocation during this week. Amen.

Notes

1. 'Sycamore trees' in the first reading

One of the annoying things about this reading is that anyone listening to it wonders why these sycamore trees need such careful looking after. We think of sycamores as big broad-leafed trees that are simply there, they do not need looking after, nor are they of any commercial importance. However, the JB has Amos 'looking after them' while the RSV has 'a dresser of sycamore trees' which immediately raises useless questions about what this is all about. The probable explanation (for we are rarely certain of how to translate plants' names) is that the Hebrew text refers to 'sycamore figs' which were used for cattle fodder. So the solution is to change the line so that it does not distract, thus: 'I was a shepherd and sought out fodder for cattle: but it was the Lord ...'

2. The shorter form of the second reading

This text, vv 3-14, is a unit. However, we have become accustomed to reading a shorter form (vv 3-10) in the Liturgy of the Hours, and this has prompted the suggestion of a shorter form today. Just because we habitually truncate this reading is not a good reason for chopping off the conclusion of a literary unity.

COMMENTARY

First Reading: Amos 7:12-5

The essential background to appreciating this reading is to recall what while we think of people called 'prophets' as outsiders (Jeremiah and Jesus being the great exemplars), for most of the time the word referred to a stable, institutional group within the religion of Israel. In actual fact, 'the prophets' (their use of the word) were not 'prophetic' (in our sense of the word), but part of the religious administration: operating the temple, keeping the rituals, performing the tasks that needed religious expertise such as examining foods or sicknesses or matters of the calendar – in fact, they were very like clergy in medieval Christianity.

What makes Amos stand out – and today's reading is at the core of his presentation of his own vocation – is the contrast between himself and this professional elite. He is the agricultural nobody, a field hand, who does not belong to any of the professional bodies, yet he acts as a prophet and tells the experts that they are corrupt. This is a paradigmatic example of vocation calling on the least expected person to act as the corrective to the divinely instituted establishment. Moreover, this story inserted into the whole of our tradition as the People of God the awareness that God's breath blows where it will and cannot be contained in human categories. There is always a 'random factor' in God's dealings with humanity which can upset any fixed idea of how God related to his people.

Psalm: 84 (85): 8-13

The verses for the psalm today do not pick up any specific theme in either the first reading or the gospel, as we read the psalm in the lectionary in The Grail translation. So why was it chosen? The answer lies in the very different tone and content of the first verse (v 8) of today's psalm in the original and its even more pronounced tone in the Vulgate: *audiam quid loquatur Dominus Deus loquetur enim pacem ad populum suum et ad sanctos suos ut non convertantur ad stultitiam* ('Oh! may I hear what the Lord, God, will speak; for he speaks peace to his people and to his holy ones, that they might turn their hearts from stupidity.') Read following the emphasis of the Latin, today's psalm is the prayer of Amos and, by extension, of any one who has a prophetic vocation – such as the members of The Twelve in the gospel, that he might hear the Lord's voice and know what he must preach.

Today is a good example of a recurring problem in the lectionary: the creators of the English lectionary just took over the numbers from the Latin *editio typica* without checking how the actual translations they have chosen relate to one another. Is there a solution? Either use the NRSV for this text or replace it with a hymn.

Second Reading: Eph 1:3-14
While often in the liturgy, especially the Liturgy of the Hours, we have treated vv 3-10 as a unit, the canticle *Benedictus Deus*, the actual unit in the letter is what we have in today's reading: vv 3-14. It is a 'blessing' hymn in a form that was clearly much appreciated in the early churches, as several examples are extant and needs to be read in its entirety to be appreciated.

It takes the form of a 'blessing' and it is God that is blessed – this is a concept we find difficult to get our heads around as we tend to think of 'praying' to God and of 'blessing' creatures (people or things) – in the sense of setting them apart and asking for divine protection for them. However, in both Judaism and early Christianity, it is God who is 'blessed' in that a 'good word' of praise for his goodness and love is spoken to him and about him. This is the notion that 'he who praises God prays well.'

So for what aspect of his goodness does this hymn bless God the Father? If we keep this question in mind and then read the text, the hymn explains itself.

First Reading > Gospel Links
The link is thematic: both readings are examples of vocation. In the first, an unexpected individual is called to proclaim God's love of justice; in the gospel, an unexpected group is called to proclaim the arrival of the good news.

Gospel: Mk 6:7-13
Mark intends this mission scene to be read at a number of levels. First, 'The Twelve' – this unique group that represent the whole of the new people are sent out and not only preach, but bring into existence, the new age of the kingdom. Thus the work of the Christ is extended in time and place by the new people. Second, this is a task that continues in the communities in that they make

the kingdom present in preaching, opening the possibility of repentance, casting our demons, and healing the sick. Third, within
the early church there were wandering preachers – such as our
evangelists – who were to be made welcome by the individual
churches. The checklist in reverse – namely a list of what they
are not to bring with them – reminds the churches of the duty of
hospitality.

The little reference to anointing the sick with oil is a glimpse
into the role the community was understood to have towards
the individuals who made it up.

HOMILY NOTES

1. Sometime between the Council of Trent (mid-sixteenth century) and the French Revolution (late-eighteenth century) a
   radical shift took place – almost without anyone noticing – in
   how priesthood, the other grades of Holy Orders, formal
   ministry, and vocation were viewed within Catholic spirituality. In effect, the notion of vocation, ministry, and order became coalesced into one package. This had the effect of removing the notion of vocation from all but priests. So, for example, if
   a man became a monk, it was assumed he would go 'all the
   way' and become a priest; meanwhile, the choice of becoming a religious brother, who was not a priest but could become one, became, for many, inexplicable. Similarly, although less obviously, individual Christians were not considered as having a vocation: they simply had jobs alongside
   of which they had religious obligations. When, in the early
   twentieth century, it was realised that a layperson might
   have a role in the work of Christ, this could no longer be
   handled with the notion of vocation, and therefore a new
   category called 'an apostolate' had to be invented. In short,
   clergy had vocations (some of which were in religious communities); women had vocations to religious life (they became nuns), while other people could have 'an apostolate'
   (but this was little more than some job or other that might fit
   with the practical agenda of the church).

2. Why this confusion arose is not our concern, but the sad fact is that the confusion is still widespread – and leads to many people not having any sense that they may have a unique role in God's plan of salvation. This confusion can be seen in the oft-heard prayer 'for an increase in vocations to the priesthood and religious life': if every one of the baptised has a vocation, how can there be an increase in the number of people with vocations? If every vocation is unique to a person, her talents, her situation, how can it be equated with a task that belongs to the very structure of the universal church? So clearing up some of this confusion is preaching the gospel. Why? Because, the message of today's readings is that every follower of Jesus is sent out to a different place to proclaim and enact the good news.

3. How does one tackle this deep-seated confusion within Catholic spirituality? The place to begin is to note that 'vocation' and 'ministry' are two distinct realities within the life of the People of God.

- Vocation relates to an individual and her/his life and work and witness. In the unique situation in time and space where I exist, I am called to be the presence of the love of God, a follower of his Christ, and a temple of his Spirit.

- Ministry relates to the services that the community of the church needs its members to perform towards one another so that it can fulfill the church's (as a single body) vocation to be the body of Christ and the People of God. These ministries are as diverse as the Petrine ministry and the person who distributes the newsletters, some relate to the sacred mysteries (e.g. the presbyterate) and some are transitory and needed in only some places at certain times.

   An individual's vocation includes her/his ministry; but one's vocation must never be reduced to being equated with one's ministry. For the individual, vocation is always more embracing, more all encompassing, and more demanding than any or all of the ministries she/he fulfills.

4. The task that faces every one of us, as baptised persons, is:

- to become conscious that we have a vocation,
- to become aware that we all have several sub-vocations linked to the various situations in which we live: as spouse, parent, child, friend, fellow worker ...,
- to discern what it calls for us to do,
- to value our unique talents,
- to grow in awareness of God's call as ever present in our lives,
- to become aware of how one's vocation changes as one's life-situation changes, and
- to pray for the help to fulfill one's vocations.

Moreover, we have to pray that we will be given the strength and perseverance that our individual path of discipleship may call us to follow. While we all hope that our vocation will not take us into extreme situations, we have only to think of the extreme situations to see how personal and all-embracing vocation can be. How often has it happened that suddenly someone has realised that his/her vocation also included martyrdom: they had lived a quiet life, now the world changed, and witness was demanded in a new and total way? How often has someone had to face suffering from a chronic disease, and there had to discover the presence of God and a new way of giving witness to the God of love? Vocation is personal, on going, and demanding.

5. Vocation is often surprising, and it is that zest in individual Christians that allows us to see the Spirit at work in the church. It is in following our vocations – and Amos is a perfect example of this – that we discover the cost of discipleship.

6. The challenge for the community of the church that is highlighted in today's Liturgy of the Word is to know how the community can help the individuals who make up that community to discover their different vocations. Alas, we put a lot of energy into recruiting ministers; we are not nearly so good in this more delicate and more fundamental task.

7. However, it is worth remembering that the vitality and joy of any Christian community is directly proportional to the ex-

tent to which its members have come to own, and respond to, their vocations. In a community made up of people with a keen sense of their vocations and their special talents, it then becomes a matter of linking skills to needs so that all the ministries that the church needs are fulfilled.

Sixteenth Sunday of Ordinary Time

Introduction to the Celebration

The desire to be in the presence of the Lord and to listen to his teaching is what draws us together each time we assemble as a church – just as we are doing now. Today we hear of early groups of people who also had the desire to be with Jesus and how he took pity on them 'because they were like sheep without a shepherd, and he set himself to teach them at some length'. Let us set the tone for our celebration by thinking about our need to listen to the teachings of Jesus so that they can bring light into our lives.

Rite of Penance

Lord Jesus, you call us to rest with you today from our comings and goings. Lord have mercy.

Lord Jesus, we hasten to you as our Teacher and Guide. Christ have mercy.

Lord Jesus, look on us with pity as our shepherd and teach us. Lord have mercy.

Opening Prayer

The alternative prayer ('Father, let the gift of your life') is to be preferred because it makes explicit reference to the theme – found in today's gospel – of the teaching of Jesus.

Headings for Readings

First Reading

The prophet utters a terrible warning against those who are sent by God to guide the people, but who instead led them astray; in contrast is the perfect teacher, the virtuous Branch for David who will be called 'the Lord-our-integrity' and whom we call 'the Christ'.

Second Reading

Jesus has brought us reconciliation: he has broken down the barriers that separate us from God and from one another. Through him everyone has, in the one Spirit, the way to the Father.

Gospel

Those who met Jesus called him Rabbi, teacher. He was the righteous teacher and good shepherd promised by the prophets: we hear of him today fulfilling this ministry of teacher.

Prayer of the Faithful
President

Having gathered us and taught us, the Lord invites us now to stand before the Father and as a priestly people intercede for ourselves, all Christians, and all humanity.

Reader (s)

1. For the whole church of God, that we will grow ever more attentive to Word of God. Lord hear us.

2. For this community, that we will have open ears for the Lord's teaching. Lord hear us.

3. For all who are teachers in this community, that they be lights to their students. Lord hear us.

4. For all who seeking truth and understanding, that their quest may bring them wisdom. Lord hear us.

5. Specific local needs and topics of the day.

6. For the dead, that they may come to the fullness of life and light. Lord hear us.

President

Father, your Son took pity on those he met and set to teaching them of your love, look on us now and hear our prayers for we make them as the disciples of Jesus, your Son, our Lord. Amen.

Eucharistic Prayer

No Preface or Eucharistic Prayer is particularly appropriate for today.

Invitation to the Our Father
Recognising ourselves to be sisters and brothers, and acknowledging that we are children of the Father, we pray:

Sign of Peace
Jesus has come among us to bring us the good news of peace: peace to those who were far away and peace to those who were near. Let us celebrate his peace by wishing the gift of peace to one another.

Invitation to Communion
The Lord gathered his people about his table and taught them of the Father's love, happy are we who have gathered here to be taught by him.

Communion Reflection
We are sitting here as the body of Christ. Let us pray that we will live in his light and bring his light into our world.

O Father in heaven, you who dwell in unapproachable light, grant us the light of your presence in our lives.

O Lord Jesus Christ, you are the light of the Father shining in the universe, you are the life and light of all, and you have said, 'I am the light of the world; he who follows me will not walk in darkness, but will have the light of life'; and you have called us to become 'the light of the world'. Grant us the strength to follow your light.

O Holy Spirit, you give light to every human heart to know the truth, in your light we see light, your light is the light of love, and you shine your light in the darkness of our minds. Enlighten now the darkness of our minds.
Amen.

Conclusion
Solemn Blessing 10 (Ordinary Time I), Missal, p 372, is appropriate.

Notes

Some of the most hidden ministers in the contemporary church are teachers: while vast amounts of energy are put into church schools, the teachers are seen as just employees who happen to be able to teach catechetics. Teachers, indeed, often think of teaching as their secular employment, and any ministry they might have as being a parallel activity. This separation of teaching from vocation/ministry is a new phenomenon in the church: most academics in universities were clerics until the nineteenth century, most founders of religious orders considered having an educational wing to be an essential part of what they did, many were founded specifically to teach. Yet, today, appreciation of teaching as a specific Christian vocation is almost nil. Today when we focus on the Christ as teacher is a good time to seek to enable teachers in the community – not just of religion or catechetics, but any subject because 'all wisdom is from the Lord' (Wis 1:1) – to appreciate their everyday work as a ministry. One way to do this would be to have them as the reader of the Lections and of the Prayers of the Faithful.

COMMENTARY

First Reading: Jer 23:1-6

This passage forms a unit within Jeremiah as the prophesy of the future king (some say that the unit extends to v 8, but the last two verses are unstable within the textual tradition and do not really link with what we read today); and should be read as one of the basic texts supporting the messianic hopes of the people. The new Branch for David is righteous, the bringer of justice (both justice in the land among people and salvation for the people) and peace (again both in the land and in terms of salvation). Indeed, justice and righteousness is so central to his agenda that this is his name: 'The Lord-is-our-righteousness.'

Psalm: 22 (23)

This is the classic 'shepherd' theme text, but the aspect of the shepherd theme that it invokes is that of the shepherd-king. This fits well with the First Reading, and so the psalm is best seen as a prayerful-reflection on that reading. However, in the gospel the shepherd is the shepherd-teacher: the one who teaches the people the way to life.

Second Reading: Eph 2:13-18
This reading captures a central element of the thought of this author: what Jesus has done profoundly affects who we are as human beings. There is now no division between Jews and Gentiles, but there is a New Man which has been brought into existence by the death of Jesus on the cross. We become part of this new humanity through our incorporation into the Christ in baptism. The meaning of this passage has been well-captured in the ancient vesting prayer: 'Put on me, O Lord, that new man who has been created after the fashion of God in righteousness and true sanctity.'

This passage has had more effect on our theology than any exegesis could express: whenever we use phrases like 'in Christ' in the liturgy, we are employing the theology of this passage to express who we are.

First Reading > Gospel Links
The link is two-fold. First, both use the language of shepherding for the function of teaching the people. The prophet speaks about the flock led astray by false teachers; the gospel speaks of the flock that needs a teacher. This is a link of prophecy finding its fulfilment in Jesus. Building on this is the second, messianic, link: the prophet promises a new shepherd-teacher who is the virtuous Branch for David, and this messianic description is then fulfilled in Jesus.

Gospel: Mk 6:30-34
Today's passage is the prologue to the story of the feeding of five thousand men with five loaves and two fish (6:30-44) – a story whose perfect form is found in Mark. As the prologue, it is there to establish the reason why the people were there and in

need of feeding. As a distinct element within the story, it shows us Mark combining the images of shepherd (one who guides and protects), teacher (one who feeds understanding and guides) and the one who cares (feeds with food and looks out for the people) in the person and work of Jesus.

The opening verses of this passage 'come away ... and rest awhile' have launched a thousand retreats – but with scarce respect for the actual meaning of Mark's text. The whole point of Mark's story is that while it might be nice for Jesus and the disciples to have time 'away from it all', that is not to be for the simple reason that there is a people in need of pity which manifests itself in teaching.

HOMILY NOTES

1. The gospel is so simple that it seems hardly worth preaching about it. Living in an age of celebrity we are used to the idea that people like to go and see where the 'action' is. Everyone who sets themselves up as having answers or a 'lifestyle guide' – no matter how bizarre – has a following. And one of the ways you show that someone is unusual, special, a curiosity, or a 'star' is to make sure that the 'groupies' get to each photo opportunity and that the paparazzi are anxious to be there all the time. Could it be that this is what we have just read – and that Mark is just glad that Jesus had such groupies?

2. On a practical level there is nothing remarkable about the scene: it all takes place over distances of just a couple of miles along the shore of a small lake and there were plenty of lonely places just behind the small village settlements that are referred to in the gospels as 'cities'. Moreover, we are so used to hearing of miracles or healings or exorcisms – all of which can cause us to wonder 'what was that really like' or which make us feel uneasy; or hearing bits of Jesus's preaching we find hard to apply to our own lives, that we are apt to dismiss something like today's gospel as an irrelevance!

3. However, the fact that 'Jesus took pity on them ... and set himself to teach them at some length' contains a lesson for us

that is of the first importance. This is what we must explore in the homily today.

4. It is very easy to think of Jesus taking pity on people. Sinners, poor people, sick people, hungry people, people in mourning, paralytics, outcasts such as Zacchaeus (or some other tax-collector), people possessed by evil spirits: in each of these cases we can think of Jesus taking pity and then either doing something about it or teaching us about our duties of pity. He pitied sinners and forgave them; he pitied the sick and healed them; he pitied the widow and raised her son to life; he had pity for outcasts and made them welcome at his table; and he preached that we, his disciples, should take pity on the hungry, the poor, and those who are suffering. But the pity he shows today does not fit this pattern. He takes pity on the whole people – rich and poor, healthy and sick – and the form that his pity takes is teaching.

5. The idea that Jesus takes pity on people because they are like 'sheep without a shepherd', and the idea that teaching could be an expression of pity/mercy, are two ideas that are very alien to us. On the one hand, we do not like the idea that we need to be taught: we are in love with the notion of our own autonomy. This is expressed in the atheist sentiment: don't walk in front, I may not follow; don't walk behind, I may not lead; let's just walk beside each other! On the other hand, teaching conjures up someone who knows what we do not and tells us – implicitly showing up our imperfection – and teaching also seems to be just a technical skill: imparting boring skills be they how to cook, do arithmetic, a language, or car-maintenance. Teaching is no more than 'transferring skills' – to use modern educational jargon.

6. But these notions of autonomy and of our human need to be taught are incompatible with the basis not just of Christianity, but all monotheistic belief. It is our belief that the universe – be it the outer universe of atoms or galaxies or the inner universe of our human existence – cannot be understood without reference to God. God is the maker of all that

is, seen and unseen, and without thinking about God and the divine origin and purpose of the universe, there is something lacking in our understanding, in our judgements on how we should act, and in the depths of our hearts. As Augustine said: 'You, O God, have made us for yourself and our hearts are restless without you.'

7. Yet, modern society tries to live in a God-free zone and make out that the divine is an optional extra, no more than a personal choice. While, at the same time, the 'body, mind, spirit' shelves of bookshops groan under the number of books by lifestyle consultants that promise happiness by a mix of diets, mind-games, and ways of re-arranging the furniture in your home. The God-free zone is also a happiness-free zone.

8. We only become fully human when we recognise that there is more to life than the sum of the bits we can manage, the bits we can cope with, and the bits we can see. This recognition is rarely a blinding flash of understanding that there is a 'God-shaped aperture' in our existence, rather it is, more often than not, a painful discovery that we would almost be glad to avoid. Yet in this discovery we need also to appreciate the wisdom who teaches us – here lies the mission of Jesus the prophet and teacher. He teaches us to become aware of the deeper needs of our humanity: to see ourselves as the Father's children, to work together to build the kingdom, and the need to journey through life towards our true home. Jesus both teaches us of our fundamental dependency on God, and of the love that God constantly offers us.

9. We as a community continue that teaching: not just transferring skills such as how to pray or how to help the poor, but teaching in the sense of bringing people to wisdom. This is the wisdom that knows that our lives are incomplete without acknowledging who we are as creatures within a God-given universe.

10. The people hurried after him, and he set about teaching them at length. Here is a hard question: are we willing to sit as students (the same word as 'disciples' except it is less pious) at the feet of Jesus – and be taught at length?

John's Gospel in Mark's Year

I am the living bread which came down from heaven; if any one eats of this bread, he will live for ever; and the bread which I shall give for the life of the world is my flesh (Jn 6:51).

In the middle of the Year of Mark in the Lectionary we read from John 6 – the Bread of Life Discourse – over a period of five Sundays. These are:

Sunday 17:	Jn 6:1-15	2 Kgs 4:42-4
Sunday 18:	Jn 6:24-35	Ex 16:2-4, 12-5
Sunday 19:	Jn 6:41-52	1 Kgs 19:4-8
Sunday 20:	Jn 6:51-58	Prov 9:1-6
Sunday 21:	Jn 6:61-70	Jos 24:1-2, 15-8

Although these readings do not form an 'official' unit as the Lectionary groups the Sundays – they all fall within the nine-Sunday unit of Jesus manifesting himself that runs from the fifteenth to the twenty-third Sundays – they do have a distinct theme and a distinct flavour (if for no other reason than it is the only time in the whole three-year cycle when we are called to preach on John over such a sustained length of time).

It is useful to address three questions regarding these gospel readings.

(1) Why have they been used?

It is sometimes suggested that these readings from John were simply added because there were not enough texts in Mark for thirty-four Sundays. This is simply not the case, there is more than enough text left 'unused' in Mark to have provided five more gospels. The answer lies in the relationship that exists between Mark's gospel and the Bread of Life discourse (Jn 6). There is an almost unconscious habit of linking Matthew, Mark, and Luke together ('the synoptics'), and then treating John as a singleton. Now while there are good reasons behind that instinct, we have also to remember that there are links between

186

portions of John and one or more of the others. Here is a case in point.

Now given that Mark is presented in the lectionary over Sundays 15-23 as 'Jesus manifesting himself' and this stage covers this particular 'overlap' between Mark and John, if there was a good reason for adding John, then this would be the time to do it. The reason for adding John is quite simple: in the synoptics the reflective theology of the Eucharist is focused on the Last Supper event, and then it takes the form of an origin account of the Christian meal. These accounts are used every year as part of our annual Paschal celebration, and so do not 'fit' with the Sundays of Ordinary Time (by the same token we do not read the passion nor the resurrection accounts outside of the celebration of Easter). Only John presents his theology of Eucharist outside the events of the final week of Jesus's life (although he does invoke a paschal context, see Jn 6:4: 'Now the Passover, the feast of the Jews, was at hand') so if we are to have access to this theology of the Eucharist for reflection at our regular weekly Eucharists – and without all the other concerns of Easter – then these texts have to be read somewhere in Ordinary Time. So the question now becomes: where in the three-year cycle should this crucial part of the preaching of the gospel be located?

(2) Why have they been inserted here?

Of the three years, Mark was the most suitable because of the connections between Jn 6 and parts of Mark, and so they have been dovetailed in this way.

John	Mark	Lectionary
		Sunday 16 (Mk 6:30-34) prepares the scene for the Jn readings: Jesus steps ashore from the Sea of Galilee and begins to teach.
6:1-15	6:30-44	**Sunday 17** replaces Mk 6:35-44 with the parallel passage in Jn.
6:16-24	6:45-54	Jesus walks on the sea: not used in the Lectionary in this cycle.

6:25-34	8:11-13	**Sunday 18** uses Jn 6:24-35 The much shorter Mk parallel is not used in the Sunday Lectionary.
6:35-59	8:14-21	This section of Jn is split into two: **Sunday 19** we read Jn 6:41-52; **Sunday 20** we read Jn 6:51-58. There is an overlap between these lections which makes Jn 6:51 the key to the whole Jn section of the Lectionary. The Mk parallel is not used in the Sunday Lectionary.
6:60-69	8:27-30	*Sunday 21 uses Jn 6:61-70.* The Mk parallel is used on Sunday 24 but with a different focus.
6:70-71	8:31-33	The Mk text is used on **Sunday 24.** The Jn parallel is not used in the Sunday Lectionary.

Given that these Johannine readings fit so well into Mark, it is perhaps preferable to think of this as a 'transfusion' of John's theology rather than a set of 'insertions'. We can justly claim that John's reflections on the Eucharist's place in the life of the church develop Mark's narrative rather than being simple something 'tacked on.'

(3) Do they present any special opportunities in a pastoral setting?
The introduction to the Lectionary states that:

> One important particularity is that the Lectionary [for this year] includes a major insert from the gospel of John (Sundays 17-21: John 6 – the sermon on the 'Bread of Life'). This fits well into this part of Mark's gospel, which is concerned with Jesus' revelation of himself, and is known as 'the Bread section' (p li).

But how can we make best use of 'the Bread Section'? St Augustine once remarked on how his own congregations reacted to the liturgy: 'What we do everyday, bores us!' It is a remark that would find an echo not only in the hearts of many in an average congregation, but also in the hearts of many clergy. One has only to be thrown off track by something unexpected happening – I saw it happen recently when a poster fell off the wall with a crash – to see how often we preside on auto-pilot! Equally, people participate on auto-pilot: change the setting to a wedding or a funeral when 'the pillars of the parish' are not there to take a lead in the responses and people, who are regular 'church goers', are thrown off their stride and cannot remember the prayers. In a community that uses hymnbooks there is a simple test of how much change and evolution there is in the liturgy: how old are the hymnbooks, and are there some pages with soiled corners from sweaty thumbs, and some that are clean?

On the other hand, stability is a value in the liturgy: part of the wonder of ritual is that it frees us from having to feel our way into a fresh situation each time. Its regularity, and indeed its boredom, means that we do not have to waste energy each occasion we gather finding out what is happening and what is expected of us. You can see this in the way franchise fast-food outlets work: the first time you use one, you have to learn a new way of queuing and ordering – a new ritual – but once you have been through this once, you know how it goes, you 'know the ritual' and can get your fast-food (if it can be called 'food') fast and go! So it does not matter whether you are in Beijing or New York or your home town, the familiarity with the ritual breeds comfort rather than contempt.

Our celebrations of the Eucharist have to strike a mid-point between the lifelessness of autopilot on the one hand, and the lack of ease that is the result of the un-familiar on the other. The usual way we deal with such 'have your cake and eat it' situations is to use the device of the regular 'review'/'check-up'/ 'audit'/'renewal'. The focus of John's preaching was the actual gathering at which he was preaching: he was asking his audience to reflect on why they had gathered for a meal and what this meal meant to them in terms of the mystery of the Christ.

Since this is the way we use these texts in this year, they are an ideal opportunity for a 'triennial review' of how our community is celebrating and what it means to us.

Like all reviews, this has to be driven by questions. Here is a sample:

- How well do we celebrate?
- Is it a real celebration or simply a religious exercise?
- Is it characterised by integrity between our words and our actions in celebrating?
- Is our celebration just a matter of ritual tokens?
- How can our celebration be improved?
- How true is it to our vision of the Eucharist?
- Is it an exclusivist affair or the work of the whole community?
- How interested are we in its music?
- Can we make the communications during the Liturgy of the Word more effective?
- Can we make the eating and drinking we speak about an actual fact?
- Can we establish links between this meal and those who cannot or do not come to it?
- How can our banquet reflect our care about the global food-situation and the environment?
- Do we need more ministers at our gathering charged with various tasks?

The list can go on – as it should reflect the particular situation of the community.

A community that meets each week should be willing for a short period every three years to stop and take a look at what it is doing – such review processes are taken for granted in every other area of life – and 'the Bread section' is an ideal occasion once every three years.

Seventeenth Sunday of Ordinary Time

Introduction to the Celebration

We have assembled for our weekly Eucharist – as we do every week. But why is this important to us? And although we do it every week, how well do we as a community engage in this activity of celebrating the Eucharist? Giving thanks to the Father, in union with Jesus, while being empowered by the Spirit, is an activity: how well do we do this as the group of disciples who form a church here each Sunday?

These are important questions for us. So, over the next five weeks we are going to be reading passages from St John's gospel on the Eucharist, and these will challenge us to reflect on what we are doing when we gather, why we are gathering for this meal, and how well we are celebrating it.

Let us reflect that we are gathered in the Holy Spirit, and about to celebrate the Lord's meal, and with him offer thanks to the Father.

Rite of Penance

Lord Jesus, you gave thanks over five barley loaves and fed all who had gathered about you. Lord have mercy.

Lord Jesus, you instructed the disciples to gather up all the fragments so that nothing would be lost. Christ have mercy.

Lord Jesus, you were acclaimed as 'the prophet who is to come into the world'. Lord have mercy.

Headings for Readings
First Reading

The servant of God, Elisha, provided bread for the God's people as the demonstration of God's care for his people: all ate and there was some over.

Second Reading
This reading calls on us to remember who we are as a church, the unity that should exist among us, and on what that unity is founded.

Gospel
The Son of God, Jesus, provided bread for God's people as the demonstration of God's care for his people: all ate and there was some over.

Prayer of the Faithful
President
Gathered in the one Spirit, we are one Body in the one Lord, and now we call on the one God who is Father of all, through all and within all.
Reader (s)
1. For the whole People of God scattered across the globe, that we shall draw new life from our celebrations of the Eucharist this Sunday. Lord hear us.
2. For this community that our gatherings may be celebrations of joy and thanksgiving, that they may renew us in Christ, and strengthen us to be his disciples. Lord hear us.
3. For our sisters and brothers in Christ for whom gathering for this holy meal is no longer an important part of their lives, that we, and how we celebrate, may help them to know the Lord's invitation to share in his supper. Lord hear us.
4. For all peoples, that we may appreciate and be thankful for all God's gifts, use them wisely, and use them in ways that promote justice and peace. Lord hear us.
5. For all those who do not have access to the food they need, that we may learn to share our bread with the hungry. Lord hear us.
6. Specific local needs and topics of the day.
7. For those who have died, that having shared in the Eucharist on earth they may come to its fullness in the banquet of heaven. Lord hear us.

President

Father, when we gather to give you thanks we know that we depend on you for all. Hear these prayers we make to you for we confess that there is one Lord, your Son, one faith, one baptism, and one God, you who are Father of all, through all and within all. Amen.

Eucharistic Prayer

There is no preface nor Eucharistic Prayer that picks up John's theology of the Eucharist as expressed in today's gospel.

However, P48 (Preface of the Holy Eucharist II) can be adapted to fit these Sundays when we reflect on the Eucharist (but without tying the Eucharist to the Last Supper event – a tying down that John wished to avoid) by omitting the paragraph that begins: 'At the last supper'. Instead, read or sing the preface thus:

Father, all-powerful and ever-living God,
we do well always and everywhere to give you thanks
through Jesus Christ our Lord.
In this great sacrament you feed your people
and strengthen them ...

Then use Eucharistic Prayer II and concentrate more time on the fraction and the sharing of the loaf and cup.

Invitation to the Our Father

In the power of the Spirit, and in the words of the Son, let us pray to the Father:

Sign of Peace

There is one Lord, and we are one Body. Let us express to each other the bonds of love that the sharing in the Lord's banquet creates between us.

Invitation to Communion

The Lord Jesus asked the crowds to sit and he shared the loaves among them; now he bids us to share this loaf and become one with him. Lord I am not worthy ... .

Communion Reflection

Give an introduction to a formal period of silent reflection with something like this:

> Gathering, listening to the Word of God, thanking the Father, breaking, sharing the Bread of Life, drinking the cup of salvation, reflecting on what we have done, then departing. This is the pattern of our weekly assemblies: so now is our time to reflect on our becoming the Body of Christ in this gathering.

Conclusion

The Lord fed the people who gathered to hear him, and now he has fed us at his table, may this food strengthen us to be his disciples this week. Amen.

The Lord took the loaves and the fish and gave thanks to his Father. Now we have given thanks with him. May this attitude of gratitude to God continue in us during the coming week. Amen.

When the people were fed with the five loaves and the two fishes, they recognised the Lord to be the prophet come into the world. May we be his witnesses until we gather again at this table. Amen.

COMMENTARY

First Reading: 2 Kgs 4:42-44

The Elisha Cycle (2 Kgs 2:1-8:29), that has as its core yet another cycle of ten miracle-stories (4:1-8:15) – one of which we are reading today – is not nowadays a very popular part of scripture. However, one has only to look at how these miracles/wonders/signs form the background for later miracle stories, be they in the gospels or in the lives of saints, to see that our taste is out of harmony with that of most of our ancestors. While we find these stories obscure and rarely come across them, they were familiar to people at the time of Jesus in the way that we can take it for granted that people can pick up on allusions to *Star Trek*. And, it is this story that we read today that stands behind the feeding the multitude stories: if Elisha the great powerful prophet fed the multitude by wondrously multiplying twenty barley loaves for a hundred men (with some over), then the greatest prophet can multiply five barley loaves for five thousand men (with some over)!

Psalm: 144 (145)

This is a basic hymn of thanksgiving, and as such is well suited to a gathering who formal name is 'the thanksgiving'.

Second Reading: Eph 4:1-6

The letter was written in Paul's name, some time in the later first century, to churches in the Lycus valley in western Asia Minor (near the west coast of modern Turkey). One of the concerns of the author is the danger of factions breaking out in the churches through festering disagreements. In that context he comes up with some of the basic sound bites of ecclesiology: one Lord, one faith, one baptism. It is a formula that is influenced by Paul's style in dealing with the same problems in Corinth in 1 Cor 10:17; and one that works just as well today as when it was first used.

However, if the phrase 'one Lord, one faith, one baptism' is a catchy sound bite, we should not forget that in this letter it is the conclusion of a very significant way of viewing the church as the work of the Spirit. The unity is not just the fact of 'sticking together' because it is of practical utility, rather unity is an essential feature of the church because it is the Spirit's gift which transforms the individuals into the one body of the Lord. To act in a way that destroys unity is to reject the work of the Spirit, to deny the nature of the church, and, indeed, to put one outside the 'one body'.

First Reading > Gospel Links

The link is continuity of activity by the prophets/servants, whereby the care of God is manifested to the people. If we look at the stories told about the prophets of old, we are enabled to appreciate the nature of Jesus from his actions: it is because they know stories like that about Elisha that they are able to recognise that Jesus 'really is the prophet who is to come into the world.'

Indeed, the original 'feeding story' of the kerygma (which was in circulation before Mark preached his gospel) is modelled on this Elisha story: so we have the liturgy today presenting us with the basic background story we must know if we are to understand the gospel.

Gospel: Jn 6:1-15

We know that the story of the miraculous feeding of a vast crowd was part of the fundamental kerygma for it surfaces (with various numbers) in no less than six places in the gospels: here, in Mk 6:30-44; 8:1-10; Mt 14:13-21; 15:32-39; and Lk 9:10-17. However, in John it is the opening event of the entire discourse on the bread of life, and this means that the actual feeding must be read, in this gospel at least, as a part of John's theology of the Eucharist. Once that connection is made, the context given in the gospel about being on the edge of the Sea of Galilee becomes just scenery: the real location is the community who are sharing a single loaf of bread at their gathering as the Lord's gift of the bread of life to them.

These two feedings, in the story being heard and in the meal being celebrated, are characterised by the loaf being heavenly food, and each event (the story and the Eucharist) being free of the normal limitations of space and time. Here a small amount of material food can supply the wants of a multitude, a portion of a loaf and a mouthful from a common cup can transform a meagre meal into an anticipation of heaven. Likewise, in both the story and the community's meal, the initiative rests with Jesus: he knows what he will do, he is the one who thanks the Father and shares the food, and all are his guests. Only after sharing the heavenly food do the people recognise him as the messianic prophet/king, but from the group in the story he then retreats for this recognition is partial and confused; among his audience, by contrast, John expects that they will recognise Jesus as the true prophet/king whose 'kingship is not of this world' (Jn 18:36).

HOMILY NOTES

1. Today is not a day for 'giving' a homily, much less 'preaching' – both assume an agent (the speaker) and an object (those who are spoken to). Rather, this is a day for trying to create a mood of just settling back and reflecting on what we are doing. What we are doing by gathering each Sunday, what we are doing when we celebrate the Eucharist, what we are doing as God's People.

2. One way to do this is to set the scene before reading the gospel. The scene can be set in this way (if the gospel is read by a deacon, then the president could set the scene; if the president himself has to read the gospel, then someone else could do it; it is better done while people are sitting down before the gospel acclamation):

We gather here each Sunday – this is the day when we recall the resurrection of Jesus; it is for us the first day of the week.

At this gathering we always recall something of our Lord's life and teaching. This takes the form of reading a part of one of the four gospels – and today we are going to read from the gospel written by John.

Then we gather around the Lord's table for the meal of the Lord, when we give thanks through Jesus to the Father over the gifts of bread and wine. Then by sharing those gifts we are transformed into the Body of Christ.

This is what Christians have done since the very beginning, and were doing this even before the gospels were written down.

Today we recall a story told by John at a gathering for the Eucharist on a Sunday over 1900 years ago. John knew that when the gathering heard the story it would help them understand the sacred dimension of the meal they celebrated together each week. We will now read that story.

3. Then when people have settled down again after the proclamation of the gospel, this reflection could be offered:

Like the crowds we have gathered here to hear the message of Jesus.

Like those crowds we have gathered here to be fed from his hands.

Like on that hillside, Jesus takes our loaf, gives thanks to the Father, and gives it to all of us who are sitting around ready to be fed by him.

Like on that hillside, we know that this food with which he feeds us is precious, and that it is the food for the whole world.

Like those people who acclaimed him as 'the prophet who is to come into the world', we acclaim him as our priest, our prophet, and as our king – not a king whose kingdom belongs to this world, but as the king who presents the kingdom of truth and life to our Father in heaven.

Eighteenth Sunday of Ordinary Time

Introduction to the Celebration

We have gathered to offer thanks to the Father for his care and love in our lives. And we make this thanksgiving in union with Jesus who is the wisdom of God and our brother. But today our reflection on the Father's goodness holds, as it were, a mirror up to this relationship that the Father has established with us in Jesus, and we are reminded that the Father's greatest act of love was sending Jesus to us. Our fathers in the desert long ago thanked the Father for the gift of heaven-sent bread, but we thank the Father that heavenly life and wisdom have come down to encounter us in Jesus. In Jesus we see our God made visible and so are caught up in the love of the God we cannot see.

Rite of Penance

Lord Jesus, you are the bread of life, Lord have mercy.

Lord Jesus, anyone who goes to you will never be hungry, Christ have mercy.

Lord Jesus, anyone who believes in you will never thirst, Lord have mercy.

Headings for Readings

First Reading

The Lord heard the needs of his people and cared for them with the gift of bread from heaven.

Second Reading

If we wish to call ourselves Christians, then we have to be willing to adopt a different set of values in life from those prevalent in the society in which we live.

Gospel
As we listen to this gospel it is useful to keep in mind this question: who is this Jesus whom we follow, whom we call our teacher and Lord?

Prayer of the Faithful
President
Gathering in the presence of Holy Wisdom, let us look towards the Father for our needs.
Reader (s)
1. For the whole church – all who call upon the name of Christ – that we may encounter anew each day the wisdom that comes from the Father. Lord hear us.
2. For the church gathered here – all of us who form this community – that we may encounter the Christ who brings us the fullness of life. Lord hear us.
3. For those in need – all who search for healing, for justice, for truth – that they may encounter the Father's gift from heaven and in meeting the Christ may their lives be transformed. Lord hear us.
4. For all who have died searching for goodness, justice, peace, and truth – all whose faith is known to God alone – that they may enter into the fullness of life. Lord hear us.
5. Specific local needs and topics of the day.
6. And lastly, for ourselves gathered at the Lord's table, that our encounter with the bread of the Eucharist may be for us an encounter with the bread of life. Lord hear us.
President
Father, you answered the prayers of our fathers in the desert with the gift of manna. You answered all our human hopes and prayers in the gift of the true bread. So now, answer these prayers for they are made in union with your highest gift, Jesus, your Wisdom, our Lord. Amen.

Eucharistic Prayer
See the note for the Seventeenth Sunday.

Invitation to the Our Father
It is the Father who gives us the bread from heaven, so now let us pray to him:

Sign of Peace
We are sharing the bread of heaven at the table of the Lord. It would be wholly inappropriate to stand here and not be willing to make peace with each other. Let us now express that willingness to one another.

Invitation to Communion
Behold the bread of God which comes down from heaven and gives life to the world. Happy are we who share this meal.

Communion Reflection
Jesus says:
> Do not labour for the food which perishes,
> but for the food which endures to eternal life,
> which the Son of man will give to you;
> for on him has God the Father set his seal.

Jesus says:
> Truly, truly, I say to you,
> it was not Moses who gave you the bread from heaven;
> my Father gives you the true bread from heaven.
> For the bread of God is that which comes down from heaven,
> and gives life to the world.

Jesus says:
> I am the bread of life;
> he who comes to me shall not hunger,
> and he who believes in me shall never thirst.

Conclusion
Prayer over the People 18 (Missal, p 382) is suitable.

COMMENTARY

First Reading: Ex 16:2-4, 12-15

This is the classic story of the manna with which God fed the people during their wilderness journey from Egypt to 'the Land'. The story is a piece of spirituality written to present an image of a people who are totally dependent on God for good things, who are loved by God and lavished with gifts as part of their covenant.

The origins of the story, within the larger origins myth of the wanderings in the desert, and how it was received within the tradition before the time of Jesus is a long and fascinating one. However, such background is irrelevant to the liturgy today. The reason being that we are reading the Exodus account not as a story in itself, but through the lens of its use within John's gospel. So what did it mean for John?

Moses gave the people signs in the desert, the manna being one of them, that God was caring for them; now the people have a new sign in their midst: Jesus, the one on whom the Father has set his seal.

Moses was the lawgiver who showed the people what they must do if they were to do the works God wants; now the people are turning to Jesus with this same question: he is the new Moses, the author of the new Law – and at the heart of that covenant is the call to the people to believe in the one sent by the Father.

Moses is linked with the bread from heaven understood as the token of all that the Lord provides for his people; now there is the even greater gift, the Bread of Life, which is the sustenance for eternal life.

The whole of the old covenant/testament/relationship is summed up in the image of Moses, the manna, and the people; the new covenant/testament/relationship is that Jesus is the Bread of Life, the gift of the Father, that offers eternal life to believers.

Psalm: 77 (78):3-4, 23-25
The story of the Lord's goodness is the basis of the tradition, and this is seen in the gift of the bread from heaven. This psalm is the perfect link between the first reading and the gospel: it is a development of the theological understanding of the story found in Exodus and the psalm is quoted in the gospel: Jn 6:31 is taken from Ps 77:24.

Second Reading: Eph 4:17, 20-24
This reading is one of the places where the relationship of the Christian to the life she/he is called to lead is depicted in terms of putting on clothing: the new life must have a new outward fashion. The use of the clothing imagery may very well reflect the baptismal liturgy of the churches of eastern Asia Minor in the later first century. It was the final verse of this reading that has always been appealed to with reference to the white garments of the newly baptised (and therefore, by extension, it formed the basis of the old vesting prayer for the surplice!).

The aim of the pericope is to present vv 20-24, and v 17 is used simply as an introduction. However, by omitting vv 18 and 19 no great benefit is gained but, by contrast, the sense is given that this reading is really just a sound-bite: hear vv 20-24 as a piece of advice, without having to bother about the larger scheme of the author.

First Reading > Gospel Links
The relationship exists at two levels. At the level of communications, the first reading provides necessary background for understanding the gospel. However, no doubt the reason the first reading was chosen is that it is seen as the 'antetype'/foretaste to the gospel, which is seen as perfection. This sort of relationship built on continuity (both the desert bread and Jesus the Bread of Life are the Father's gifts) and discontinuity (the desert bread was imperfect in that people hungered again, the Bread of Life is perfect in that it gives eternal life) has not just been at the heart of much Christian exegesis down the centuries, but indeed

was active in the very first communities – as we see in today's gospel – whereby they sought to make sense of their experience as Christians by relating the Christ-event to the tradition of the faith of Israel.

Gospel: Jn 6:24-35
Reading the Bread of Life section of John's gospel can often be a frustrating experience if at the same time one is preparing to preach on the text at the Eucharist. Why is this the case? The problem seems to lie in failing to take account of two misleading assumptions that have become part of our general thinking without recognition of the fundamentally different approach of John.

The first assumption is that when we hear phrases such as 'I am the bread of life' it can be directly related to the Eucharist (or indeed the Blessed Sacrament). That we should make this assumption is readily explained: for centuries we have used phrases from Jn 6 to provide imagery for the cult of the Eucharist. I grew up in a parish where the 'day-cover' for the altar cloths had emblazoned upon it in fancy letters: *Ego sum panis vitae* (Jn 6:48). That cloth stood for most of the day just in front of the tabernacle, and its legend served to identify the tabernacle's contents. Just so, for many people hearing any references to the 'Bread of Life' seems to be as simple as just one more name for the Eucharistic bread. However, John's theology is both richer and more complex than any such simple identification. We can avoid this assumption by remembering that while the bread we eat at the Eucharist can be identified with the Bread of Life, the Bread of Life cannot be identified with the Eucharistic Bread (it is another of those situations where 'all admirals are sailors, but not all sailors are admirals').

The second assumption is to read parts of Jn 6 as the symbolic presentation of a mystery and parts of it as if it were a simple code that borders on fundamentalism. In this reading when we hear of the manna in the desert we think of it as a symbol, but when we hear 'he who eats my flesh and drinks my blood has eternal life, and I will raise him up at the last day' (Jn 6:54) we read it as if to question what it means is tantamount to denying the reality of Christ's presence in the Eucharist. Because we actually eat and drink at the Eucharist, we extend the metaphor and think of the Eucharist as eating flesh or drinking blood. This has a long, and sorry, history in popular theology with stories on the one hand of the doubting priest who suddenly saw the wafer he was holding ooze blood, and on the other, the charge that accepting 'real presence' would be tantamount to cannibalism! This might seem far-fetched, but that approach to Christ's Eucharistic presence, termed 'physicalism', is often unwittingly preached as a way of explaining 'real presence'; and indeed many Catholics have rejected any notion of 'real presence' – this rejection usually comes in an unwillingness to have 'real presence' presented to their children around 'First Communion' – as they assume that it means talking about eating flesh and drinking blood in a ghoulish manner. When we read the Bread of Life discourse, we have to read the discourse in its entirety as the presentation of a mystery through symbols – always remembering that the only way we humans can enter into the mysteries of faith is through symbols.

The next step is to ask what range of symbols, or to put it another way: what symbolic language, lies at the heart of Jn 6? This range is determined by (1) the language of Exodus – and the feeding with manna in the desert; and (2) by the language of divine wisdom – the wisdom that abides in the very 'heart' of God – in the Wisdom Literature. This is the range of imagery we must use to plumb John's meaning. Only when exegesis is complete, can we then take that symbolic survey of the mystery of the Christ, and extend it to help us have a deeper appreciation of the Eucharist.

So the sequence is that:
- the Old Testament helps us to understanding Jn 6;
- Jn 6 helps us to understand the mystery of the Christ;
- and new appreciation of the mystery of the Christ gives us a new appreciation of our meal as a community.

Lastly, there is a strong temptation to try to make all the different symbolic languages that we use in relation to the mystery of the Christ, the mystery of the church, or the Eucharist into a single language. This takes the form of assuming that language Paul uses for the Eucharist in 1 Cor fits perfectly with the language used of the church in Ephesians or the language of the Last Supper theologies of the synoptics and the Bread of Life language of John – and then, hopefully, get these to fit with the scholastic language in which Eucharistic controversies have been fought. This attempt to have a theological Esperanto is not only doomed to failure, but should not be attempted. It is doomed to failure as there is no end of different ways that the early Christians tried to make sense of who they were following and they all have different starting points. The same is true about the Eucharist: they were faithful to Jesus's practice of eating together from a common loaf and drinking a common cup while blessing (i.e. praising and thanking) the Father, and they came up with any number of different theologies to explain its meaning, significance, and importance to them. So imagining that all the different bits and pieces on Christology (or on the Eucharist) are just segments of a single consistent theology fails to take account of the historical reality of how our theology originated. Moreover, searching for a single language should not even be attempted for it assumes that a mystery can be tied down in a single theology or a single set of metaphors or a single set of symbols: the mystery is always greater not only than our languages or even our imaginations, but greater than our ability as creatures to even approach the divine. As John himself expressed it: 'But there are also many other things which Jesus did; were every one of them to be written, I suppose that the world itself could not contain the books that would be written' (21:25). Put bluntly, anyone about to read Jn 6 should repeat to her/himself several times: *Deus semper maior!*

How, then, should we interpret today's section of the Bread of Life discourse? The answer lies in recognising that Jesus is the new, and greater, Moses; and that this gift of God is greater than that most obvious of God's loving gifts under the old Law: the gift of the manna which sustained the people in the desert.

The source of all gifts is the Father: it was the Father, not Moses who gave the manna, just as it is the Father who has given Jesus to his people. Manna was a gift from on high that sustained the people for a day; Jesus is the gift from on high that sustains them for eternity. The manna was the bread of life for a wandering people; Jesus is the bread of life in a newer and truer sense: he gives life to the world.

Now in the wisdom literature we have the notion that God's Wisdom comes down and so satisfies those who receive it that it is like food after which one is never hungry and drink after which one is never thirsty. Look at these few texts: 'Come, eat of my bread and drink of the wine I have mixed. Lay aside immaturity, and live, and walk in the way of insight' (Prov 9:5-6 which is read on Sunday 20); 'She [Wisdom] will feed him with the bread of learning, and give him the water of wisdom to drink' (Sir 15:3); and 'Those who eat of me [says Wisdom] will hunger for more, and those who drink of me will thirst for more' (Sir 24:21). With these as background, John is identifying Jesus with the Wisdom of God, and that one who enters into a relationship with Jesus is encountering, and being united with, the divine Wisdom. The human who encounters Wisdom 'will never be hungry' and who believes in Wisdom 'will never thirst'. Where does one encounter Wisdom? In Jesus. How does one unite oneself with Wisdom? By believing in Jesus.

HOMILY NOTES

1. One can write the story of humanity as the story of our searches for our needs: for food, for water, for security, for pleasure, for comfort, for power; but also for happiness, for understanding, for love, for friendship, for wisdom, and for a reality beyond all these: the reality to which we give the label 'God'.

2. These searches are also the basis of our joys, our hopes, our disappointments, our frustrations, and our fears.

3. To be a disciple of Jesus is to believe that many of these desires, these searches, find their fulfilment in him and his
   teaching because he is the supreme gift of the Father to humanity. He is the Wisdom of God made fully accessible to us.

4. As food satisfies our human hunger, as water satisfied our
   human thirst, so Jesus satisfies our desire for wisdom and of
   access to life in its fullness. To assert that he is 'the true bread'
   is to assert that in him the needs that are greater than the immediate and the physical find fulfilment: he gives us true life,
   he gives us true joy, he gives us happiness that exceeds
   human happiness.

5. He who believes in him will never thirst. So how do we express our faith in him? We express this faith in him as the
   Father's gift when we gather as his community, the community founded upon him, the community inspired by his
   Wisdom, the community that shares his bread and his cup.

Nineteenth Sunday of Ordinary Time

Introduction to the Celebration

In today's gospel we hear Jesus describe himself as 'the living bread that comes down from heaven, anyone who eats this bread will live forever.'

We have gathered here around this table so that he can share with us his Living Bread. We have gathered for his meal at which his food is his own life: life that he shared with us to sustain our lives as children of our heavenly Father.

Rite of Penance

Lord Jesus, you are the Bread that came down from heaven, Lord have mercy.

Lord Jesus, you are the one sent by the Father, Christ have mercy.

Lord Jesus, you are the Bread of Life, Lord have mercy.

Headings for Readings

First Reading

The Lord sustained his prophet so that he could carry out the mission entrusted to him.

Second Reading

The Holy Spirit has set his seal on us, marking us out as children of God, and we are called to live in a way that reflects this love that we have received.

Gospel

Jesus is for us 'the bread of life'. To say this is to recall that he is one sent by the Father, who invited us to draw eternal life from him.

Prayer of the Faithful
President
The Lord Jesus is the Bread of Life: he sustains us by sharing his life with us, he is our Wisdom, and we are his disciples. Now, sustained by him, and in union with him, let us pray to the Father.

Reader (s)
1. For the church, that we will draw strength for our mission to the world from the Bread of Life. Lord hear us.
2. For this community, that we may become a people who bear witness to the presence of God's gift of life to our society. Lord hear us.
3. For those who hold power in the world, that they may seek out the wisdom of God in their actions. Lord hear us.
4. For all who are seeking the fullness of life, that their search for life and wisdom may reach fulfilment. Lord hear us.
5. Specific local needs and topics of the day.
6. For sisters and brothers who have died, that having encountered the Bread of Life they may live forever. Lord hear us.

President
Father, hear the prayers of your people, for we assemble here professing faith in the One you have sent, Jesus Christ, our Lord. Amen.

Eucharistic Prayer
See the note for the Seventeenth Sunday.

Invitation to the Our Father
Nobody has seen the Father, except the one that comes from God, so in union with Jesus we now pray:

Sign of Peace
As disciples we are made one in Christ, so let us express our willingness to live out that unity by offering each other a sign of peace.

Invitation to Communion
Jesus is the Bread that came down from heaven; happy are we with whom he shares his life.

Communion Reflection
We have eaten the Bread of Heaven.
We have eaten the Bread of Angels.
We have eaten the Bread of Life.

We have drunk of the cup of salvation.
We have drunk of the cup of the Lord.
We have drunk of the cup of life.

We are united in a broken loaf.
We are united in a common cup.
We are united in the Bread of Life.

We move onwards as Christ's presence.
We move onwards as his witnesses.
We move onwards as his Body.

We look forward to the banquet of heaven.
We look forward to the fullness of joy.
We look forward in the Bread of Life.

Conclusion
Prayer over the People 18 (Missal, p 382) is suitable.

COMMENTARY

First Reading: 1 Kings 19:4-8
This is the story about Elijah: he is the prophet who places his trust in God, is sustained by heavenly food, and then with that sustenance can perform his vocation. Elijah's heavenly food has been read as the model of placing total trust in God – God's gifts rather than human labour become the very basis of life; it has been read as an example of wisdom – with this food he can go up the mountain of God; it has been read as a type of the dependence of the Christian on the Bread of Life who is Christ – which

is how we read it today in the liturgy; and it has been read as a way of understanding the Eucharist in the on-going pilgrimage of Christian life.

Psalm: 33 (34): 2-9
The key to this psalm's use here – and over these weeks of Mark's year – is the sentence: 'Taste and see that the Lord is good.' We use the imagery of eating to express the transformation that comes over us when we unite our lives with the life that God offers us.

Second Reading: Eph 4:30-5:2
The Spirit of God dwells in each Christian, and when a Christian fails in his/her duty of discipleship this is a cause of sadness to the Spirit. How then is discipleship understood in this passage? It is the imitation of God as seen in Christ, loving as one has been loved. This life of loving is the Christian sacrifice.

First Reading > Gospel Links
The relationship is one of 'part' to 'whole', and invokes two classic notions of how the new covenant is hidden within the old. First, there is part and whole in terms of divine gifts. The prophet is sustained by a gift of bread from heaven to fulfill his earthly mission: it is heavenly bread but an earthly destination; Jesus is not simply offering bread from heaven, but *is* the Bread of Life: heaven itself giving a heavenly destination. Second, there is part and whole in that in the first reading it is just one man who is sustained by the bread from heaven, while in the gospel it is the whole People of God.

Gospel: Jn 6:41-51
Continuing with the image of Jesus as the Bread of Life, John develops the argument: reliance on Jesus is the very core of faith, the central confession is that he is the one who has been sent by the Father. This seems fine for such should be the relationship with the new Moses and with divine Wisdom, but the task of

faith is that this new Moses, this Wisdom is also the boy from up the street! John's discourse invites us to affirm the whole reality of Jesus: an individual like ourselves in all the particularity of our individual humanity, but also the Wisdom who sits by the throne of the Father. Wisdom has been given to us in Jesus. Indeed, it has come so close as to share our humanity.

HOMILY NOTES

1. It is tempting to think of being a Christian in terms of striking a deal with God. I, for my part, will do this and that, these actions will show that I trust in God, 'love God' (whatever that means), and profess that I believe all things I ought to believe (just tell me what I am to believe and I will do it – and if you want me to sign something to that effect, I will do it!). If I do all this, then God will reward me with eternal life, or, at the very least, stop me going to a place of eternal punishment.

   We, preachers, have often connived with this sort of presentation of faith: its simplicity as a piece of communication for the 'simple faithful' seemed to justify its blasphemy of placing God and the creature on a single plane of commutative justice. It was connived at in little 'pious practices' which were let be understood without any of the subtle distinctions found in learned books in Latin. The practice of 'the Nine [First] Fridays' was one such: if you did these, then it was understood you would not die without a priest; and then once the priest got to you, you could confess, be absolved, and everything would end up all right.

   In this sort of presentation, faith is a deal rather than a relationship; it is something that occurs at fixed moments in the way one visits a service station rather than a pilgrimage; it is on the edges of ordinary life rather than at life's core; and it is an individual matter of survival rather than relating to the whole community of the People of God.

2. So the first task in getting a congregation to hear today's gospel is to try to alert them to how we all fall into these false

images in relationship with God.

    We all, to a greater or lesser extent, tend towards:

- reducing faith to doing a deal with God;
- reducing faith to fixed moments in life;
- reducing faith to being peripheral to life;
- and reducing faith to being a matter of individual survival.

3. Then the task is to see how Jesus presents the relationship of being a Christian in today's gospel.

- The Father has not struck a deal with us, but in his love has sent his Son among us: we are called to a relationship of love with God.

- A relationship with God is on-going: he loves us at all times and without exception, so we cannot think of 'holy moments' and 'ordinary moments': God's love abounds and envelops every aspect of our lives. Jesus, the Son of the Father, has come among us and lives with us as one of us.

- Jesus is the Bread of Life: it is he who sustains us throughout our pilgrimage of life.

- It is a community that ate the manna in the desert, and it is a community that is sustained by Christ the Bread of Life – this is why we gather and we pray and we eat and we drink.

4. Discovering the whole extent of God's loving involvement in our lives is the task as great as life itself. We can never fully grasp this mystery while we live; but we must be careful never to betray it by reducing that life-long and life-giving relationship to miserable meanness of human dealings.

5. We can grasp the horror of reducing faith to commerce by noting how jarring this sentence is: The Lord has come offering life in abundance, Love's gift; he did not come selling tickets for places in a life-boat.

Twentieth Sunday of Ordinary Time

Introduction to the Celebration

'Anyone who eats this bread will live forever.' These words of Jesus from today's gospel set the tone of our celebration today. We who share this meal share in the life of Jesus. And as he says: 'As I draw life from the Father, so whoever eats me will draw life from me.'

This is not some magic formula, rather it is the mystery that our sharing here is not simply joining us to one another in the way that every common meal unites those who participate in it, but that in our sharing here we are caught up into the life of God. We are caught up into the life of the Father, who has sent his Son among us as our source of life and wisdom, and who has sent his Spirit into our hearts.

Rite of Penance

Option c. vi (Missal, p 394) is appropriate.

Headings for Readings
First Reading

Wisdom is like food: to accept it into one's life is to become transformed. The divine wisdom came among us in Jesus and he invites us to take his wisdom into our lives and become a new people.

Second Reading

Christians are called to offer a model of sensible living to the world, and to offer a sacrifice of thanksgiving to the Father. It is to fulfill these twin vocations that we gather here each week: seeking to grow in knowledge and seeking to sing psalms and hymns as part of our thanksgiving sacrifice of praise.

Gospel

We are called to make Jesus the centre of our lives. He is to be the source of our lives, and from him we draw life and peace and happiness.

Prayer of the Faithful

President

In baptism we have declared Jesus to be our Bread of Life; so united in him and empowered by the Holy Spirit we can now pray to the Father.

Reader (s)

1. That Jesus, the Son of the Father, may become the Bread of Life for all who call upon his name. Lord hear us.

2. That all those who seek the source of wisdom and life will have the quest rewarded in God's presence. Lord hear us.

3. That this community may draw ever closer to the Bread of Life through our sharing in this Eucharist. Lord hear us.

4. That all who are hungry may be fed and be given new life. Lord hear us.

5. That all humanity may grow in our awareness of God's gifts in the creation and our duty to use them wisely. Lord hear us.

6. Specific local needs and topics of the day.

7. That all who have died having shared in the Bread of Life may live forever. Lord hear us.

President

Father, you have sent Jesus among us as our Bread of Life, hear our prayers and sustain us today and every day of this coming week. We ask this of you in the power of the Holy Spirit, and united as the people of Jesus, your Son, our Lord. Amen.

Eucharistic Prayer

See the note for the Seventeenth Sunday.

Invitation to the Our Father

Through baptism in Christ Jesus we have become the children of God; and so in confidence we pray:

Sign of Peace

We are to be always ready to give thanks to God who is our Father in the name of our Lord Jesus Christ. So likewise we have to be always ready to forgive one another and build peace. Let us offer each other the gift of peace.

Invitation to Communion

Jesus said: 'I am the living bread which has come down from heaven', and now he invites us all to share in this, the Living Bread of our thanksgiving sacrifice to the Father.

Communion Reflection

Silence can be unnerving; yet only in silence can we hear what is going on within us and set what we do at the liturgy in context within our lives. So having a structured silence – which is a lot more than simply time when nothing appears to be happening – should form a part of every liturgy.

Conclusion

Prayer over the People 18 (Missal, p 382) is suitable.

COMMENTARY

First Reading: Prov 9:1-6

This text is the opening of a passage that runs from 9:1 to 9:18 and the seeker of wisdom – the wise holy man – reflects on the choice that life constantly presents between wisdom and folly. Both are personified as women: Lady Wisdom offers a house, indeed a many-columned palace, and presents her gifts as food which, if eaten, bring understanding and life.

By the time of the early church, this figure of wisdom had become an aspect of the divine presence in the world: wisdom came to be seen as a sharing in the divine life, and the image of that sharing was that of eating food and drinking wine. As the healthy individual had good food and drink, and through that food had life, so sharing in the food that is wisdom, the individual has true life and a share in the divine life. It is this understanding of wisdom that is the key Bread of Life discourse in Jn; then, in turn, it becomes another key to our eating/drinking at the Eucharist as a sharing in the life of Jesus.

Psalm: 33 (34):2-3, 10-15
See the note for Sunday 19.

Second Reading: Eph 5:15-20
The churches of the Lycus valley, in what is now western Turkey, were all too familiar with the wilder excesses of Greco-Roman religious cults which, in some of these cities, focused on sexual orgies and wild ecstatic experiences. The [truly] Spirit-filled body of Christ was to be made up of much more sober members: intelligent, rational service of God and neighbour, and their liturgy was to be offering of thanks (not wild antics) and the singing of hymns (not bizarre rituals).

First Reading > Gospel Links
The relationship is that the first reading is part of the theological background of Jn 6. Wisdom in both readings is imagined as food.

Gospel: Jn 6:51-58
Having established that Jesus, the Wisdom sent by the Father, is the Bread of Life, then the question becomes how are the disciples to imagine their encounter with this wisdom. The encounter is in eating and drinking: the community's meal is the sacrament of the Christ, and by eating and drinking in that meal, they are sharing in the banquet of Wisdom, and sharing the banquet of Wisdom is to become united with Wisdom.

In this section of the Bread of Life discourse there is a truly Eucharistic dimension, but note that it is a sacramental dimension built upon the reality of the community's meal, and not simply 'getting Jesus' or 'getting communion'. The link between the Bread of Life christology and the eucharistic theology, which reflects on the community's eating and drinking at its common meal, is formed by the imagery of the Banquet of Wisdom.

HOMILY NOTES

1. When I wander around a supermarket I can buy any food I fancy, from anywhere in the world, at any time in the year. While it might be hard to buy a Christmas Cake in July, virtually anything else I fancy – and can afford – is available all the time. I can choose a menu every day based on what I want, what I like, or what the latest television cooking sensation decrees is what stylish people eat. It could be a wintry day in January, yet I might want a salad and can find all that I need to make it: seasons no longer count, and I might have exotic flavours – all fresh – from three continents. We are less than a generation from when we marvelled that one could get 'new' potatoes all year round, yet in this world of maximum consumer choice we simply cannot grasp the full significance of Jesus describing himself as the bread of life.

2. For most of human history – and history begins with the settled agricultural life of Mesopotamia – the key to life is a ready access to storable carbohydrates: grain which can be turned into bread weeks, months or even years after the harvest. The regularity of the grain harvest was at core of settled, urban life; and it was at the centre of religion in that temples were, *inter alia*, at the centre of urban life in that they were grain stores. So running right through the history of civilisation and/or religion is the issue of having enough grain and avoiding being without it. Grain meant bread, bread meant life; its absence meant famine and death. It is in this context we have to hear the old adage: 'Bread is the staff of life.'

3. This dependence on bread was not some obscure item of economic knowledge: everyone understood it and felt it. The fear of having no bread caused riots, made kings look foolish, made clergy look ineffective, and obtaining grain stood behind a whole range of exertions. One has only to think of the riots over food at the time of the French Revolution or the fear of famine that stalked Irish memories after the famine of 1847. Food and survival are linked in a way we cannot, thankfully, understand.

4. In today's gospel Jesus presents himself as the heavenly equivalent of bread. To survive in this life one relies on bread; to survive in the presence of God one is called to rely on him. Jesus sums up in himself the whole of the faith of Israel: each member of the People is called to rely on him as 'the bread of life'.

5. To have the whole of the Law and the Prophets and the traditions of the fathers all focused on this one individual – he is the one the people are to depend on for survival – was indeed a hard saying. Could it be that this individual's way was the whole of the Law? Could it be that this way was more than the temple? Could it be that this individual's way was what all the prophets had longed for? The answer for us is simple, and we use a hundred titles to express it: Jesus is the way, the truth, the life, the temple, the altar, the sacrifice, the priest, the new Moses, the giver of the new Law, the final and greatest prophet, the Bread of Life, the son of man, and the Son of God. But in today's gospel we glimpse those who could not accept that this one man, Jesus, was all they were waiting for, and we hear John preaching to us the question: Is Jesus going to be your Bread of Life?

6. Accepting Jesus as the centre upon which life, true life, depends is no easier for us than for those who first heard the gospel. Placing Jesus at the centre of life is easy to say, but not easy to do. So we are left with two questions: first, is Jesus our Bread of Life? And second, what image for our dependence on him would you come up with to express the meaning of Jesus, the Bread of Life?

Twenty-first Sunday of Ordinary Time

Introduction to the Celebration

Rather than give an introduction, say something like this:
We are gathered here as sisters and brothers, members of the Body of Christ, so let us introduce ourselves to each other.

Rite of Penance

> For those times when we have failed to accept the teaching of Jesus, Lord have mercy.
>
> For those times when we have failed in faith and hope and love as disciples, Christ have mercy.
>
> For those times when we have not looked to Jesus for the message of eternal life, Lord have mercy.

Headings for Readings

First Reading

In this reading we recall that faith in God is not just 'going with the flow', something that we just happen to do because we have always done it. Faith is the decision to enter a relationship, a covenant, with God. And this relationship involves recalling his goodness, living according to his law, and offering him praise.

Second Reading

Understanding who we are as 'the church' is far more difficult than saying we follow a common teaching or are members of a club: we are the body of Christ. And to try and tease this out, the author of the letter to the Ephesians borrowed from his experience of marriage to explain the relationship of Jesus and the church. We may find his views of marriage are very different to our own, but we have to see through them to try and grasp what he is saying about his real subject: who are we as 'the church'.

Gospel

On the need for an introduction to today's gospel, see notes.

When some disciples heard Jesus claiming that he was the Bread come down from heaven – in other words he was the Father's gift which would give eternal life to those who accepted him – they could not accept this. They imagined that God's ultimate gift to humanity had to be something more spectacular than the man, Jesus, they saw before them. Faced with those who would not accept his words, Jesus put this challenge to the whole group.

Prayer of the Faithful
President

We have been called to be the people whose love and unity spreads a new harmony and purpose within humanity. So, my brothers and sisters, let us pray for the unity of God's people on earth, that we will grow in our awareness of our mission, and that we be given the courage to fulfill it.

Reader (s)

1. For the whole church, all the baptised, that we will recognise the need to work for unity and harmony with each other. Lord hear us.
2. For all communities that are gathering to celebrate the Eucharist this day, that in our sharing at the Lord's table we might discover the unity to which Jesus has called us. Lord hear us.
3. For all who seek to follow Jesus, that the Holy Spirit who gives us life may give us the gift of unity and make us one people proclaiming one Lord. Lord hear us.
4. For all those who lead communities, and all who teach the Christian faith, that they may be inspired by a new vision of the church as God's People and work for its unity. Lord hear us.
5. Specific local needs and topics of the day.
6. For all those sisters and brothers who have died, that we may all be united in Christ at the heavenly Eucharist. Lord hear us.

President

Father, as we gather for this meal at which we offer you our thanks for all your gifts, hear too our needs, for both our petitions and our thanksgivings are made in union with Jesus Christ, your Son, our Lord. Amen.

Eucharistic Prayer
Preface of Sundays in Ordinary Time VI (P34) fits with Peter's confession at the end of the gospel. Then use Eucharistic Prayer II and concentrate more time on the fraction and the sharing of the loaf and cup.

Invitation to the Our Father
Let us stand before the Father and pray to him as disciples of Jesus:

Sign of Peace
The Holy One of God is among us. Let us express the peace and joy towards one another that is fitting for us who gather in his holy presence around his holy table.

Invitation to Communion
Behold the Holy One of God, behold him who takes away the sins of the world, happy are we who are called to his supper.

Communion Reflection
The weeks of reflecting on the Bread of Life discourse should also be a time when a community reflects on how it actually celebrates the Lord's meal and shares in the loaf of bread and cup of wine of the Eucharist. The fundamental imagery is that scattered bits, grains of wheat, are transformed into a greater unity – a loaf of bread which can then be broken so that each of us has a share of it. The same imagery applies to the wine: grapes – which as individual little bunches of fruit (remember wine grapes are not like our dessert grape) are unpalatable, are transformed into a new reality, wine, which is very palatable indeed. A single loaf shows us all sharing a single source of life, and drinking from a common cup is sharing a common destiny. These images – long before we reflect theologically – can speak

volumes to us. So why not get some grain (health food shops stock it), a living loaf (i.e. not unleavened bread), a bunch of dessert grapes (although not what wine is made from, they are familiar and more visible), and a glass of red wine and just remind people of the basic human realities of the meal they have just shared.

Then leave some time for the Spirit to help them do the theology.

Conclusion
Prayer over the People 18 (Missal, p 382) is suitable.

Notes
1. Dropping the Second Reading
The early Christian view on the relation of the sexes, invariably framed in the form of 'men and their wives', always generates antagonism today when it is read. Paul (or in this case 'Deutero-Paul') is on the hit list of long-dead males who have had a hand in the oppression of women. This is unfair in that Paul is seen as promoting the view of women as '*Kinder, Kirche, Kuche.*' But it should be pointed out that virtually all classical writers would have held it was 'sex, sons, and service'. However, fair or not, we have to face two facts:

First, the social views of early Christians on marriage are massively different from our own. Therefore, we must be careful that they are not presented as socially normative, which is a species of fundamentalism.

Second, like it or not, people will be antagonised by this reading. That antagonism can then create a 'blockage' between them and the liturgy, between them and the church, and even within their relationship of prayer with God. If that happens, then the proclamation of the Word has become counter-productive.

So what should we do? The simplest answer seems to be to drop the reading and just pass over its problematic effects. There are cases where this is probably the best course of action: in both the Eucharistic Lectionary and in the Liturgy of the Hours we have dropped the cursing psalms – and the problems they caused have gone away. However, should we do this with the classic ecclesiology of Ephesians? This reading presents one of the most sophisticated ecclesiologies found in any early Christian source, and without it we are not presenting the range of our wealth on the crucial question 'Who are we as the church?'

One solution is to shorten the reading by omitted the most 'offending' verses (21-24) and begin the reading as v 25: 'Husbands should love their wives ... '

Then make sure that it is given a proper introduction which can act as a 'health warning' which stresses that this is about the church, not about relationships between spouses.

Then make sure that it is read by a woman, so that the communication does not appear to be a male defining the role of women. And make sure that she has had time to think about the reading and is happy with the task of reading it.

2. Introducing the Gospel

Even if you are not in the habit of introducing the readings, this is a day when you should consider it for, at least, the gospel. Today's gospel assumes that the group have just heard the teaching that some disciples found intolerable. Now while we might imagine that people will remember what last week's gospel was, in practice few, in any, will be able to recall it. Therefore, today – if this gospel is to make any sense when it is heard – there must be some quick reminder of what has gone before. Think of this introduction as the equivalent to the opening lines of a serial on TV which begins: 'in the last episode ...'

COMMENTARY

First Reading: Jos 24:1-2, 15-18

The Book of Joshua belongs to that idealised history of Israel that we refer to as 'the Deuteronomistic History'. The key word here is idealised: it is theology being presented as history teaching by example. The work was composed within circles that were seeking to develop a far more consistent, and theologically more sophisticated, Judaism that was radically distinct from the religions of the surrounding peoples – a theme that surfaces in this reading. This process of inventing a history that neatly and perfectly reflects a theology may seem strange, but it is worth remembering that the exact same processes were at work in Christian hagiography until relatively recently, and the process continues today in film where our secular myths find perfect expression in any number of Hollywood movies.

In most idealised histories there is a crucial moment of decision: the hero challenges the people to decide between the right way and the wrong way, and this moment of decision comes in Joshua in the renewal of the covenant at Shechem. The moral is clear. The good and righteous people long ago made the right choice, and now the decision is yours: are you going to do the right thing and follow the ways of your fathers? Given that the story is told within a tradition – where the key virtue is to keep in the paths handed down to you – the decision is really a non-event. Rather, the point of the narrative is that the community (who have been listening to the story) re-affirms its commitment to its own identity as the children of those righteous people who made the historic covenant.

Psalm: 33 (34):2-3, 16-23
See the note for Sunday 19.

Second Reading: Eph 5:21-32
This is not a statement on Christian marriage: the use of 'should' is based on the belief that these are common assumptions in the society, this is a state of affairs: what else would/could a woman do but submit to her husband – indeed, in his culture, it would be ridiculous to think of her not doing so. Well, if that is the norm in life, it should be reflected in the attitude of dependence that is the relationship of the church to Christ. However, even this analogy is defective: the relationship is beyond anything we can imagine.

Lastly, when this reading is read, someone always (in a Catholic context) murmurs that this is another case of celibates telling people about marriage! Well, no one is telling anyone about marriage – it is about the church identity in the Christ; and the writer was not celibate – in the churches that came in the wake of Paul, celibacy was highly suspect (just look at the Pastoral epistles).

First Reading > Gospel Links

The link is one of similarity of situation: the people had to choose which way they would follow when they stood before Joshua who represented the covenant; now the people have to choose as they stand before Jesus who is the new covenant.

Gospel: Jn 6:60-69

When the community hears this passage, be that the community listening to John thousands of years ago or the community who hear it read at the liturgy today, it is the intention that they identify themselves with the confession of Peter. They, the listeners, are those who have decided that they should go to Jesus – and there is no one else to go to; and they are those who believe that Jesus is the one with the message of eternal life; and that Jesus is the Holy One of God.

This text appears to be a challenge to those who are hearing the message of Jesus (just as Joshua appears as a challenge to the Israelites) and appears to be a situation: now you must choose: Jesus or not! However, in fact it is not a challenge as the assumption of John is that if you are listening to this, then you have already chosen. So, in reality, it is a statement of identity.

This fact about the narrative structure of both this first reading and this gospel has important consequences for preaching. It is all too easy to imagine that the preacher must now hold a challenge to the congregation: are you for Jesus? This is neither useful nor appropriate. It is not appropriate in that the community is there in Christ as baptised brothers and sisters, not some loose assemblage of people vaguely interested in what Jesus has to say. It is not useful in that it misses the point John wanted to make: know who you are, you are those who belong to the covenant, those who know that Jesus is the Bread of Life, the Holy One of God.

Lastly, the natural unit of text extends to v 71 but the last two verses have been omitted, correctly, because (1) this heightens the dramatic effect of Peter's confession, and (2) the last verses do not make sense when this passage is read as a lection in Mark's Year.

HOMILY NOTES

1. Avoid making challenges!

2. Ask this question: Who are we as a people, what unites us, what draws us here, what makes us live the lives we do?

3. We are the community who assert with Peter that there is no one else, but Jesus, who has the message of eternal life.

4. We are the community who assert with Peter that Jesus is the Holy One of God.

5. Now let us stand up and state that formally in our profession of faith.

Twenty-second Sunday of Ordinary Time

Introduction to the Celebration

We gather here because Jesus has made us welcome. He has called us, he has chosen us, he desires that we love one another around his table.

This is our great religious gathering: we affirm who we are, what we believe, we ask the Father for our needs, and we thank him for our lives and all our blessings.

So what are the characteristic human qualities with which we should approach God? For many, it is some notion of being 'clean', or having observed all the minute rules, having done and said all the correct things connected with religion. Today, Jesus lifts us completely out of that view. In order to be able to stand here in the presence of the Father, we must be people whose lives bring forth good for others, who do not injure others, and who seek to care for others.

Rite of Penance

For those times when we have only offered God lip service. Lord have mercy.

For those times when we have not worshipped God from the heart. Christ have mercy.

For those times when we have let wicked deeds and thoughts come from within us. Lord have mercy.

Headings for Readings
First Reading

A life that is based on following the ways of the Lord will bring wisdom and understanding.

Second Reading

We have been made children of the Father, and we serve him when we care for those in need such as widows and orphans.

Gospel

We are called to praise God from the depths of our hearts in every action of our lives. In this way we will become the Lord's holy people.

Prayer of the Faithful

President

As a people made holy by our incorporation into Jesus Christ, now let us stand in the presence of the Father, and pray.

Reader (s)

1. Let us pray for the whole church of God, scattered around the world, that it may be truly holy, and reflect the glory of God to humanity. Lord hear us.

2. Let us prayer for this church gathered here, that it may be holy and be the presence of Jesus in this society. Lord hear us.

3. Let us pray for ourselves, that we may act in ways that bring goodness, peace, and love to those around us, and make us a people worthy to bear the Lord's name. Lord hear us.

4. Let us pray for all humanity, that we will act with justice and responsibility in all our actions, knowing that what we do always has effects far beyond what we can see. Lord hear us.

5. Specific local needs and topics of the day.

6. Let us pray for our sisters and brothers who have gone before us marked with the sign of faith. May they find in God's presence light, happiness and peace. Lord hear us.

President

Father, may our worship not be worthless. May we praise you not only with our lips but with all our deeds, and may you hear these prayers we make as your holy people gathering in Christ Jesus, our Lord. Amen.

Eucharistic Prayer
No Preface or Eucharistic Prayer is particularly suitable for today.

Invitation to the Our Father
Now let us stand before the Father, as the holy people of Jesus Christ, and in the power of the Spirit, say:

Sign of Peace
From the depths of our heart can come the peace that builds our human family and the kingdom. Let us express that peace to one another.

Invitation to Communion
Behold the Lord, behold him who calls us to eat and drink at this banquet with clean hands and clean hearts, and with him to offer thanks to the Father.

Communion Reflection
Repetition often means that the second time we hear something we are able to absorb it more deeply.

Have some of the last verses of today's gospel read slowly, without any introduction, while people sit and listen. Here the text is laid out in sense-lines to facilitate reflective reading:

Listen to me,
All of you,
And understand.
Nothing that goes into someone from outside makes a person unclean.
It is what comes out of someone that makes a person unclean.
For it is from within,
From people's hearts,
That evil intentions emerge.

Conclusion

May your lips bring forth true worship of the Father during the coming week. Amen.

May your hands collaborate with Christ in building the kingdom of peace and justice. Amen.

May your hearts be filled with the Spirit and be the source of good deeds. Amen.

Notes

Today's gospel reading, in any of the translations found in lectionaries, contains masculine language (e.g. 'nothing that goes into a man ...') when in reality 'man' here is used to cover both men and women. Many clergy dismiss such worries as if they only belong to a 'lunatic fringe' and hold that concern over 'sexist language' is 'simply political correctness' – and that it makes no difference. Alas, there will be many people in any average congregation who will not accept such dismissals and will find this language in the lectionary deeply offensive. Whether or not you agree with them is not the issue; the issue is that celebrants are charged with communicating the Word of God, and if some detail in the medium stops reception, then it has to be removed with the same care that a booming echo in a microphone system is removed.

The simplest way to deal with today's reading is to replace (without comment) 'man' with 'person'; and replace 'men's' with 'people's'.

COMMENTARY

First Reading: Deut 4:1-2, 6-8

The book was written as part of a theological reflection on what the destruction of the temple in the sixth century could mean for Israel. The response was the creation of the new law book that would regulate how the people could return to re-possess the land, to form a new people, and build a new temple. In this reform, this book, this 'Second Law,' suitably located within the life of the greatest lawgiver, Moses himself, played a key role.

Here is the scene the hearers of Deuteronomy are asked to imagine: their wandering in the desert for forty years are over, it is the eve of entering the land promised them, so now, just before his death, Moses gives them one last sermon setting out the demands of God and declaring them to be as unchanging and binding on them as those laws written in stone.

The passage we read today is the opening exhortation of the whole book: it sets out the need for the law, its excellence in comparison with other laws, and its results. If the people keep the law, then they will keep possession of the land, and by being able to remain in the land they remain with the range of the temple.

The text is well edited for reading: omitting vv 3-5 does not affect the reading. However, given that the gospel actually cites Isa 29:13, it is a pity that was not used as a first reading.

Psalm: 14 (15)

This text has to be read as a preparation for the gospel: it is purity of heart that establishes the person who can dwell on the Lord's holy mountain.

Second Reading: Jas 1:17-18, 21-22, 27

These verses, edited here so that they might be seen as a bunch of sound bites, reflect James's concerns that faith find expression in the practical action of Christian living. For James, any preaching which does not include this practical dimension is a deception.

First Reading > Gospel Links

The link is obscure. The first reading is a general exhortation on the importance of the law; the gospel is a radical reinterpretation of what constitutes the 'cleanness' of the group. One possible link is that the first reading could be seen to illustrate why legal discussions, such as encountered in the gospel, were significant.

Gospel: Mk 7:1-8, 14-15, 21-23

This text has always proved problematic for Christians. Mark's basic incident, no doubt tied to a memory going back to the events in Jesus's life, is a dispute with some Pharisees on what makes a group clean/unclean. This was a religious category that rapidly disappeared among the Greek-speaking churches: clean and unclean became meaningless, and the emphasis shifted to be up-right before God. Hence the incident was wrapped up in Mark into a larger discussion on the importance of the commandments (omitted in today's gospel) that makes the whole story hard to follow. The lack of sympathy with the incident can then be seen in that it was radically changed by Matthew in his preaching (Mt 15:1-20), while Luke dropped it altogether.

The key is to note that cleanness is not an individual virtue, but a religious quality of individuals as members of a group, be that the group of the disciples of a teacher, a family, a gathering for worship, or a gathering in a house for a meal. The group would not want someone with them who could make them 'unclean' (think of 'uncleanness' as a spiritual infection which impedes entry into the sphere of the holy); while a clean individual would not want to be contaminated by associating with an unclean group.

This is a religious category that had/has a prominent place in many religions, but is at the very limits of our understanding. Here lies the value in reading today's gospel. It shows us the dangers of reducing the text to our own size and our own culture. Such reductions commit the intellectual crime of colonisation, and the religious crime of fundamentalism.

HOMILY NOTES

1. This gospel's message can seem trite to the point of irrelevance. Our society takes three things for granted – indeed, it makes them the basis for much of its thinking about religion in general and about Christian observance in particular. First, active morality is more important than religious ritual. Second, intention is more important than following prescriptions about details: following conscience is the high road to moral integrity. Third, what's really important in what reli-

gious leaders, such as Jesus, have taught is basic human morality: so avoiding murder, theft, and avarice are more important in living a good life than regular prayers or obeying rules on 'observances'. All that 'mere ritual' can be put to one side, so long as we behave morally towards others. There is much truth in all of this – so is today's gospel simply Jesus's affirmation of this position?

2. If this is so, then this piece of gospel, good news, is not really good news at all! Moreover, in the early communities where this was preached they were careful about regular prayer, gathering for the Eucharist, and conveying a new style of living – so is this gospel really saying that all that activity was really irrelevant, and that so long as people conscientiously followed a way of respecting others, then the 'religious bits' were dispensable? That is how many would read or want to read this gospel: care of others is fine, care of the planet is fine, some spirituality (as a private commodity) is fine. But 'religion' with its group observances, its gatherings, and its demands is just old hat! And, according to the way that many people read this gospel, it seems that Jesus agrees.

3. Therefore, this is a very good day to point out just how easy it is to hear ancient scriptures, imagine that one understands them, and then go off with totally the wrong idea. The essence of all fundamentalism is to take ancient writings from another culture, another way of thinking and understanding, and to colonise them so that they mean what we think they mean in our culture. Therefore, preaching today should have two objectives. First, to show the gathering just how easy it is to read a text and take completely the wrong message from it – and, thereby, to show them the dangers of biblical fundamentalism. The second objective is incidental: to show how this gospel still has a key message for us, and how we might get at it.

4. Showing the dangers of fundamentalism is something that has to be done in a number of steps.

   Step 1: To show that a 'simple', so-called 'obvious' 'plain' reading of the text, leads to a contradiction. Namely: if it is the case that the 'religious bits' can be just sidelined in favour of being kind to one's neighbour, why did the early Christians who first heard this gospel – and were in a far better position to understand it that we are – pay such attention to those very religious bits?

Step 2: If the 'plain, simple' reading leads to a contradiction (i.e. 'it just does not add up'), then are we missing something in today's gospel? We should note that the Pharisees do not accuse Jesus's disciples of being bad people, nor do they accuse them of being unjust, or even of lacking in holiness. What they accuse them of being is unclean.

Step 3: We still use in everyday life the notions of being just/unjust (this is a quality of individuals); we also use the notions of being caring/uncaring (again, a quality of individuals); and we even, sometimes use the notion of being 'holy' – but we tend to think of it in terms of individuals so we say X or Y is a holy person, but we have difficulty nowadays in thinking of a collectivity as holy as in 'the holy church of God.'

However, we do not use the notion of clean/unclean as a category for people.

So to understand today's gospel, we must first discover what the notion of clean/unclean (alien concepts in our culture) meant in a culture that is very foreign to our own.

Step 4: Clean/unclean are not individual virtues, but social qualities: the real danger of someone doing something unclean is not what it does to the person as an individual, but what it does to the whole group to which the person belongs. This is a very different way of thinking to how we think: the whole group is affected by what we think of as purely private actions. The reason that the Pharisees are worried about what the disciples are doing is not because they are concerned for the souls of the disciples, but because they are concerned for themselves! The impure actions of the disciples is making everyone – who is gathered in the same place as the disciples – unclean!

We can barely understand this type of thinking. Perhaps the nearest we come to it is when there is a flu bug about and people are asked to stay at home, not because it will make them better, but because it will stop it spreading and make the larger group unwell. Uncleanness is like a contagion: the whole group suffers because of the carelessness and lack of group awareness and group care of individuals.

Step 5: Knowing that, how are we to understand this gospel? Jesus does not dismiss the notion of uncleanness, he changes the list of actions by which an individual can damage the whole group, and its ability to stand before God as a holy people. The actions of individuals that damage the whole group, its ability to be the people of God, its ability to stand before God and ask for its needs and the needs of humanity (as we will do in the Prayers of the Faithful) and its ability to reflect God's love to the world is the list given at the end of the gospel.

Step 6: Each hearer of the gospel gathered today (especially clergy in the aftermath of child sex-abuse scandals within the church in recent years) have to ask how his/her individual actions have not only damaged them as individuals, but have had the effect of making the whole people unclean, unholy, unfit to stand before the world as the Body of Christ.

5. Discovering how easy it is to slip into fundamentalism is something that takes most people by surprise: and it is a lesson we have to learn over and over again. Discovering the 'deeper' meaning of the gospel – as opposed to a trite message that suits us – can also be a painful surprise: today is a case in point.

Twenty-third Sunday of Ordinary Time

Introduction to the Celebration

The Rite of Blessing and Sprinkling Holy Water (Missal, p 387) is appropriate because the gospel is that of Jesus restoring hearing and speech to the deaf man with the speech impediment.

A more focused introduction could take this form:

Dear friends,

Today's gospel reminds us that when we were baptised,

the Lord touched our ears to receive his word and our mouths to proclaim his faith.

Now we have gathered together to listen to his word and to proclaim that faith.

So, let us ask God to bless this water, which we will use to remind us of our baptism, and to keep us faithful to the Spirit he has given us.

Headings for Readings

First Reading

The prophet looks forward to the time when God will visit his people and redeem them: then the blind will see, the deaf will hear, the lame walk, and the dumb sing. As we listen to God's promise we might recall that we are those who often are blind to truth and injustice, we are those who are often deaf to God's word or the cries of the oppressed, we are those who stumble in our discipleship, and we are those who often fail to open our lips in praise of God.

Second Reading

The social miracle of the early church was that people of every class – in a highly stratified society – came together: their new relationship as sisters and brothers in Christ cut across social divisions. In this reading, James reminds the church that this new social reality is not an optional 'add-on' to Christian faith, but belongs to the essence of faith. To believe in Jesus is to belong to a new people who act in a new way.

Gospel
In the gospel Jesus reveals himself as the one who carries out the tasks of the Messiah: he restores hearing and speech to a disabled person, and those who see this recognise that these are the signs that a new prophet has been sent by God.

Profession of Faith
Use the Renewal of Baptismal Promises from the Easter Sunday liturgy (Missal, pp 220-1). In the introduction, omit the line: 'Now that we have completed our Lenten observance.'

Prayer of the Faithful
President
At our baptism we became the children of God receiving the right to call God our Father in the midst of the church, so now let us ask him for our needs.
Reader (s)
1. For the whole church, that we will hear the word of God and courageously proclaim it. Lord hear us.
2. For this community, that our ears will be opened to hear the word of God in this assembly and our mouths enabled to offer praise. Lord hear us.
3. For all who are disabled and have difficulties in communicating, that they may experience God's love. Lord hear us.
4. For all who work in the media, that they may be attentive to the truth and willing to communicate it. Lord hear us.
5. For all who have difficulties with faith, that their ears may be opened to hear God's word in their lives. Lord hear us.
6. For all who have difficulty in praying and in offering thanks to God, that their mouths may be opened in praise. Lord hear us.
President
Father, we have gathered to listen and to offer praise, hear the

people the Holy Spirit has gathered here in union with Jesus Christ, your Son, our Lord. Amen.

Eucharistic Prayer
Today's gospel reminds us that the ability to hear God's word and to offer praise is, itself, a gift of God; this is expressed well in a preface that most people never hear: Preface of Weekdays IV (P40) – so today is a good day to use it. No Eucharistic Prayer is particularly suitable.

Invitation to the Our Father
Let us open our lips in prayer and praise to the Father:

Sign of Peace
If we are to hear the word of God, we must be willing to be peacemakers. Let us now show that willingness to one another.

Invitation to Communion
The Lord made the deaf hear and the dumb speak. He has done all things well, and now he invites us to share in his supper.

Communion Reflection
We have listened to the word of God.

We have opened our lips in praise and thanksgiving to the Father.

May this food strengthen us to continue our journey over the coming week with ears open to God's word.

May this drink give us the gift of opening our mouths in praise and thanksgiving.

May our communion with Christ enable us to say to others who cannot hear or pray: 'Be opened.' Amen.

Conclusion
Solemn Blessing 7 (Easter Season), Missal, p 370, is appropriate if you have used the mystery of baptism as a theme linking various parts of the liturgy.

Notes

1. A renewal of readers

The action of Jesus in today's gospel has become an action of the church in the little ceremony of 'the Ephphatha'. Indeed, it is that action of the church that sets the tone for reading the gospel in the way that Mark, most probably, intended it to be read: the deaf man is a symbol of all of us: we need to have our ears un-stopped and our mouths opened. Moreover, in receiving this gift we recognise Jesus as the Christ. However, very few people notice the ceremony at baptism, and many will never have seen it. Therefore, the task today is to make this tradition visible within the community; and if this is seen, and it becomes part of the memory, then this gospel will have been preached effectively.

The question is now: how should this action become visible? One solution might be to have a baptism at today's Eucharist – if there is one pending within the community. However, this draws attention – as it should – to the whole mystery of baptism, rather than this particular ritual.

An alternative solution would be to call on adults who are preparing for baptism to receive this ritual today – but this sup-poses there is/are such person/s in the community; and doing this can become simply a demonstration for its own sake, and it can smack of classroom re-enactments.

A more creative solution is to see today as a day when the ministry of those who read at the liturgy is formally acknowl-edged as a ministry – not just a job that needs doing – in the midst of the community that hears them. The instruction on the lectionary assumes that anyone who reads/proclaims the word of God, must already be a hearer of the word of God, and grow-ing in her/his attentiveness to the word of God. So one could celebrate this with as many readers as are present in the assem-bly today. The ceremony could take this form:

Assemble the readers/psalmists in front of the community.

'Brothers and sisters, you have been called from this commu-nity to proclaim to us the word of God and to lead us in praising him in our singing of the psalms.

Let us remember what the church teaches us about the word of God in our celebrations:

That word constantly proclaimed in the liturgy is always a living, active word through the power of the Holy Spirit. It expresses the Father's love that never fails in its effectiveness towards us.

You are the messengers of that love, and when you were baptised we prayed that your ears would be opened to hear that word and mouths opened to proclaim that word.

We make this prayer again today,

asking the Spirit to renew you through your ministry among us, so that your ministry / service among us may bear greater fruit.

Silent prayer for a moment.

Then touch with your thumb the ears and closed lips of each reader using either the formula rite of infant baptism (omitting the word 'soon'):

The Lord Jesus made the deaf hear and the dumb speak. May he touch your ears to receive his word and your mouth to proclaim his faith to the praise and glory of God the Father

Or the formula from RCIA:

Ephphatha: that is be opened, that you may profess the faith you hear to the praise and glory of God.

Then the group return to their places. Then move to the renewal of baptismal promises or preach.

2. Ephphetha or Ephphatha?

In today's lectionary this Aramaic word, retained by Mark, is spelled 'ephphatha' and this is the correct form for it transliterates what is found in the Greek text of Mark. The word is best pronounced as eF – faa (as in far) – thaa (as in that). However, in liturgical books it is always spelled 'ephphetha' (and pronounced: ef – fay – tha) which is derived from early Latin translations which mis-transliterated the Greek text as *eppheta*.

It is best to stick to one spelling and one pronunciation, and the obvious choice is the accurate transliteration: 'ephphatha.'

3. *The Second Reading and Inclusive Language*

Many people in the average congregation will find the two references to 'brothers' off-putting; unfortunately, such people often do not bother to mention this, unless asked, as they imagine that mentioning it would be a waste of time. Then, in turn, many church leaders imagine that concerns over inclusive language is restricted to a few vociferous 'extremists'.

So in the opening and closing verses of today's reading, simply add 'and sisters': 'My brothers and sisters, do not try ...'; and 'Listen, my dear brothers and sisters: it was those ...'

COMMENTARY

First Reading: Isa 35:4-7

Chapters 34 and 35 present a vision of Israel's glorious future and the joy of the redeemed. It is the perfect time of the messiah when all will be restored and 'put right'. And within this broad sweeping vision of messianic times – which exercised a profound influence on those who followed Jesus as Mark's gospel shows us – these verses form a little set-piece: it will all be wonderful, every problem, big and small will be removed. At the same time, nowhere is it made more clear that the joy of the messianic times is the gift of God and the messiah's coming an expression of his love for his people of the covenant.

Psalm: 145 (146)

This psalm emphasised that the Lord is the giver of all good things: his love restores, protects, and heals. It is the ideal prayerful response to the first reading.

Second Reading: Jas 2:1-5

The Greco-Roman world in which Christianity appeared was a society organised around an honour system: everyone knew exactly where he was fixed in the pecking order of the household, the village, the city, and the wide world (women, on the whole did not figure in this pecking order, but took their place from the male responsible for them (father, husband, owner) except they were inferior to that male. This was something far more deep-seated that our notions of class-distinction: it was the very structure within which life was lived.

Into this came Christianity with its notion of the radical equality of slaves and free, male and female in Christ as children of the Father: equality expressed in the very way the group met and organised itself. Indeed, at the meeting, all ate from one table as equals, shared a common loaf, and, horror of horrors, they even passed round a common cup!

However, all this stuff about being brothers in Christ was just too much: and already by Paul's time it was causing problems in Corinth. By the time of this letter, probably a generation later, there was an even more profound dissonance between the basic teaching and the actual practice at the Christian meals (what in the second century would be termed 'Eucharists'). It is in this context that the letter makes its teaching crystal clear: favouritism and class-distinctions are incompatible with Christian faith. And, then as the examples illustrate, this new social behaviour that goes with faith must find expression in the way their meals are celebrated. Those who organise great official occasions when the Eucharist is used as if it were simply a convenient ritual format, and then arrange all the VIPs in order in their special seats, and then have special escorting 'chaplains' for politicians, should read this whole section (2:1-13) with care!

First Reading > Gospel Links

This is a straight-forward case of prophecy-fulfillment; indeed, Mark's miracle event is modelled on today's passage from Isa 35. Today we have a perfect combination of first reading and gospel.

Gospel: Mk 7:31-7

This healing, which follows the pattern of healings in Mark, is intended to be read as one more indication of the arrival and nature of the messianic times. Each healing and each miracle is like a pointer to one more aspect of Jesus as 'the christ'.

At the end of the healing, the crowd's reaction and amazement is a direct allusion to the reaction described in Isa 35:5-6; and for Mark, the healing taken with the reaction is an indication that the glorious future, which was long awaited, is already a reality in Jesus. But there is still the 'messianic secret' when Jesus orders them to tell no one of the miracle, yet the more he tells them this, the more they ignore him. Mark is anxious that no one should think of Jesus just as a healer: the messiah only becomes truly visible in the cross and resurrection.

Since this miracle is only found in a much cut-down form in Matthew (15:29-31), this is a very good place to see just what a distinctive theological voice Mark had. Moreover, the details of the Ephphatha, which has had such a profound impact on the liturgy of baptism, is only found here.

HOMILY NOTES

1. Better than just a homily today is to have a little ceremony of ephphatha (see notes), and then perhaps say a few words. However, if that is not possible, then here are some notes.

2. There is a little ritual in the rite of baptism – alas it is often omitted – whose name and form is taken from today's gospel: 'The Ephphatha'. The celebrant touches the ears and then the lips of the one to be baptised saying: 'The Lord Jesus made the deaf hear and the dumb speak. May he soon touch your ear to receive his word and your mouth to proclaim his faith …' This simple ceremony captures not only what is the kernel of today's gospel, but a most profound aspect of our faith: its 'giftedness'.

3. In the first reading we hear the prophet describing the people in terms of their disabilities: stumbling, hard of hearing, with poor sight – the sad reality of the human condition. But holding out the promise of God's help, and aid, and mercy: the gift of the Promised One will be the gift of new sight, new hearing, and new lips. And the miracle in today's gospel is a demonstration that this time has come: Jesus is the gift of the Father to us.

4. The gift of new sight shows us the true nature of the creation: the universe exists in dependence on God's will; we human creatures exist because of his love, and our destiny is not within the creation, but in union with God.

5. The gift of new hearing allows us to hear the word of God in our gatherings, in the situations and ups and downs of life, and in our consciences. We can come to know that God loves us, cares for us, and calls us to be his ministers and his witnesses.

6. The gift of new speech allows us to praise him in prayer, to proclaim the truth to sisters and brothers, and to announce the good news of Jesus.

7. God's gift to us is the gift of receiving and the gift of transmitting. We are enabled to hear the word of God, and we are empowered to communicate the word of God. In opening our ears and lips, Jesus gathers us up into his own divine life.

Lectionary Unit III.I

This unit consists of eleven Sundays (Sundays 24 to 34 inclusive) whose overall theme is the Mystery of the Son of Man. It is made up of three stages:

I.   The 'Way' of the Son of Man.

II.   The final revelation in Jerusalem.

III. The fulfilment of the mystery.

The first stage runs from the twenty-fourth to the thirtieth Sunday. It opens with Peter's confession of faith and then the narrative that immediately follows in Mark.

Twenty-fourth Sunday of Ordinary Time

Introduction to the Celebration

This year we have been reading the gospel of Mark each Sunday. Today we come to its centre: Mark built his whole story around the moment of declaration by the disciples about who they believed Jesus really is: 'You are the Christ!' Once, the disciples had recognised his full identity, they were ready to be presented with the demands of being disciples, people who had chosen to follow his way. Today, this gospel presents us with the same challenge. By assembling here we are declaring our belief in the identity of Jesus as the Christ, the Son of the Father. But having declared that faith, we now have to face the challenge of following his way. This way is the way of renouncing self, of taking up our crosses, and of being prepared to see in his way a radically different way of living.

Rite of Penance

O Anointed One, O Son of Man, give us strength to follow in your way. Lord have mercy.

O Anointed One, O Son of Man, give us strength to renounce ourselves, and take up our crosses, and follow you. Christ have mercy.

O Anointed One, O Son of Man, give us strength to lose our lives for your sake and the sake of the gospel. Lord have mercy.

Headings for Readings

First Reading

The prophet announces that the Anointed One of God will suffer as a result of seeking to do the Father's will.

Second Reading

Faith is not about warm feeling and good intentions: if we are disciples of the Christ, then we must be taking care of the needy, the poor, those who are suffering. Belief without action is dead.

Gospel

This gospel poses to all who declare that Jesus is the Christ, the Anointed One, the challenge that we must not simply believe, but embark on the way of discipleship.

Prayer of the Faithful
President

Gathered in the presence of Jesus, the Christ, let us now stand before the Father and pray for our needs, the needs of all Christians, and the needs of all humanity.

Reader (s)

1. Let us pray for the church throughout the world, may we declare that Jesus is the Christ before our world. Lord hear us.

2. Let us pray for all Christians, that each of us may have the strength to carry our individual crosses and follow the way of the Son of Man. Lord hear us.

3. Let us pray for those for whom life is full of sorrow and whose crosses are breaking them, that God may offer them strength and move human hearts to help them with their burdens. Lord hear us.

4. Let us pray for this community, that each of us will not only confess that Jesus is the Christ with our lips, but live that faith in action towards our sisters and brothers in need. Lord hear us.

5. Specific local needs and topics of the day.

President

Father, we confess that you have anointed Jesus with the oil of gladness as our priest, our prophet, and our king. Hear us now for we are the people of Jesus Christ and we make these prayers in his name. Amen.

Eucharistic Prayer

Preface of Lent III (P 10), Missal, p 413, could be a paraphrase of today's second reading and the latter part of the gospel; and therefore is most suitable for today. Moreover, since this is a preface for the weekdays of Lent it is a text that few in any congregation will have any familiarity with. Because it is a short preface, it fits very well with Eucharistic Prayer II.

Invitation to the Our Father
We are the people who have confessed that Jesus is the Christ, and he has sent his Spirit into our hearts to enable us now to call on the Father:

Sign of Peace
As fellow travellers on the way of discipleship, let us resolve to live in peace with one another.

Invitation to Communion
Let us behold the Christ, the Anointed of the Father, whose Spirit gathers us about this table; happy are we who are called to his supper.

Communion Reflection
Only in reflection can the full implications of discipleship become apparent to us; so have a structured silence with this as the theme. Introduce it with some formula like this:

> Silent reflection is part of our lives as Christians – only in reflection can we grasp the implications of discipleship for us personally. Let us reflect for the next sixty seconds on what the way of the Lord means for us.

Then measure 60 seconds on your watch, and conclude the silence by standing and saying 'Let us pray.'

Conclusion
On this day when we recall the disciples' confession that Jesus is the Christ, may he strengthen you to be his disciples during the coming week. Amen.
On this day when we recall the disciples' confession that Jesus is the Christ, may he strengthen you to carry your cross in the days ahead. Amen.

On this day when we recall the disciples' confession that Jesus is the Christ, may he strengthen you to confess in the coming days his way as the way to eternal life. Amen.

Notes

This is one of those days when quite by chance there is a clear overlap of ideas between the second reading and the latter part of the gospel. While it would be foolish not to make use of this overlap in having a clear theme to communicate today, this should be done without references that explicitly link the second reading and the gospel as this would simply reinforce the widespread notion among people that the three readings 'must somehow join up'.

COMMENTARY

First Reading: Isa 50:5-9

This is the third of the so-called 'Servant Songs' and differs from the others in that the servant and the speaker are the same person: 'For my part I made no resistance, neither did I turn away.' The servant sees suffering as his duty, he does his duty, and then the Lord comes to his help and before the Lord no one condemns him.

This has usually been read by Christians as a song in the mouth of the Christ, and it is as such that we read it today in the liturgy: just as in the gospel – picking up its theme from this text – Jesus says that the Son of Man must suffer grievously, so here the Word says the very same thing as an expression of his mission of obedience to the Father. This christological reading, building on how the first generations of Christians searched their common memory to make sense of the ministry of Jesus, has inspired many of the most beautiful liturgical creations of the Easter liturgy, perhaps most notably the '*improperia*' drama that is still part of the Good Friday liturgy, though, since it became optional, it is now rarely used. However, this christological reading is also highly problematic: it can be read – as it has so often been read in western Christianity – as if the Father is extracting a punishment, blood-price, for reconciliation. In brutish form it runs like this: the Father knows that humanity deserve a punishment for their sins; the Son wants to save them, so he must redeem this penalty; therefore he must suffer the cross to pay the penalty. This notion, far more widely diffused at the popular level than many would admit, makes nonsense of the whole of the rest of the Christian message: God is a stern Father who needs to be appeased, propitiated with sacrifice, and what would make a suitable sacrifice – the bloody suffering of his 'beloved' Son! Regrettably, this is actually quite an accurate exegesis of this text. The text arose in the New Year Festival liturgy in Babylon where the king – the sacral figure who linked the people to the gods – had to be ritually tortured to make reparation for the failures of the people to give due honour to the gods during the past year: the king's suffering as the anointed one restored the people, and started life, the new year, anew. This ritual also influenced the Jewish Day of Atonement liturgy (Lev 16), except that here the suffering was not that of the king or high priest, but of the scapegoat. The scapegoat took the sins away, and the people started afresh. So here the servant is the scapegoat.

But while it may have been inevitable that the Christ should suffer (because his way would upset the ways of sinful humanity); it is a very different thing to present that as destined by the Father because of his 'need' for a scapegoat. Therefore, any use of this text must acknowledge just how problematic it is when read christologically, and use it with great care. We hardly serve the God who is love by making the Father a projection of all that is worst in a tyrannical parent extracting vengeance on her/his child.

Psalm: 114 (116)

This is read as the song of the disciple: s/he cries out to the Lord in distress, but with faith that the Lord will care for her/him, and let the disciple walk in the land of the living.

Second Reading: Jas 2:14-18

This is the first part of a section that runs to v 26; and it is the passage that created controversy at the Reformation with its clear endorsement that faith without works is dead. For Luther and Calvin it was the text behind the whole 'erroneous' doctrine of works rather than relying (which is what they say as the act of faith) on grace to be saved. When we take this passage out of such arcane debates, we see a text that speaks directly to the situation of the earliest churches and, indeed, to us today. Christianity was unique among ancient religions in that it spread among many strata of a very stratified society: in particular, we find it among the merchant class (e.g. Corinth); the labourer class (e.g. Rome); and even among slaves. Yet, all these groups were to see themselves as a single community, a new people. So one could not be part of the community, have wealth, and ignore compassion for the poor. It is this real, practical concern that is a function of Christian belonging that is the object of James' argument using a series of hypothetical cases.

Given that there are still poor brothers and sisters in every community, and the whole community worldwide, the arguments still hold good.

First Reading > Gospel Links

This is not a relationship of 'prophecy-fulfilment,' although it looks very like it. Rather it is a case that both readings refer to the same reality: the sufferings of the Lord's Anointed One which both readings prophesy. So the relationship is one of the continuity and consistency of the Lord's revelation in the two covenants.

Gospel: Mk 8:27-35

Today's gospel is presented by Mark as a single scene taking place at Caesarea Philippi (the scene extends from 8:27 to 9:1); but it is made up of three parts: first, the confession of faith that Jesus is the Anointed One (vv 27-30); second, the prediction of the passion, death, and resurrection (vv 31-33); and, third, that the disciple can expect his/her life to follow the same pattern as that of the Christ (vv 34-35). All these elements of the scene are present also in Matthew and Luke, but the way they follow on from one another in Mark – almost like logical consequences – is found most clearly in Mark and gives this gospel an unique tone.

We tend to break them apart: one bit is 'christology', another is about 'encouraging the twelve', and the other is about discipleship – but for Mark this passage is a unity and it is at the very centre of his preaching. Here it all becomes plain: who Jesus is and his task and his people. Following is about who one follows, who that leader is and what he does, and about what is expected for those who come in the wake of the leader. For Mark, here we have his message in a nutshell. Yes, the Christ will rise, but before that there is the experience of being with him and the cross: his cross and one's own. Once we see this as Mark's core message, it is easier to see why his preaching, in its original form, ended with the death and burial of Jesus. Resurrection is but a promise for the future for those who are, as disciples, carrying their crosses.

HOMILY NOTES

1. The gospel presents us with a single message in two stages: if you acknowledge that Jesus is the Christ, then you embark on a life of discipleship. However, that is too complex a notion to try to communicate to an average congregation of people in various stages of life, with differing levels of religious commitment, a variety of listening abilities, educational backgrounds, and Christian spiritual 'awareness' – all in less than 10 minutes! So it is perhaps better to focus on a single aspect of the gospel and try to explicate that and help people come to a deeper understanding of that one aspect of today's gospel.

2. Two themes come easily to mind. The first is a homily built around 'the challenge' of discipleship. In its crudest form it sounds like: if you believe, then you must be ready to die for your beliefs. The problem is that unless one is in an extreme situation, this is just 'hot' rhetoric that excites a few hotheads

in the congregation, but switches off most as a harangue. We can all offer challenges – and they are offered *de facto* in the liturgy today, but preaching needs to tap into something more reflective. Moreover, if preachers throw out challenges, then it has to be transparent that they are ready to be as daring themselves. Most clerics are seen by the congregations as anything but that: they are company men who keep the show running but are not prepared to offer challenges to their own leaders about discipleship, so why are they willing to throw out challenges to their flocks. So, unless there is a pressing need to adopt the challenge model, leave it alone.

The second is based on the theme of 'faith without words is dead'; and takes the form that belief must involve making a practical difference in the world around you, faith is not 'pie in the sky when you die' but social engagement. However, that can become a simple exhortation to moral or social work rather than a homily which helps people hear what the Spirit is saying (which includes the notion that an incarnational faith must engage with the world around us). To preach that discipleship involves works is either to state the obvious, or else requires that there is some very specific task that a community needs to undertake as part of its particular discipleship – but even then care must be taken that a homily does not become simply an advertising slot for some specific task.

3. An altogether different approach is to focus on the notion of the cross which lies at the heart of Mark's preaching today. Most preachers are so familiar with the cross as a concept, a liturgical object, or even an item of decoration, that we fail to appreciate just how off-putting many people – many Christians included – find it as an object, icon, image, and symbol. The notion of glorifying the image of a tortured, contorted body on an instrument of execution seems to smack of the grotesque. It can appear to glorify all that is vile in human nature, to rejoice in suffering for its own sake, and to be life-rejecting, joy-rejecting, and convey a message that religion is a dismal, dour business.

4. Many apologists then jump up and shout that that is not what it means, that is not how Christians see the world, that is not the message of the cross! Yes, this is all true; but the problem with symbols is that they communicate with us *before* we hear what they mean. And, in a culture where faith-meanings are not absorbed simultaneously with the faith-symbols, we have a problem.

5. Tackling that problem in the homily situation is a two-step process. First, acknowledge the problem. This will come as surprise to many in the congregation, but it will be useful for that group to realise that many fundamental Christian symbols are no longer 'obvious to all'. However, there will be some people in every gathering who will share this cultural unease with the cross and having that unease openly spoken about is often a great help: the individual is not alone in finding this aspect of faith/liturgy difficult.

6. The second stage is to ask why the earliest Christians focused on the cross as one of their basic symbols – along with baptism and the Eucharist? Why, when they preached that Jesus is risen as their basic message, did they bother with the cross? Christians focus on the cross because of a realistic assessment of what living a life of discipleship will cost. Working honestly, working justly, working for reconciliation is not only difficult, it generates opposition, and often provokes ridicule from others. In every generation Christians have realised that if they seek to follow the way of the Son of Man, then they will encounter the cross.

7. Using it as a symbol is a declaration of what living as a disciple of Jesus will involve. Using it, we can never be accused of making false promises under a 'trade descriptions' act'!

8. This sort of homily is not a theology of the Holy Cross, rather it is following up the notion of the cross as used in today's gospel, and as part of a low level programme of apologetics: giving sisters and brothers answers to the questions round about us.

Twenty-fifth Sunday of Ordinary Time

Introduction to the Celebration

Each week when we gather here we renew our commitment to being disciples: to following the way of the Lord on our pilgrimage through life. And as a pilgrim people we have been listening to Mark during this year as he reminds us of the demands of discipleship. Today we hear Mark reminding us as disciples that the core of the mystery we celebrate is that Jesus, the Son of Man was arrested, put to death, and rose again. This is the mystery of faith. But we also hear him warning us about how we can be distracted in our discipleship: instead of seeing this community as the group which must model the way God's people should live, it can all too easily degenerate into being a group where people argue and compete for honours and position. We as disciples have to both be focused on the Lord and recognise how often we fail as disciples.

Rite of Penance

> Lord Jesus, Son of Man, you were delivered into the hands of men and suffered. Forgive us when we have argued over precedence amongst ourselves. Lord have mercy.
>
> Lord Jesus, Son of Man, you were put to death on the cross. Forgive us when we sought to dominate rather than serve one another. Christ have mercy.
>
> Lord Jesus, Son of Man, you rose again on the third day to give us life. Forgive us when we have failed to welcome the poor and the needy. Lord have mercy.

Headings for Readings

First Reading

The one who seeks to do the will of God must be prepared to suffer at the hands of Godless men; as we see in the life of the Son of Man, the price of obedience to the Father may be suffering and death.

Second Reading
We are a people who claim to have wisdom. So what is Christian wisdom like? The wisdom that comes from above is, first of all, pure, peace-making, kindly, considerate, compassionate, and shows itself in doing good.

Gospel
In this gospel we do not hear Jesus the preacher, but rather the master instructing those, the disciples, who were prepared to travel with him.

Prayer of the Faithful
Use General Formula 1 from the Sample Formulas given in the Missal, p 995.

Eucharistic Prayer
Preface of Sundays in Ordinary Time IV (P32) has the same history of salvation that is outlined in the first part of the gospel; none of the Eucharistic Prayers is particularly suitable.

For the proclamation of the mystery of faith, use the formula 'Christ has died ...' as it closely resembles Mark's teaching in today's gospel.

Invitation to the Our Father
We stand here together as children of the Father, so now let us pray:

Sign of Peace
The wisdom that comes from above makes for peace: let us act as people who possess the wisdom of Christ and share peace with one another.

Invitation to Communion
The Son of Man was delivered into the hands of men, put to death, and has risen. Now he is with us and he gathers us to his table; happy are we who are called to this supper.

Communion Reflection

We have gathered to celebrate the sacred mysteries.
We have proclaimed the mystery of faith.
The Son of Man will be delivered into the hands of men;
they will put him to death;
and three days after he has been put to death he will rise again.
Christ has died;
Christ is risen;
Christ will come again.

We have gathered at his table.
We have assembled for his banquet.
We hear him say:
If anyone wants to be first,
he must make himself last of all
and servant of all.
Anyone who welcomes one of these little children in my name,
welcomes me.

We are the pilgrim people of God.
We are sisters and brothers,
the Father's children,
disciples.
We have become one body in Christ
And we hear him say:
Anyone who welcomes me,
Welcomes not me,
But the one who sent me.

Conclusion

Prayer over the People 20 can be adapted (to reflect the second reading) thus:
May God bless you with every good gift from on high. Amen.
May God keep you pure and holy in his sight at all times. Amen.
May God bestow the riches of his grace upon you,
bring you the good news of salvation,
and always fill you with love of all people. Amen.

Notes

A central and obvious plank of Jesus's teaching, as seen in today's gospel, is that his community was to be radically egalitarian: if we are to be brothers and sisters of God the Father, and were to meet one another in the presence of the Father about a table rather than a temple, then equality in status of every person becomes part of the good news. And, from the start this was both welcomed and ignored by his followers. On the one hand, we have the great miracle of early Christianity: in a society defined by the social strata of an honour/shame system, we have the radically new communities that included rich and poor, slaves and free, and all looking to the kingdom. On the other hand, we have plenty of evidence that churches were dividing along the lines of social dignity: it was fine to be associated with Jesus the Saviour who promised the heavenly banquet, quite another to feel one was no better than – or to have to share one's food with – those smelly people from down the road. The fact that Mark had to include this passage in his preaching is testimony to the fact that Jesus's notions of service were controversial even among the first generations. What eventually emerged was the notion of 'hierarchy', that holiness flowed down through intermediaries who while they were considered 'servants' where actually higher in a chain of command, with God, the angels and the apostles at its top. The clergy were the servants, but they were also the essential intermediaries: verbal loyalty coupled with existential contempt for the notion of the love that is to bond the kingdom.

In a society where those clergy were also the only experts, there was little to challenge this notion: the clergy became the model for the civil service and all 'clerical' work. But where there were alternative experts, the dissonance between the notion of being servants and being hierarchs jarred and came to be seen as fraudulent: it is noteworthy that the Reformation of the sixteenth century emerged and took deepest root in those places where there were elaborate civil structures – usually based on trade – and where the clergy were expected to concentrate on their spiritual roles. Today, that situation is well nigh universal: the priest is often not even considered to be one of society's experts. In this situation, displays of hierarchy are (at best) invariably seen simply as pomposity and ritual displays seen as a childish love of 'dressing up'. At worst, they are seen as a self-aggrandising betrayal of the message of Jesus or a cover-up for people who have really little to offer. This is a painful message for many clergy, in many church traditions, who have been socialised since their student days within hierarchical structures.

This has practical implications for today's liturgy. Given that the assembly is hearing in the gospel of how those who want to be 'first' are to be servants, then look through the liturgy and see if it is sending out conflicting signals either explicitly or by implication. For example:

- This is not the day when 'Father' can do all the readings because someone has not turned up. How many voices are heard in the liturgy? Is the presider's voice the 'default' option?
- Are there going to be announcements made by someone using the 'Father knows best' style of communication: e.g. 'Father wants us to sing hymn X' – are such announcements appropriate?
- Is the entrance procession really a statement that now the liturgy can begin because the important people have arrived, and they have been greeted by standing up?
- Should the presider's hands be washed at the Preparation of the Gifts by servants? Today is a day to let him use a finger bowl or simply drop this survival from the time when he moved quantities of food that were presented for blessing at the Eucharist.
- Is this a day when only the presider drinks from the cup? A cup drunk by one but not by the rest of the assembly is a very clear statement of hierarchy.

A recently as the 1950s books on the priesthood were happy to use the simile of the 'officer corps/other ranks' distinction to justify the position of clergy in society, their role in the church,

and the way 'the laity' were to relate to them. That world is gone
– and today's gospel makes plain that we should not regret its
passing.

COMMENTARY

First Reading: Wis 2:12, 17-20

The Book of the Wisdom [of Solomon] is today a 'Cinderella' in
biblical studies as a result of the decision by the Reformers in the
sixteenth-century that it was not canonical, and this has meant
that even for Catholics it has slipped into a kind of 'second class'
obscurity (the so-called 'Deuterocanon'). However, it is one of
the most remarkable works of the period just before the time of
Jesus and its theodicy – part of which we read today – became
central to Christian orthodoxy on why 'bad things happen to
good people.'

The book's argument is that the wicked act with foolishness
and by their actions invite death for themselves (the 'sin is its
own punishment' approach which Karl Rahner championed in
the twentieth century). However, in their foolishness they find
themselves conspiring against the righteous – those who seek to
act as children of God (see v 13 which the lectionary omits) – because the righteous make life inconvenient. So while the wicked /
foolish invite death, in the meantime the servants of God have to
be ready to accept suffering as part of their discipleship.

Sometimes the editing of verses in the lectionary is wholly inexplicable unless there was a morbid fear of adding an extra 45
seconds to the reading! Here is one such case. Verses 12 to 20
form a unit, including the 4 omitted verses, and if these are included the relationship to the christological theme of the gospel
becomes even more clear. Look up the entire passage, and you
may decide that it is better to read the whole eight verses without omission.

Psalm: 53 (54)

The opening verses of this psalm are an individual's petition to
God to be saved. The righteous petitioner asked to be saved 'by

your name' because he has been acting in the name of God as his servant. Traditional Christian exegesis is at work here in the choice of this psalm for today's liturgy. It was seen as the prayer of the suffering Jesus to the Father, and so it is a link between the first reading and Mk 9:31 in today's gospel (see the note on First Reading > Gospel Links).

Second Reading: Jas 3:16-4:3

Claims to 'knowledge' (*gnosis*) and 'wisdom' (*sophia*), or the desire for these gifts, were part and parcel of ancient religion and so, not surprisingly, they were also sought after by Christians. We can think of *gnosis* as 'having the inner track on the universe' or having access to 'programming' of the mind of the deity. Regarding *sophia*, it is better to think of this as the sort of 'lifestyle' advice for happiness that is to be found on the 'body-mind-spirit' shelves of an airport bookshop rather than philosophical wisdom of the sort one finds in Aristotle's *Nicomachian Ethics*. It was in this world of 'instant success,' 'quick wisdom,' and alternative secret lore, that James – ever the practical hard-nosed preacher – gives his advice on what are the qualities of Christian wisdom. The wisdom that is 'from above' is made to sound as if it is very much concerned with the 'world below' – it is not a secret esoteric code, but about doing, and the doing takes place in the world around us of people and situations. True divine wisdom is seen in peacemaking, in building harmony between people, and carrying out the tasks of discipleship.

If the work of peacemaking is taking place, and the community is acting with the wisdom from above, then the community's strife should cease, and then the community can pray for what it should truly desire. One can hear James's frustration even in translation! If the community gets on with the practice of being disciples – and this he links with peacemaking in the same way that it is linked in Mt 5:9 – then the other problems will settle down in their true perspective.

First Reading > Gospel Links

In effect the relationship is between the first reading and Mk 9:31 ('the prediction of the passion'). The link appears to be one of continuity of teaching: in the first reading we have the Wisdom tradition warning of what will happen to the righteous man who seeks to be obedient to God, then in the gospel Wisdom, himself, announced the same message.

Given the overlap between the milieu that produced the Book of Wisdom – only decades (if that) before the time of Jesus – and the milieu from which the first followers of Jesus came, the use of these two texts together in the liturgy is most appropriate. It was with these patterns of thought that Jesus, and his followers, faced the increasing opposition they incurred, and then saw the resurrection as the Father vindicating his servant.

Gospel: Mk 9:30-37

This is a unit of teaching in Mark – we can see this in that it supposes the same locality and the same activity of walking along the road to Capernaum while talking and teaching – but it is made up of two elements: (1) the so-called 'second prediction of the passion' (using this designation, the 'first prediction' occurred at 8:27-33); and (2) the dispute about greatness. But while splitting these verse into two like this makes great sense if one wants to study the gospels using the three synoptics together, it is less than useful if we want to hear the distinctive voice of Mark. For Mark these are not separate items of tradition just cut and pasted together, rather they are distinct lessons in what is the master-class on discipleship (today's gospel opens a section of Mark's gospel devoted to discipleship that runs to 10:31).

All the stories on discipleship are intended by Mark to correct false notions about discipleship: the first being that the Christ will be a triumphant figure in history – for Mark he is an historical failure who is arrested and put to death, but whose resurrection after three days is the hope of the church. Mark has now abandoned – he is presenting this as Jesus's open teaching to the disciples – the notion of the Messianic Secret, and so the disciples have to come to grips with the reality of the historical destination of discipleship: the cross.

If the cross is the place to where discipleship leads, then the jockeying for position in an historical Jesus-run administration is all the more ridiculous – and so the second correction of false notions of discipleship. Mark's staccato examples have an elegance lost in the prolixity of Matthew and Luke: discipleship is about the cross, great discipleship means service, not rank or position.

For the ecclesial contexts within which Mark preached this material on discipleship, see the homily notes below.

Care should be taken in making any comment on the phrase 'he took a little child' as attitudes to children have so changed in recent centuries that it often produces a very false reading of this text and its parallels (Mt 18:2; Mk 10:15; Lk 9:47 and 18:17). Our culture sees children as valuable and who symbolise innocence, purity, and humility. In the world of Jesus and his followers, the words for 'child' and 'slave' were interchangeable. In the gospel, the child is a representative of the 'no-body', someone without dignity or worth. In fact, the same point could have been made by choosing a slave, or a domestic servant, or, indeed, a woman. Read in this light, the teaching on the disciple as 'servant of all' (*pantón diakonos*) takes on an even sharper significance.

HOMILY NOTES

1. Is there ever a case where straight forward exegesis should form the content of the homily?

    The vast majority of modern preachers would argue that exegesis belongs in the classroom or is too boring for the average congregation: the homily should be lighter, inspirational, and more like a communications soundbite. On the other hand, it is the gospel reading that is the centre of the Liturgy of the Word and an important reason for the reform of the liturgy after the Second Vatican Council was to ensure a more prominent place for scripture in the liturgy. Hence the purpose of the homily is to explicate the readings as the

Word of God – and this necessarily involves exegesis. Most of us find a middle way: a homily that tries to draw the gospel into our human situation but which is influenced by exegesis or, at least, does not fly in the face of what formal exegesis can tell us about the meaning of the text.

However, there is much to be said for occasionally preaching a homily that is a piece of exegesis: where the text can be explained without complex biblical background, and without a well-stocked larder of general knowledge about the scriptures, and where that exegesis will say something useful to an average person about their life, and where that exegesis helps bring out something distinctive about how one of the evangelists preached the gospel, because it was the richness of that variety that inspired the three-year cycle.

2. Today's gospel is one that lends itself to a little bit of formal exegesis.

3. What does that gospel mean?

• Let us begin with a basic observation:

• What Mark, and each of the other evangelists, selected for their preaching was to a large extent determined by the information their audiences needed to live as proper disciples of Jesus.

• We see this in two ways in today's gospel.

• First, over the last few months we have been reading each Sunday extracts from Mark's gospel. One of the distinctive things about his gospel is that very often after Jesus has performed a miracle or a healing in front of all the people, there is little command that 'He wanted them to tell no one.' What Mark was saying by this little device was that people should not think of Jesus just as a healer, or a teacher, or one who could perform miracles. These miracles were exceptional glimpse of how God loves us: to know Jesus is to know the one who was arrested, put to death, and who now is living in the church. To think only of the nice bits, was, for Mark, to get the whole picture wrong. Only when you looked at teaching and healing and dying and rising, could you say you knew the story of Jesus.

- Look at the contrast with today's gospel: we are clearly told that he is with his own people away from the crowds: 'He did not want anyone to know, because he was instructing his disciples.' And Mark sees what he is preaching to the churches as the same as what Jesus was telling the first disciples moving along the road. Now what was this inner teaching that Mark wanted his audience to know? To know who Jesus is, the very kernel of our faith, one has to come to grips, just as his first disciples had, with this:

- 'The Son of Man will be delivered into the hands of men; they will put him to death; and three days after he has been put to death he will rise again.'

- Mark wants there to be no confusion about the central mystery in the communities where he has been preaching: this is what no disciple can be left in any doubt about.

- The second way we see him presenting the teaching of Jesus in a way that it made sense to the first churches is in the rest of today's gospel. It is a fact of human life that we are competitive and there are people who want to be the VIPs in any situation. We may talk about 'fraternity' and 'equality' but we all can identify the sentiments of the pigs in *Animal Farm*: 'All animals are equal, but some animals are more equal that others.'

- The radical message of Jesus was that each of us are children of the Father, hence we are brothers and sisters. As disciples, we are to love one another, share our gifts with one another, and our central common action is this gathering where we are each given a seat at the Lord's table. Yet since the very beginning there have been people who do not like this aspect of discipleship, who want to preserve their worldly status within the church, and those within the church who want to compete for position as if this were just some other club. We know that such disputes were tearing apart the community in Corinth about the time that Mark wrote. We know that it still happens, and we can suspect that it happened in several of the churches where Mark preached. His preaching is by example: you may be full of factions over who is the leader, and which people are the most significant. Well, it was so also in the first group; now listen to what Jesus said when he heard of these arguments. Now go and take that message to heart.

- The test of discipleship is service to one another, and being willing to welcome those who are poor, needy, and from whom you can expect no return. This is typified in Jesus setting the child before them as an example.

- Here we have a little bit of the earliest preaching: we still need to hear it to help us note precisely what is the kernel of the mystery we celebrate, and to be reminded just how easily our arguments within the church can be at odds with the vision of the new humanity Jesus preached.

4. Having given an exegesis. people need to be able to absorb the text again in a more enriched form. So pause for a moment, and then announce:

- We shall now hear that gospel read again, but this time we should be listening out for what Mark wanted his first audience to hear – and which still today we need to hear.

    Then read the text aloud at a slightly slower pace than usual – or, better still, get someone else to read it aloud while you sit down and listen.

5. Lastly, it is good to consider this description of the difference that exegesis makes: it is the difference between 'hearing' and 'listening out'!

Twenty-sixth Sunday of Ordinary Time

Introduction to the Celebration

We gather here as a community, but we are not a club. A club is a group of like-minded people who see themselves or their interests as distinctive from others. We are a community whose deepest desires are pursued by every human being of good will. Whoever is seeking to do what is right; whoever is seeking peace; whoever is bearing witness to the truth; whoever is caring for the creation; whoever is helping the poor – with all these we make common cause and, gathered here, we commend them to our heavenly Father.

We desire to accept Jesus' inclusive vision that all who are not against us are for us, but know that often we fall short of this calling. So now let us reflect on how we live as disciples and recognise our need of forgiveness and healing.

Rite of Penance

Lord Jesus, for those times when we have placed obstacles in another's path towards faith, Lord have mercy.

Lord Jesus, for those times when our hands or our feet have caused us to sin, Christ have mercy.

Lord Jesus, for those times when our eyes and minds have caused us to sin, Lord have mercy.

Headings for Readings
First Reading

This reading reminds us that the Spirit cannot be confined. The Spirit works in every human mind offering enlightenment and guidance towards the fullness of life – if only we accept it.

Second Reading

We often hear people saying that Christians must have a 'preferential option for the poor'; opponents of this concern for the poor often insinuate that this is a trendy politically-inspired message. This reading reminds us that desire for justice for the poor has always been part of our good news. If we are the community gathered to share the banquet of the Lord around this table *(point to the altar)*, we must also share the banquet of the Lord's gifts with the poor.

Gospel

Jesus proclaims, 'Anyone who is not against me is with me'; we have to note how different this good news is from the usual default setting of human beings (which we can see in the disciples and in ourselves): 'Anyone who is not with me is against me.'

Prayer of the Faithful
President

Standing before the Father, let us pray for ourselves and all people of good will; that we may all be strengthened in our good work within the creation.

Reader (s)

1. That we, and all humanity, will respect the integrity of the creation which God has given us as our earthly home. Lord hear us.
2. That we will learn to use wisely the resources of God's creation, recalling that all these resources are God's gifts. Lord hear us.
3. That we will recognise the new responsibilities that our technological abilities place on us with regard to the creation. Lord hear us.
4. That we will commit ourselves to protecting life and all creation, be it water, earth, or air, and know the limits set by wisdom. Lord hear us.
5. Specific local needs and topics of the day.

President

Father, your Son has shown us how to live and work within the creation, to welcome all who do what is right, to recognise that all goodness comes from you and returns to you, hear us now as we pray to you in union with your Son, Christ Jesus, our Lord. Amen.

Eucharistic Prayer
Eucharistic Prayer II for Masses of Reconciliation picks up the theme of inclusiveness and healing from the gospel.

Invitation to the Our Father
We have been transformed into brothers and sisters of Jesus, and now let us pray to our common Father:

Sign of Peace
The Lord has shown us a way to peace in proclaiming that all who are not against us are with us, so let us celebrate our common discipleship by exchanging the sign of peace.

Invitation to Communion
We are gathered here, included on the Lord's guest list, because he who is not against him is for him; thankful for his loving inclusive mercy, let us pray: Lord I am not worthy ...

Communion Reflection
You call us to your banquet;
You include us around your table;
You adopt us as your sisters and brothers;
You transform us into your body;
You make us brothers and sisters of each other;
Lord Jesus, you have included us;
Lord Jesus, you have made us welcome.

Grant that we may be a people who include others;
Grant that we work with all people of good will;
Grant that we promote harmony not discord;
Grant that we foster reconciliation;
Grant that we become peacemakers;
Lord Jesus, you have included us;
Lord Jesus, you have made us welcome.

May our inclusion here make us welcoming;
May our common food make us caring for the poor;

May our common drink energise us to love others;
May our community here extend peace to strangers;
May our joy radiate outwards to those in need;
Lord Jesus, you have included us;
Lord Jesus, you have made us welcome.

Conclusion
Solemn Blessing 12 (Ordinary Time III), Missal p 372, is appropriate.

Notes
1. Preaching inclusion/practicing exclusion
It is always problematic to preach on the inclusiveness of the love that Jesus models for us as his followers. The problem arises in that there will be some people in every assembly who are not feeling included, indeed who feel they have been marginalised within the church: divorced people, gay people, Christians of other churches who attend with their families but feel excluded from participation in the Eucharist. This exclusion is more felt today than a generation ago because we have moved – to some extent – from the materialist notion of the Eucharist that emerged after Trent: in that view, 'Communion' was a sacred commodity one either qualified for, or not; and attendance at Mass was a distinct activity which all Catholics had to observe even if only a small minority 'took communion'. Now that we point out that Eucharist is an activity in which we engage in union with the Christ, and the form of the engagement is a meal, then exclusion becomes obvious: most eat and drink at each gathering and it is the expected behaviour. It is now all too easy to feel the hurt of being allowed to be present at a meal, yet told that eating is not an option. That this produces a certain feeling of vague absurdity is not due to some modern religious relativism; rather it is part of our hard wiring as human beings. As such, meals are central to us and have their own inherent grammar: to be at a meal is to be welcome and to eat and drink; and conversely, one cannot not eat and drink and not feel rejected.

So if one is going to mention 'the inclusive love of Christ' one must do one of two things: (1) let everyone know that they are welcome, as baptised brothers and sisters, to eat and drink if they believe that sharing with us is a sharing in the body of Christ and sharing with us today will give them strength to continue as disciples in the coming week; or (2) have a story ready for afterwards for those people who point out that they are always hearing about 'welcome' and 'inclusiveness' and yet when it comes to practice, it is all just words!

2. The importance of first readings

It is instructive today to note how the choice of first reading can act as a focus for the gospel: by the choice of Num 11 we have highlighted for us the opening section of the gospel (vv 38-41). However, the second section of the gospel actually cites Isa 66:24, and so Isa 66:18-24 could also have been the first reading. If that choice had been made, it would have given a completely different environment in which we would hear, and react to, the gospel. We are apt, at times, to ignore the importance of the first reading in providing a focus on the gospel; today reminds us of its importance!

3. The social-justice agenda

In every community there are those groups who champion the church's concern with social justice. These are often people whose ministry does not get seen within the liturgy by contrast with lectors, teachers, or ministers of the Eucharist. However, the community that has gathered to share the banquet of the Lord must also share the banquet of the Lord's gifts with the poor. Rarely does that agenda receive such a clear endorsement in the readings as in today's second reading. Today, therefore, is an occasion when that aspect of the community can be highlighted and 'show cased' as a reminder to the whole community.

- At the simplest level this could be by making a special note that the reading is read by one member of such a group, and introduced by another.
- It could then be followed by noting that the collection originated as care for the poor not for the maintenance of plant and personnel.

- There could be gifts for the poor presented with the loaf and cup.
- One or more people concerned with this aspect of disciple-ship could make a presentation after communion highlight-ing how having shared at the Lord's table, we must work so that all humanity can share in the table of the creation.

COMMENTARY

First Reading: Num 11:25-9

This self-contained little story probably originated as a 'proof of authority' story (the Christian equivalent would be texts of an-cient privileges jealously guarded by chapters of canons which gave them impunity from incompetent or over-zealous bish-ops!) of some small group of prophets who wanted to remain in operation at a time when prophesy was being organised around an 'official' band of prophets connected with the temple. This group proved their right to co-exist by claiming descent from (the otherwise unheard of) Eldad and Medad whose distinctive authority came directly from Moses himself, no less. This story was then edited with a few other random tales to form this sec-tion of Numbers (11:4-35). The tales are then given an historical scene: right out in the desert in the early part of the long wander-ings.

The text is a lovely example of how pseudo-history (the orig-inal privilege story is transformed into the larger pseudo-history of the exodus and the wanderings in an ideal desert and then formally recalled within the further pseudo-historical scene of Mosaic authorship) and theological imagination combine to pro-duce a text that touches something deep within monotheistic faith: a God who is creator is always larger than the created structures within which we seek to know and serve him – *Deus semper maior.*

Psalm: 18 (19)

It is not clear how this psalm relates to either the first reading or the gospel.

Second Reading: Jas 5:1-6

James is concerned about the religious significance of poverty / wealth throughout his letter (1:9-11; 1:27; 2:1-7; 2:15-17; 4:10; 4:13-16), and in this little unit of text that concern reaches its highpoint. Discipleship cannot be separated from justice towards the poor and concern for a just distribution of resources; and his message comes without compromise. When we hear this we are reminded of the concern for social justice that was part of the message of the prophets, but equally we should remember that many of the earliest churches were not well-provided-for 'house churches' (the equivalent of our 'middle class'), but tenement churches among the poorest workers. It was among these groups that the social miracle of the spread of early Christianity occurred.

First Reading > Gospel Links

Similarity of events / teaching: in the first reading the Spirit is not confined to the group of the seventy, and those outside that group are not to be stopped; in the gospel, the Spirit is likewise not confined to the visible group around Jesus and, likewise, that exorcist is not to be stopped. Through this similarity of events / teaching, the continuity, in both Covenants, of our understanding of God's working is expressed.

Gospel: Mk 9:38-43, 45, 47-8

Today's lection is made up of two distinct pieces of Mark's story: first, the incident of 'the stranger' exorcist (vv 38-41); and second, teaching on temptations (vv 42-8). The 'link' in Mark's eyes presumably being the reference to 'his reward' in v 40 acting as an introduction to various ways by which one could lose one's reward. However, neither Matthew nor Luke understood Mark's linking of the two passages as each responded to the two sections differently from Mark (and one another).

The first section is by far the most interesting as it gives an insight into 'open' attitude of Jesus to the whole work of inaugurating the kingdom (a kingdom that for Jesus is characterised by healing, forgiveness, and restoration, rather than the advent of judgement and retribution). This is the very opposite of a sectarian view: you do not have to join the right huddle in order to be part of the coming kingdom of God. This openness is the antithesis of most of the preaching of the time: the people in Qumran believed one had to go off and live in a separate settlement; John the Baptist preached the need to become associated with the special group that was distinguishing itself from the sinful mass of the people by a baptism of repentance; the zealots were preaching a political sectarianism, the Pharisees a distinctiveness of precise adherence to the law. Now Jesus tells people that the Father's love knows no bounds and extends to everyone who seeks him and, therefore, this stranger is as much a member of the kingdom as the visible group. This openness was too much for the more sectarian minded in the early church: Matthew simply ignores the incident and then, at a suitable point, has Jesus preach the opposite position (Mt 12:30).

The second section is a single piece of teaching expressed through a fourfold repetition of a warning: any amount of physical suffering is better than sin or causing others to sin. It is with these highly visual warnings that Mark rounds off his teaching on discipleship. The examples show how the early church took over the imagery of a place of continual torment, Gehenna (rendered in our translations as 'hell'), awaiting those who accept a sinful way of life. The most gruesome image is that of 'where their worm does not die, and the fire is not quenched' which is a quotation from the final verse of the Book of Isaiah (66:24). In Isaiah, this was read as the final destiny of those who had rejected the reign of God; now the image is invoked as the alternative to discipleship. Placed immediately after the statement about people being rewarded for the smallest acts of mercy (v 40), the combined text has a very particular flavour. On the one hand, the least acts of mercy can bring one into the kingdom of God, but, by contrast, to deliberately lead 'little ones' – this refers to the poor and the marginalised, and not simply children – astray leads to death.

Technical Note

From looking at the gospel reference-numbers given for today's reading, it would appear that this is a heavily edited piece of text where verses 44 and 46 have been cut out. However, if one looks at any modern edition (e.g. JB, RSV, NRSV) one finds the text exactly as in the lectionary. The strange numbering indicated that vv 44 and 46 have been dropped in modern editions are they are simply repetitions of v 48; and this late copyist's error just happened to be in the text that became normative in the west in the later middle ages. This little blunder should serve as a reminder to everyone that the scriptures survive in the memory of the church, and as a part of that memory, rather than as the Christian 'Holy Book' (where the 'book' is seen as God's revelation). This attitude, that the book is the revelation – and, therefore, that the truth of God's communication is somehow linked to the book's 'truth' – is so common in our society that it affects all Christian groups to a greater or lesser extent. The blunders of scribes are concrete evidence that our 'holy book' is but an *aide-memoir* (prone to all the faults of bits of paper), while it is the memory of the church, living people seeking the face of God in their lives, that communicates the Word of God even though that too has to be passed on from one earthen vessel to another.

HOMILY NOTES

1. 'Inclusiveness' is a modern virtue! We are told of the importance of 'inclusive language,' sales people and politicians stress that all references to people must be 'inclusive': we are this, we are that, and we are moving forward. As soon as any person or group is not 'in the loop' or consulted or mentioned, then there is trouble. Every decision must be inclusive because if someone or group is excluded, then there will be trouble. In this simple world nice people are inclusive and nasty people are exclusive. But this desire to be inclusive is often only a façade, a marketing ploy, or formulaic adherence to political correctness.

2. 'Exclusiveness' seems also to be virtue! A chic, expensive

restaurant where people want to be seen is an 'exclusive restaurant' – 'exclusive' is an adjective of quality and approval. 'An exclusive holiday destination' is where only a few, 'the better people' – just like us, go. In an exclusive resort there will be no riff-raff! An 'exclusive offer' for this or that comes with every postal delivery: it means we, just a few of us, are special. Unlike the great-unwashed mass of humanity, we appreciate such an exclusive opportunity and, indeed, being the special sort of people we are, we deserve this exclusive offer. Exclusiveness is even a desirable quality in tinned fish: 'It is the fish John West rejects that make John West salmon the best.'

3. Exclusion as a tool within society is deeply programmed into us. The tribe is defined by the people who-do-not-belong. Then they become 'the others' and because they are not 'with us,' they are opposite us, and so they can easily be seen as opposed to us, and a threat. The others must be kept in place, they must be controlled, excluded from power, made subject to us and, if necessary, be destroyed. Exclusiveness is ideal as a means of making us united, but then can often destroy us in the conflicts and wars that it makes possible. How many leaders down the centuries who, when they found themselves without any positive vision with which to lead a people, turned to exclusiveness and preached the fear of others, and held sway by the threat of the others.

4. We can see this demonising of 'the others,' the pernicious attitude that only 'we' are OK/saved/normal, in the way countries are run (e.g. apartheid), in the way churches are run (e.g. sectarianism), or how some club or association is run (there must be careful 'screening' of who joins the residents' association lest the area's value be undermined). We see it at work in today's gospel: someone was doing the same things as the disciples, but because the person was not inside the group, then he was a threat; therefore he was to be stopped.

5. The reply of Jesus clearly shocked them: he who is not against us is for us. This is the very opposite of exclusiveness,

this is true inclusiveness – not simply a façade to make an impression. This is the inclusiveness that is based in the infinity of God's goodness and love, and it is that openness and generosity that we are called to imitate.

6. Sadly, it was just too shocking for the disciples, and the record of the churches ever since has not been very honourable. It shocked the first followers because it was reversed in Matthew (12:30) to become: 'He who is not with me is against me!' Matthew wanted a neat little world where people 'knew where they stood' and if they were not with Jesus, then they must be against him. Matthew's clarity is all too human; Mark's statement could only come from someone who fully embraced the world with love. And, the church has been closer to Matthew than to Mark: we are very good at noting who does not belong, who should be excluded from communion, who is to be seen as a threat. Equally, we have been very good at dividing up the Body of Christ into exclusivist sections: clergy – lay; those with 'authority' and those who are supposed to be led. An inclusive love that sees each Christian, indeed each human, as someone called by God to participate in the growth of the kingdom seems utopian. Yet, it is just such a communion of love that we, as the church, are to model to faction-riven humanity.

7. Today's gospel calls all of us to examine our behaviour. Does it reflect inclusive love: anyone who is not against us is with us; or, is it that all too human exclusivist vision: anyone who is not with us is against us?

8. In that shift in perspective lies the difference between religious observance as an aspect of human life and true discipleship of Jesus.

Twenty-seventh Sunday of Ordinary Time

Introduction to the Celebration

We gather each week to form the church: the community who follow Jesus as the way to the Father, and who encounter Jesus, and become one with him, when we gather about his table. It is this encounter with Jesus that makes this a sacred place and a sacred event. At our gathering today we are reminded in the gospel that one of the other sacred places where we can encounter the Son of God is in marriage: the union, indeed, of a married couple is the image of the bond that exists between Jesus Christ and us, his church.

Rite of Penance

Option c. vii (Missal, pp 394-5) is appropriate.

Headings for Readings

First Reading

Here is a little piece out of the story of Adam and Eve – a story we have used for thousands of years to remind us of some basic, and often unpalatable, facts about our human condition as God's creatures. This bit of the story reminds us that marriage is part of God's plan for the happiness and fulfilment of the creation.

Second Reading

In this reading we have an answer to that basic question of Christians: who is Jesus whom we follow? This reading gives us this answer: Jesus is the 'one who was for a short while made lower than the angels' but who is 'now crowned with glory and splendour'.

Get the reader to add 'and sisters' at the end of the reading.

Gospel

The shorter version is preferable.

This gospel reminds us that for us, Christians, a marriage is not just the union of the couple, but is the work of God.

Prayer of the Faithful
President
We have gathered as the church, the people united to Christ in a bond so close that it can be compared with the union of a married couple, so with Christ we now place our prayer before the heavenly Father.

Reader (s)
1. Let us pray for the whole church of God throughout the world: that it will be ever more aware of the mystery of its union with Christ, its bridegroom. Lord hear us.

2. Let us pray for all married people, that their marriages may be happy, bring them fulfilment, and bring them into the presence of God. Lord hear us.

3. Let us pray for this church that we may be united with one another in peace and love, and be united with the Christ who has given us his love. Lord hear us.

4. Let us pray for all those people whose marriages have not worked out, that the Lord will bring them healing, peace, and happiness. Lord hear us.

5. Let us pray for ourselves that we, and all humanity, will respect the integrity of the creation which God has given us as our earthly home. Lord hear us.

6. Specific local needs and topics of the day.

7. Let us pray for all who have gone before us marked with the sign of faith, that having being united with Christ in this life, they may rejoice in union with him in the heavenly marriage feast of the Lamb. Lord hear us.

President
You, O God, are the loving Father of the world of nature; you are the loving Father of the new creation of grace; hear us your children when we call on you in Christ Jesus, our Lord. Amen.

Eucharistic Prayer
Of the three prefaces of marriage, Preface of Marriage II (P73,
Missal, p 476) is the most suitable for use on a Sunday as it pre-
sents marriage from within the mystery of the new covenant
and the saving mystery of redemption. It works well with
Eucharistic Prayer II.

Invitation to the Our Father
Gathered together we form the church, and united with Christ,
we pray to the Father:

Sign of Peace
Every community, every relationship, needs from time to time
reconciliation and a renewed willingness to live in peace. Let us
now express that forgiveness and that desire to one another.

Invitation to Communion
Looking forward to the great wedding feast of the Lamb in the
age to come, we are now invited to share in this banquet of reconciliation and love.

Communion Reflection
George Herbert's poem *The Call* (Breviary, vol 3, p 786*).

Conclusion
Solemn Blessing from Wedding Mass C, Missal, p 775, is very
suitable for today. In the first invocation change 'bless you and
your families' to 'bless you all and your families'.

Notes
1. Preaching on divorce
There is a perceptible shudder in most congregations when this
gospel on divorce is read: the subconscious expectation is that
now 'we are in for it' – an harangue on the evils of divorce, why
it is bad for society, and why it must be opposed at every turn.
There is a popular folk memory of such 'pulpit thumping' that is

far larger than probably the real extent of such preaching in the past, and despite the fact that few people under sixty can even remember seeing a sermon delivered from an actual pulpit. So the first thing to remember today is that there is a lot of deep-felt resentment about such harangues in any community, and it creates a tension and dissonance between people and their hearing of the good news. It is part of the task of every preacher of the good news to seek to remove that tension.

However, quite apart from the fact that harangues on a topic like divorce simply do not work (indeed, they are counter-productive in that people resent them), there is a deeper reason why they are wholly inappropriate at a celebration of the Eucharist. Imagine a situation where a preacher was on a soapbox in a public place (it could be a blog on the internet or a column in a local newspaper) and is arguing the church's stand on divorce. Here the communications dynamic is that the preacher is explaining the church's position to all-and-sundry, some, many, or perhaps all are outsiders to the church and the gospel, and who may be inquirers about our position or who may be detractors of Christianity and for whom this message is an explanation. However, the situation at the Eucharist is completely different: we are meeting as the church, our gathering makes us the church, and as an intimate family meal of sisters and brothers in Christ, we cannot hear the church's teaching as if we were outsiders to that teaching – alas much actual preaching fails to recognise this! The communications dynamic at the Eucharist is that we are a group made into a sacred unity as the body of Christ, and we hear this message as intimates. So we hear the gospel as good news about ourselves and our chosen way for the pilgrimage of faith and life. Any preaching which starts off on the premise that the Eucharistic congregation needs to be told what 'they should know' about 'the church's position' on this or that (which silently assumes that the gathering and 'the church' are distinct realities), is based on a false ecclesiology and ignores the nature of the task the liturgy entrusts to the homilist.

What practical steps, therefore, can the president of an assembly take to allay the fears of many that they are going to be harangued?

- First, concentrate on marriage as part of God's loving plan of salvation, rather than starting from the failure of marriage at the point when divorce looms on the horizon.

- Second, since marriage is part of human experience, recognise that a celibate speaking on marriage sounds as convincing as someone offering to service your car because he has bought the manual although he has never worked in a garage! Preaching on marriage by a celibate has as much integrity as an plutocrat preaching on the option for the poor: the lack of integrity stems from the fact that there is not the combination of thinking, experiencing and feeling that is the hallmark of true human knowledge/wisdom.

- Third, get someone to give the homily who can help the community reflect on marriage from within their own Christian experience. Obviously, if there is a married deacon, this is a day when he should preach. Otherwise, begin the homily by inviting someone, or a couple, to address the gathering, and conclude by having a moment to reflect on what they have shared with their brothers and sisters. Every community has someone with some theological training or who has some experience with one of the many groups that act to support Christians in the marriages.

- Fourth, there will be people in the assembly for whom 'regular' marriage is not an option, or for whom marriage has failed. So whoever addresses the community needs to be reminded that presenting some 'ideal' marriage as covering all and as being assured of success if only some criteria are met is not only false witness, but can be deeply hurtful. No one should leave the Lord's banquet of love feeling hurt – this is a basic Christian principle.

- Lastly, watch out in using the word 'sacrament': most people think of an event (e.g. a baptism ceremony) or a thing (e.g. the Blessed Sacrament) rather than of an on-going mystery when they hear the word. So 'the sacrament of matrimony' is the wedding. It is a waste of time to try to correct this: our task is to communicate the good news, not to make sure that people are aware of the correct use of theological jargon.

2. The shorter version of the gospel

There are two reasons for opting for the shorter form of the gospel today. First, the two topics are really distinct and reading both just creates confusion. Second, we live with the on-going effects of the abuse of children and vulnerable people by clergy. Reading this longer text, unless you are prepared to openly talk about the wickedness of the crimes of the clergy involved – some of whom may be well known to everyone in the assembly – seems like obfuscation and denial. If that is the message that is sent out, then the good news has not been preached.

3. The reader of the first reading

The passage from Genesis 2 is one that many women object to as they note in it that the author believes women should be subordinate to men (see the commentary). This in itself creates difficulties in the liturgy, but these are only exacerbated if this lection is read by a man to the women in the assembly. So this is an occasion where one should try to ensure that the reader for this reading is a woman.

COMMENTARY

First Reading: Gen 2:18-24

This is part of the second creation account, from the early narrative source we designate 'J', which sees the woman – whom the man will name 'Eve' – being created in order to fulfill the man's needs for a worthy companion. As an ancient near eastern origin story it is quite remarkable:

- the human couple is the direct and special work of the Creator of the universe (not the result of either divine warfare or divine promiscuity);
- the fate of the man is so precious in the sight of the Creator that he is even concerned that he should not be lonely – and this earthling made of matter, this creature, even knows the personal name of his creator: 'YHWH';

- this creature is to consider himself the centre of the creation and be in charge of it which is what we see in his being given the opportunity to give names to every creature – this is in contrast to cults in the surroundings which had gods in the images of animals (for the J author, animals are simple lesser creatures under the dominance of the man);
- and, finally, sexuality is a divine creation – not a principle of chaos – which is there to meet the needs of the man and of the divine purpose of populating the earth;
- however, the J author is also very clear that the woman is subordinate in creation, purpose, and authority to the man.

So we have the curious historical irony: this myth was revolutionary as a piece of theology in the early first millennium BC, but today it is one of the most problematic pieces of text that we have – partly because the 'story of Adam and Eve' is part of general common knowledge and so still has a prominence in our imaginations. The problem is twofold. First, of all the myths in the scriptures, this one raises hackles most because it is just seen as 'wrong,' 'false', and 'primitive'. Trying to explain that a myth (which, to many people, is a synonym for a lie or a falsehood) can still be theologically valuable (even if it is wholly divergent from what we know about paleontology) is a difficult task. Second, it does not have any notion of the equality of men and women, women are subordinate materially and spiritually – and only fundamentalists try to get the text to read otherwise. This was already a problem for the P-author who assembled the Book of Genesis as we know it, and it has been commented upon (e.g. by Aquinas) long before the rise of feminist theology. Therefore, the reading of this text (and of texts which depend on it such as Tobit 8:4-8 or today's gospel) provokes a great deal of anger: why are we reading a text whose view of women we would not accept? There is no convenient answer to this for it throws into relief the whole question of reading ancient texts as media for the Word of God in the liturgy. However, it can help to point out that this problem has long been recognised by Christians (as early as the eighth century) and it provoked this 'workaround' from St Thomas: why did God make the woman from man's side rather than from his head or his feet? If she had been made from his head it would indicate she was to be in charge of him; if from his feet, that he was to dominate her; but by making her from the side it was to indicate they were to stand side-by-side in friendship, and friendship, as Aristotle pointed out, can only exist between equals. This is not an answer to the problems posed by this text and others like it when used in the liturgy, but it does show that concerns of those who are shocked by the implications of the 'spare rib' view of women are not simply a recent development in the tradition.

Psalm: 127 (128)

A man's happiness (note it is a *man*'s happiness, not a human being's happiness) is to be the head of a large family and to be settled in the midst of the holy city.

Second Reading: Heb 2:9-11

Within the structure of the letter, this passage belong to a section (2:5-18) that deals with it being 'convenient' to God to bring Jesus to exaltation through abasement – by taking this 'route' Jesus can enter glory with the rest of us in his entourage, and so we can be called his brothers.

There are three problems with the reading: first, the general problem that the theology of Hebrews is alien to most congregations' ways of thinking about the Christ; second, this snippet is really too short to try 'to get into it'; and lastly, make sure to add 'and sisters' at the end of the reading.

First Reading > Gospel Links

The relationship is one of continuity of God's law over the whole of creation: Jesus in the gospel appeals to the text of Genesis as the witness to the continuity of his own teaching. We then read it as 'the background' to the gospel and, by reading it, assert that we too are in that continuity.

Gospel: Mk 10:2-16 (shorter form: 10:2-12)

The first point to note is that the teaching on divorce was always controversial among the followers of Jesus: Mk 10:1-12 is only followed as a piece of narrative by Matthew (19:1-12) who adapts it in several ways; but while the narrative is omitted by Luke, he does have the 'punch line' at 16:18. Moreover, that punch line ('Every one who divorces his wife and marries another commits adultery, and he who marries a woman divorced from her husband commits adultery') is also found in another place in Matthew: 5:32. By contrast, the little scene of Jesus blessing the children is wholly unproblematic: it is found in all three synoptics without alteration. Moreover, this controversy about divorce was not just among the followers of Jesus, but was a controversial problem within several strands of Judaism at the time, hence the fact that it is a topic on which the Pharisees set out to question Jesus.

Given the fact that divorce was a controversial matter for every community (for those to whom the evangelists preached as much as for Jewish communities) at the time – and the matter has never been uncontroversial – is there any need to say anything more: here is Jesus's position, pure and simple? In fact, if we read the narrative found in Mark noting how the answer seems so convoluted, we should immediately suspect that there is something more going on in this text. Why would Jesus not simply give his teaching on the matter, why did he wrap it up in a curious rationale as to why Moses taught in the way he did? The actual fact is that this encounter with the Pharisees is really not about divorce at all; their intentions lay elsewhere and a question on divorce was only a suitable occasion to try to trap him.

The trap lies in the fact that Moses in the law had permitted divorce and the questioners make clear reference to the basic statute: Deut 24:1-4. However, there was also this statement in the prophet Malachi: '"For I hate divorce," says the Lord the God of Israel, "and covering one's garment with violence," says the Lord of hosts. "So take heed to yourselves and do not be faithless"' (2:16). If Jesus sided with Deut, then he was denying a prophet's authority citing a direct oracle; if he sided with Mal, then he was denying the whole of mosaic authority. The issue from the point of view of the Pharisees was one of a perfect contradiction, in the eternal present of the lawyers: heads Jesus loses, tails they win. Jesus does come down on one side of the argument, but does so with a brilliant defence that could not be challenged: the law of Moses can be seen as reflecting the mind of God, but not in an absolute way outside times and circumstances. It was not God's original design, but only an accommodation to their faithlessness (an implicit reference to Malachi). Moreover, Jesus supports his interpretation of the law by appeal to Moses himself (in his citation of Genesis).

The trap was sprung, but Jesus was not caught. Jesus demonstrated a unity between Moses and Malachy, and also that there was no contradiction among the authorities.

HOMILY NOTES

1. It is a basic principle of communication that one should not start with a negative: is there anything more off-putting than someone approaching you and you already know they are only going to tell you about problems? Likewise, with today's gospel: the question was put to Jesus about divorce, yet it is an understanding of marriage that is the real issue. But that raised another issue: given that their marriages are the most complex area of the lives of most of the community gathered, what can be said that is not trite in the course of five to seven minutes?

2. If you are not going to appeal to your own experience of marriage as a place where the risen Christ is encountered – i.e. a sacramental place – then it is perhaps best to offer some texts for the community to reflect upon such that the homily becomes a guided meditation.

3. Introduce the meditation with some phrase like this:

   This passage from Mark's preaching reminds us that marriage is part of God's loving plan for the creation, and people who are married can, in their marriages, encounter Jesus who renews the creation, brings healing from discord, and who gives us strength to be people of love. Here are some passages to reflect on which express in prayer how we view marriage.

4. Use these texts from the prefaces of marriage:
   'You [O God] are the loving Father of the world of nature;
   you are the loving Father of the new creation of grace.
   In Christian marriage you bring together the two orders of creation:
   nature's gift of children enriches the world
   and your grace enriches also your church.'

   'You created man [and woman] in love to share your divine life.
   We see [our] high destiny in the love of husband and wife,
   Which bears the imprint of your own divine love.
   Love is [our] origin,
   Love is [our] constant calling,
   Love is [our] fulfilment in heaven.
   The love of man and woman
   Is made holy in the sacrament of marriage
   And becomes the mirror of your everlasting love.'

   These two texts (from Prefaces 72 and 74 respectively) should be enough, if read slowly with pauses, to create a space of reflection.

5. Some may object that offering a poetic reflection is 'dodging' a sermon, but this fails to grasp the fact that what is called for is a homily – a communication event that allows the assembly to come into contact with the Word of God (something alive and active, and not to be confused with the words in the gospel's text) in response to hearing the preaching of the evangelists. In a noisy, busy world – a world that is so frenetic that it is well to remember that in every gathering there will be one person who has forgotten to turn off their mobile, and many others who are worried that they are missing calls

while their mobiles are 'off' – deliberately creating spaces for reflection may be a necessary precondition of people hearing the Word.

Renewing Eucharistic Symbols

'Good celebrations foster and nourish faith; poor celebrations weaken and destroy faith.'[1] This simple statement seems so trite that we are apt to forget that it is a basic principle of Christian practice. Indeed, many of us who are involved in the celebration of our faith through symbols become so familiar with using the liturgy that we fail to notice that unless we are regularly checking the quality of our celebrations, and the way we use and respond to symbols, then the liturgy becomes tired, misshapen, and liable to cause the exact opposite result from that which is intended.[2] In short, liturgy like any other human work needs regular renewal if it is to succeed in being more than 'Christian doings' and be the mystery that gathers us into the Paschal event of Jesus.

Reflecting on that statement of the American bishops we see that it points us towards this truth about the human search for the divine at several levels. As human beings we are symbol-making animals. We live through making and interpreting signs that, if the signs are wholesome and well made, build us up. An example would be symbolic events that remind us of the unity of humanity. While signs can also be the bringers of suffering, can destroy us, and lead us into chaos. An example would be the ritual systems of racism and extreme nationalism that seek to divide humanity into opposing armed camps. As human beings we need to be conscious of the 'signs we are sending out' and recognise that most of what we value as humans is built through our imagination of how the world works and what life is for. And signs are what carry that imaginative vision, for good or ill,

---

1. US Bishops' Committee on Liturgy, *Music in Catholic Worship* (Washington 1972), 6.
2. On the principle of unintended consequences and the liturgy, see T. O'Loughlin, 'The Eucharist as "The Meal that should be",' *Worship* 80 (2006) 30-44.

into reality.[3] Insensitivity to the importance of human signs makes us boorish and dehumanizes us into isolated units of Cartesian-like consciousness. This phenomenon is not some rarified truth of semiotic theory; it can be glimpsed whenever someone forgets his or her partner's birthday. But it becomes truly pathetic when someone who has lost that sensitivity to the importance of signs for human beings then celebrates the liturgy: now the sacred mysteries become manual chores to be processed as 'efficiently' as possible.

As believers in a God who is beyond the creation, we have another interest in signs because the creation, of which we are a part, is the first word addressed to us by God. And, in the venerable patristic phrase, we are to find there 'the footprints of God'. We see the universe as containing the marks of the divine handiwork and it points beyond itself to the fullness of being.[4] This is the theme of much of Christian art and poetry, and attunes us to the dynamic of divine communication: we see the glimmer of the divine glory in the creation and it beckons us to respond in worship. So, for believers in a creator, being sensitive to signs of the divine is a sacred religious task. Again, this can go awry and we become so involved with the signs that they become ends-in-themselves rather than pointers to the mystery beyond. This contraction of vision was well captured by the author of the Wisdom of Solomon: 'They were unable from the good things that are seen to know the one who exists, nor did they recognise the artisan while admiring his works ... people in their delight in these things assumed them to be god!' (Wis 13). Such a reduction of the universe from a sign to an end-in-itself is at the heart of all idolatry – read Wis 15 – be it the ancient sort which gilded images in temples or the more modern varieties that invests fundamental significance in 'profit' or 'the state' or 'me'.

As Christians we belong to a sacramental religion for in the

---

3. For a fascinating account of how ritual and signs are present in human life, see E.W. Rothenbuhler, *Ritual Communication: From Everyday Conversation to Mediated Ceremony* (Thousand Oaks 1998).
4. See Augustine, *Confessiones* 10, 6, 9.

encounter with Jesus his followers have encountered far more
than a rabbi in Palestine: he is the fundamental sacrament. In
Jesus we are 'caught up in the love of the God we cannot see'.[5]
Moreover, in continuation of this logic of incarnation, we become, through the signs of water and his eucharistic meal, his
new 'great sign':[6] the church. And, in this great sign we encounter our head through signs that we can see, touch, and taste.
We enter into communion with one another and with Christ in
the waters of baptism and are changed in the encounter of the
Eucharist. But again, this precious treasure can so easily be sub-
verted to destructive ends: for many any mention of the church
far from pointing them towards the mystery beyond, reminds
them of hypocrisy and venality; while for many the signs of the
liturgy have become mere tokens which are tolerated as a necessary encumbrance to an individual's religion. This often happens in a curious way whereby we value the 'meaning' we abstract from a sign (as if it were a 'fact' existing apart from the
sign), but then ignore the value of the sign itself. An example is
the priest who preaches a long sermon on 'the Mass's meaning'
but then 'to get Mass finished in time' rattles thought the actual
sign; or, to take the example of David Power: 'What may one
think of inviting people ... to spend hours before the Blessed
Sacrament, while never inviting them to drink the blood of
Christ from the common cup?'[7]

It is a sad irony that repetition is the guarantor of what is
truly significant in a religious imagination,[8] yet the symbols
which we need to express that imagination contract with that
very repetition! And not only do they contract from being events
that involve us into being tokens whose meaning has to be de-
coded for us, but in becoming wizened they no longer direct us

5. Preface of Christmas I (Roman Missal, 1970, p 1339).

6. See Eph 5:32; *musterion* can be rendered as sign if we think of the way
complex signs draw us within them.

7. Cited in *Liturgy Newsletter* 2/2 (2002) 4 of the Liturgy Office of the
Catholic Bishops' Conference of England and Wales.

8. Cf J. Z. Smith, 'A Twice-Told Tale: The History of the History of
Religion's History,' *Numen* 48 (2001) 134-146.

correctly but bring unbidden other messages that may be the di-rect opposite of the gospel. An fine example of this phenomenon was the separation of Mass from Holy Communion – an attitude sadly still seen in many parishes on a Sunday morning when 'communion' is given from the tabernacle – whereby the rever-ence for the Host became so great that people feared to receive it lest they did so 'unworthily', forgetting that it was precisely those sick through sin who most needed this food to build them up – for he 'came not to call the righteous, but sinners' (Mk 2:17).

Words should help us to draw out the significant in our lives. Words should be the seeds of meaning within us and between us. Words should be precious in letting us see the wonder and goodness of the Father. Unfortunately, words also can obscure reality for us. They can bury us under so many layers of accum-ulated confusions that we struggle to see what is really import-ant. In a communications age, words can be the vehicles of disin-formation like never before and can confuse the chasm that should exist between the genuine, the true, the important, and the illusions of salesmen, marketers, and spin-doctors. Words also can so fascinate us with their own magic that we fail to move beyond them to the realities they exist to highlight for us. Words should be illuminating, but they are often like a fog, and indeed sometimes a smokescreen separating us from reality.

What has this to do with the Eucharist? Well, the Eucharist is a sacrament, a sign, a mystery; and as such it should convey meaning and truth and authenticity and life. And so it always involves words: words, firstly, in the actual celebration, the words of thanksgiving and prayer to the Father that justify the name of 'The Eucharist'; and words too that talk about what we are doing, explaining our actions to ourselves and to others. These words of explanation and exploration of meaning are what we call 'theology.' We see the process right from the start of the Christian journey: each week the community gathered and in its eating and drinking offered its prayer of thanksgiving. Then we see theologians explaining why this is significant: firstly, Paul writing to the Corinthians explaining it in terms of becoming one with the Christ, then the *Didache* in terms of the final banquet of the re-gathered Israel, then Mark explaining it in terms of a pre-existing understanding of the Passover,[9] then John in terms of the manna in the desert, and on and on and on until we reach some of the books on the Eucharist that are on our shelves or the pamphlets in a church bookrack.[10]

But today we face a problem with all these words. For many the words about the Eucharist make no sense. The gathering makes no sense; it does not enhance their grasp of life or of the goodness of God. Just think of these two facts. First, English and Welsh Hierarchy figures for Mass attendance showed a fall of 130,000 between 2002 and 2005. People are expressing their 'theology' (i.e. their understanding of what we are doing, whether it is an adequate theology or not) with their feet! Second, the fastest growing Christian groups are the evangelical churches where the Eucharist is not considered central or significant (and which in some groups is even considered superstitious). Yet the statisticians point out that between 25% (Catholics bishops' figures) and 33% (the evangelical missionaries' figures) of South Americans now formally call themselves 'Evangelicals' as distinct from 'Catholics'. And, this is a pattern of movement

---

9. And, in explaining a weekly meal by reference to an annual meal he left a theological time bomb that went off in Calvin's hands 1400 years later!

10. See, for example, the 2004 one-page pamphlet issued in the series 'CTS Essentials' and called *What happens at Mass?* (London 2004). It is a strange document for the word 'Eucharist' is never used, it has seven pictures (two of them of a bishop elevating the species) but not one of these shows the assembly, and the front picture is of pre-cut roundels in a ciborium. Meanwhile, the verbal text assumes that the primary focus of the Mass is the consecration of the species to enable the reception of Jesus in communion. The whole image created by the pamphlet is that this is the 'official position' and the bare-bones of what we believe, yet the anonymous pamphlet shows no trace of the theology of Vatican II which is embedded in the rite of 1970 (e.g. instead of the clear two tables structure of the rite, it suggests that the 'Structure of the Mass' is found in six bullet-points (implicitly a code for items of equal worth): Penitential Rite/Readings/Offertory/Eucharistic Prayer/ Communion/ Dismissal).

that is not confined to Latin America. When we consider the centrality of this meal, since the very first days of the church, that was the bonding force of the little groups with their Lord whose resurrection they proclaimed, then the poverty of such a *jejune* (literally) non-Eucharist centred theology cannot but be a cause of sadness.

That the Eucharist and its language are seen as meaningless, boring, or irrelevant either to life in general or the life of discipleship is, of its nature, a complex problem with many causes; and it is possible that it is beyond our ability to do anything about most of these causes. However, some parts of the problem are of our making and can be addressed. One of these is that many celebrations obscure the basic and original structure of this gift that Jesus gave us. This obscuring takes place in that we concentrate on all the various levels of meaning that have accumulated over the centuries such that participants cannot experience the answer to that constant human question: 'What's this about?' – nor can teachers give a concise explanation that might effectively (as opposed to abstractly) answer that question. Such accumulations of secondary issues are a normal part of human life and the constant bane of every group activity, and so common is it that we have the classic image of 'the tail wagging the dog' to describe the problem. In the case of the Eucharist this can take many forms: the celebration becomes primarily linked to the availability of a priest rather than the needs of a community; it becomes a teaching session and prayer service plus getting Holy Communion rather than the Lord's Banquet; the questions of who can or cannot receive become the central issue – and for a great many people this is the sole question that concerns them about the whole affair – rather than encountering the risen Christ; the Eucharist (the name for an action) becomes subsumed under the notion of Holy Communion (a commodity) or the Blessed Sacrament (an object); and for many, priests included, it is hard to think of 'sacrament' as the name of an *activity* of a group rather than of a 'something' usually had by an individual.

So what can one do to address the problem? The starting

point is to remember that the Eucharist is the collective meal of
the community of the baptised. So why not meet for the
Eucharist periodically in the community hall rather than the
church building?[11] Then stand around for the whole event
rather than be formally lined up in the way one might for a class
or a meeting where discussion is dominant. This is a gathering,
an assembly, a celebration of who we are in Christ, not a meeting to transact business. The ritual comparison is the way people
gather at a 'reception' (e.g. at a wedding or a reception at some
event): people stand and mingle, they get to know each other,
they recognise they have a common reason for being there and
at such events they are not seated in rows. Then they can gather
around a single table that is the Lord's. Words like 'altar' are secondary: they derive from a second-century attempt to explain
what we are doing as we gather at the one table.[12] A table is the
basic sign, 'altar' is an interpretation of that sign's meaning. It
was basic to the message of Jesus that there was a welcome at his
table, there was room there for the poor, the outcasts, the
strangers, the sinners, and unloved.[13] This gathering of those
who are reconciled and given new life (i.e. the baptised) is the
pattern for the whole life of the church, both now and eschato-
logically. So everyone should be able to gather around that
table, and know they have as much right to stand there at the
Lord's invitation as the mob of concelebrating priests one sometimes sees huddling round it. A decent-sized dining table, that is
still clearly recognisable as such (i.e. not covered to make it look

---

11. On the move from the community's room to a formal sacral space,
see R. Gibbons, *House of God: House of God's People* (London 2006), 31-48.
12. This is first found in Ignatius of Antioch, *Pros Philadelpheis* 4, 1
(*thusiasterion* is the word used), but should read against the cry 'we
have neither temples nor altars' (*arae*) of the late second-century apolo-
gist Minucius Felix (*Octauius* 32, 1). And, moreover, in Ignatius the key
point being made is that there is 'one Eucharist ... one flesh ... one cup
... one altar ... one bishop.'
13. On this aspect of open commensality, see D. E. Smith, 'Table
Fellowship as a Literary Motif in the Gospel of Luke', *Journal of Biblical
Literature* 106 (1987) 613-638.

like 'an altar'), is ideal.[14] It is also worth recalling those lines
from Eucharistic Prayer I (which may date from the time before
we had formal churches1[15]) that say: 'Remember your male servants and your female servants, indeed the needs of all who are
standing around [this table].'[16]

Then we come to the basic activity of thanking the Father in
Jesus. We often recite this as if its purpose was to ask God to con-
secrate elements on the table (and as such it becomes the skilled
work of the priest alone[17]). Presented in that light there is little
adequate answer to the question someone asked me after the
Eucharist recently: why does the priest not get all this done be-
fore-hand so that Communion is ready to give to us after the
readings?[18] It is strange how the culture of fast-food (if it is not
an abuse of language to call it 'food') outlets finds a counterpart
in the older attitudes relating to 'Mass and Communion (from
the tabernacle, of course).'[19] So there has to be attention to the

----

14. It is paradoxical that prior to Vatican II when the 'altar' was against
the back wall of churches the rubrics required four pilaster-style
columns on its front: the atrophied remnant of the time, well over a millennium earlier, when it was a table with four legs; now when it is supposed to be a real table again (it was pulled out from the back wall so
that people could gather around it) it often looks like a monumental
slab or solid rectangular block.
15. Cf. E. Mazza, *The Origins of the Eucharistic Prayer* (Collegeville, MN
1995), 266.
16. *Memento etiam famulorum famularumque tuarum et omnium circumstantium;* the *et* is not a simple conjunction as it is rendered in the official
English translation but a consecutive conjunction building the rhetorical coda through a hendiadys.
17. Hence the reason frequently given to explain the pre-Vatican II
practice of reciting the canon *secreto*: it was solely his work, so it concerned no one else.
18. The question may hide an even deeper confusion, cf. T. O'Loughlin,
'Eucharist or Communion Service?' *The Way* 38 (1998) 365-74.
19. The 2005 *General Instruction on the Roman Missal*, n 85 says 'It is most
desirable that the faithful … receive the Lord's body from hosts consecrated at the same Mass.' But this shows the level of confusion for as
long as it is possible to think in terms of many 'hosts' then the fact that
the basic symbol system of the Eucharist is a single loaf is lost, and so it
can seem acceptable, if indeed not desirable, to use particles kept over

tone of the Eucharistic Prayer that it is recited as prayer directed to the Father thanking him for all he has given us in his Son. In this context it is worth noting that in the Missal of 1970 there are no 'words of consecration', but an 'institution narrative' – there lies the heart of the renewed theology of the Vatican Council and this difference in language has major implications for how the prayer is voiced every time it is used.[20] We are recalling the Last Supper as part of our prayer and so justifying why we are now praying in this way (this recollection format is part of every collect: we praise the Father because of something that has occurred) not pronouncing a sacral formula. After all, in the final analysis, it is the gathered people that must be consecrated to become the body and blood of Christ.

Then we come to the basic form of the meal: Jesus used a single loaf from which each received a share; and passed around a single cup from which each drank. This is the basic symbolism of this particular meal: a common life as one body which is Christ (the one loaf[21]), and a common destiny (see Mk 10:38-9; Jn 18:11) which is in Christ (the one cup).[22] This eating and drinking by the gathering is, of its nature, a confusing and lengthy business, but that is fine. After all we are there to engage in just that activity!

---

from a previous celebration. This fundamental confusion even affects rubricians who deprecate the practice of using 'hosts from the tabernacle' (see P. Turner, *Let us pray: A Guide to the Rubrics of Sunday Mass* (Collegeville, MN 2006), 130-1.

20. The action of genuflecting during this narrative only entered the liturgy, possibly by accident (cf. E. Mazza, *The Celebration of the Eucharist: The Origin of the Rite and the Development of its Interpretation* (Collegeville, MN 1999), 234-5), in the early sixteenth century, and it has the effect of turning the narrative into a consecration prayer, for once the opus is 'complete' one is expected to worship the Eucharistic presence: *latria* is not equivalent to *anamnesis*. It is regrettable that so intrusive a confusion was not eliminated in 1970.

21. Cf. T. O'Loughlin, 'Translating Panis in a Eucharistic Context: A Problem of Language and Theology,' *Worship* 78 (2004) 226-35.

22. Cf. T. O'Loughlin, 'The Praxis and Explanations of Eucharistic Fraction in the Ninth Century: the Insular Evidence,' *Archiv für Liturgiewissenschaft* 45 (2003) 1-20.

Given that symbols contract through repetition, they must regularly be 'overhauled' so that their central structure stands out clearly and that once again correct our ways of using them. Such was the process initiated by the liturgical renewal movement from the nineteenth century onwards which reached a peak in the work of the Second Vatican Council. But this 'overhauling' is something that has to happen regularly at every level in the church. Impoverished symbols produce impoverished experiences among those who use them, and impoverished experience impoverishes faith. We are left with a stark choice: either revitalise the actual celebrations by looking at the central structures (a meal around a common table offering thanks to the Father over a single loaf and a single shared cup) or we adopt the route used in the Middle Ages whereby the actual rite was one matter and significance was another matter (the first linked to the second merely through allegory) while its importance (i.e. why it matters to be there) was something other again and wholly unconnected to the ritual. That latter course was rejected by many at the time of the Reformation (and for many groups the baby went with the bathwater) and it has become problematic for Catholics with the introduction of the vernacular in the 1960s. We now have a ritual that can be understood in the sense of words being heard and actions being seen by all present, but if it is not properly experienced then that 'understanding' will often conclude that all our words about the centrality of the Eucharist to Christian life is but much ado about nothing.

Twenty-eighth Sunday of Ordinary Time

Introduction to the Celebration

The Spirit living within each of us has gathered us together here. Now the Spirit unites us in Jesus Christ, and in union with him we are here to offer our praise and petition to our Father in heaven. Let us reflect on the mystery of the Spirit moving us towards Jesus. Let us reflect on the mystery of being united in Christ, forming on earth his holy body. Let us reflect on the mystery that we are about to offer thanks to the Father through sharing in the sacred banquet.

Rite of Penance

Good Master, you show us the path to eternal life. Lord have mercy.

Good Master, you teach us the way to the Father. Christ have mercy.

Good Master, you enable us to enter the kingdom of God. Lord have mercy.

Headings for Readings
First Reading

The Father is prepared to lavish his gifts upon us, and this gift of the Spirit must be welcomed. We express that welcome by prayer.

Second Reading

We often hear references to 'the Word of God' – and then imagine that this means listening to words from an old, holy book. This reading reminds us that the Word of God is the presence of Christ in our minds gradually revealing the mystery of God's glory to us.

Gospel

This gospel makes plain that being a disciple is difficult: indeed, we cannot find within our own resources the strength, energy and courage that it takes to be disciples. We can only have that strength by welcoming the Father's gift of the Holy Spirit in our lives.

Prayer of the Faithful
President

Brothers and sisters, Jesus told us in the gospel that we do not have the strength to follow him and love our neighbours without help from the Father, and for this help we must pray. So standing before the Father let us ask for his gifts for ourselves and all who seek to follow the way of Jesus.

Reader (s)

1. Let us pray for our community, and all Christians, that the Father will send us his Spirit to enable us to walk in the path of wisdom. Lord hear us.

2. Let us pray for our community, and all Christians, that the Father will send us the Spirit to enable us to become people who pray each day for the strength to be disciples. Lord hear us.

3. Let us pray for all those sisters and brothers who are being persecuted because of their discipleship, that the Father will send them the Spirit to strengthen them in their love and bring them comfort in their suffering. Lord hear us.

4. Let us pray for ourselves and every Christian who is finding the cost of discipleship a burden hard to bear, that the Father will send his Spirit to give them joy in following the path of wisdom. Lord hear us.

5. Let us pray for our community, and all Christians, that the Father will send us the Spirit to make us generous with all our riches, talents, and resources in using them to bring help to the poor by building a society of peace and justice. Lord hear us.

6. Conscious that we only enter the kingdom through God's help and love and mercy, let us ask the Father to look with favour on all our sisters and brothers who have gone before us

marked with the sign of faith, bring them into the fullness of life. Lord hear us.

President

Father, our desire to praise you is itself your gift, hear the petitions we make to you as the priestly people of Jesus Christ, the High Priest, your Son, our Lord. Amen.

Eucharistic Prayer

Given the focus today on our need for divine help, and the importance of prayer in discipleship, the most appropriate Eucharistic Prayer is EP I which has places for the silent prayer of the community for both the living and the dead. The theme of the interplay of divine grace and prayer is well expressed in Preface of Weekdays IV (P40), Missal, p 443.

Invitation to the Our Father

As brothers and sisters of one another, and as those committed to living as disciples of the Son of God, let us pray to the Father:

Sign of Peace

The Lord has given us peace and forgiveness, and called us to love one another. Let us now express that love we must have for each other.

Invitation to Communion

The Lord looks on us with love and mercy, and calls us now to share in his supper.

Communion Reflection

Today's gospel brings out the intrinsic connection between being a disciple of Jesus and practical concern for the poor; likewise that community cannot offer a thanksgiving sacrifice and a celebration of God's bounty without an act of practical love: this is the origin of the collection at the Eucharist. So have such a collection for the poor at this point. This act can be a perfect communion reflection today to bring out this aspect of the Eucharist that can so easily be obscured in our culture of individualised consumerism where we can imagine that 'communion' is something we 'get' and where people regularly explain why they attend the Eucharist ('go to church' / 'go to Mass') in terms of what it does for them.

This collection should be introduced by some member of the community, not the president of the Eucharist, who is directly involved in expressing the group's care for the poor. This collection can be introduced in some way like this:

> We can often be so embedded in the selfishness of our culture that we even approach our service of God with a consumerist attitude. We can easily say, 'I go to church because it does this or that for me.' Whereas we come here to give: to give thanks to the Father for his love; to give ear to the Word of God to teach us how to be disciples. And today's liturgy makes clear that genuine love for God cannot be separated from practical love for neighbour; to be a disciple of Jesus is to be caring of those in need; to share in this banquet requires we share our gifts with those in need. So now there will be a collection for the poor which my group ... will administer on behalf of us all.

Conclusion

Solemn Blessing 14 (Ordinary Time V) combines a theme of the Word of God from the second reading with that of discipleship from the gospel.

Notes

1. The first reading's biblical home.

There is a such a wide variety of titles for this biblical book – 'The Book of Wisdom' – in Bibles (many of the Bibles owned by readers will not include it!) that it is useful to be clear which text this is: it is 'the Wisdom of Solomon' (*Sapientia Salomonis*) and not 'the Wisdom of Ben Sira' / 'Sirach' / 'Ecclesiasticus'. It may be worth pointing this out to the readers if they are expected to look up their readings in their own Bibles. It may also be worth

noting that while many Catholic scriptural scholars have embraced the rather ill-defined notion of a 'second canon' ('deutero-
canonical') status for this book, this has no significance for the
liturgy. The only 'real' canon is that which is read within the
church; therefore, this book is fully canonical within the
church's view of the scriptures.

2. *The shorter version of the gospel*

The lectionary provides a shorter version of the gospel which
appears to have the benefit of making the 'rich young man'
incident stand out more starkly. However, a comparison of the
evidence (Mt, Lk, the Gospel of the Nazaraeans) shows that this
text has been preached as a whole unit (indeed with one more
verse: v 31) since the very earliest evangelists started travelling
around the churches; and as such represents the very earliest
strand of the tradition. This unity should be respected in our
repetition of the gospel today.

COMMENTARY

First Reading: Wisdom 7:7-11

Just as in today's gospel, the editors of the Lectionary have
missed giving us a natural unit of text, vv 7-12, by omitting: 'I re-
joiced in them all, because wisdom leads them; but I did not
know that she was their mother.'

This book was written in a Hellenistic Jewish setting sometime in the fifty years before the birth of Jesus, and so fits very
well with the theological culture of early Christianity. More than
half of the book can be seen as a series of praises of 'Wisdom';
and these are placed in the mouth of the human ideal of wisdom: Solomon. So here we are presented with Solomon praying
to God, and his prayer is answered with the gifts of Wisdom and
riches. But then as the rest of the unit of text makes clear: if you
compare riches and Wisdom, you have no comparison because
Wisdom is so much greater. The text is beautifully crafted to
convey its message: pray for Wisdom for it is greater than riches.

This 'Wisdom' is more than a quality of human judge-
ment/action or even a divine gift. It seems to be like a 'part' of

God's own life which can establish itself in the human being and bring the person into the divine presence. It is easy to see how this notion of Wisdom became identified with the Logos, and so created one of our fundamental christologies.

Psalm: 89 (90)

This psalm, which is a prayer of petition, is among other things a prayer for wisdom. As such, it effects the actual prayer for the assembly whose importance as an activity they have just heard about in the first reading.

Second Reading: Hebrews 4:12-13

The notion of 'the Word of God' – not to be confused with the Logos who is 'with God' (Jn 1:1) – was common among the earliest Christian communities who had taken it over from some strands of late Second Temple Judaism. The 'Word of God' is a very complex notion embracing among other things: (1) the reality of God communicating within the human person; (2) all that God has communicated; (3) the saving presence of God in the community; and (4) the presence of God judging human actions. Here, in this passage, we hear several of these themes along with the invitation to the community to persevere in fidelity to the new covenant established in Jesus.

Part of the importance of this passage is that it can recall that the Word of God – this is the Word we refer to when we speak about the Liturgy of the Word at the Eucharist – is not to be reduced to either a body of tradition or, what is worse, the words written down in the canonical collection of texts. The living Word can never be contained in a dead object such as a book! The Word is a living reality by which the community, and every member of the community, can become aware of God's presence communicating with us, showing us his glory, calling us to his way, and pointing out those ways of human existence that lead towards death.

It is worth noting that this passage has played its part in developing our understanding of the place of the Word in the liturgy:

That word constantly proclaimed in the liturgy is always a living, active word (see Hebrews 4:12) through the power of the Holy Spirit. It expresses the Father's love that never fails in its effectiveness towards us (*General Instruction on the Lectionary*, n 4).

First Reading > Gospel Links

The link here is not textual, but founded in a Catholic understanding of the mystery of grace. The full life to which Jesus calls each person cannot be lived by the human being alone (the gospel's 'for men it is impossible') but only with divine aid ('but not for God'). But this grace respects and builds upon our human resources, and so is invited by us to build up and transform us. This invitation for God to transform us, which is itself inspired by the Spirit dwelling in us giving us life and enabling us to seek out the Christ, is made in prayer; hence this reading today. The reading extols the importance of asking for divine wisdom. The wisdom asked for is more than enlightenment of the mind, it is the whole transforming presence of God in life – what we often refer to, using obscure shorthand, as 'grace'. And the activity of asking for wisdom is prayer. This first reading points to a very specific way of understanding today's difficult gospel text, and provides a very focused hermeneutic for that gospel and the preaching that is based upon it. Outside of Advent, it is very rare in the whole of the lectionary for a first reading to have such a specific role in fixing how we interpret a gospel passage.

Gospel: Mk 10:17-30

This gospel, for some unknown reason, has been shorn of its final verse that rounds it off as a unit of text: v 31 reads: 'But many that are first will be last, and the last first.' This final verse so changes how we hear the story of the 'rich young man' that it seems strange that it is omitted. Without the verse, the man going away sorrowful is one who is rejected; with verse 31 we are left with the possibility that even though he has gone away, there is still the possibility within the divine mercy that he will be yet brought within the fold. That logion captures so well the whole inversion of values between how we humans view the universe and the mystery of God's love.

Taken as a complete unit, i.e. vv 17-31, we have a story that can be shown to have been in wide circulation within the churches long before the time it became part of the preaching of the three synoptic evangelists. We can demonstrate this popularity thus: first, we have the story as here in Mark; second, we have the story as found in Mt (19:16-30) and Lk (18:18-30); and, third, a summary of the whole story circulated in the Gospel of the Nazaraeans. This popularity, despite its hard teaching, can be explained by its touching so many aspects of discipleship: the need to follow a strict way of life, the need to pray, and the need to care for the poor. However, in this story those themes are encountered within a more complex frame: there are persecutions, but the disciples look towards a reward. Yet, this reward is not presented as a simple contract, a *do ut des* system in the manner of many religions ancient and modern, but within the complexity of divine generosity. Discipleship is a relationship with God that is costly but does lead to the fullness of life. Down the centuries there have been many attempts to reduce this passage to systems: to express it so that discipleship cannot be seen to come from 'mixed motives'; or to present a complete separation between human effort which we might make and eternal life; or to see it as implying a commerce of good works and divine favour; but all such systems ignore the complexity of our human and divine relationships. This passage when encountered as an incident that reflects the experience of every Christian, presents this complexity to us; and its open questions – deliberately left open even for The Twelve in the story – invite us to ponder on the fundamental 'fact' of belief: within the creation of a loving God we creatures must have relationships of justice and love with each other; but creatures (characterised by finitude) are also called while living in this material creation to enter a relationship with the Creator (characterised before our finite minds by his lack of finitude).

HOMILY NOTES

1. The sadness of the rich young man who goes away from Jesus is something that every one of us should be able to identify with to some extent. We know what it would take build the kingdom of God, to pursue holiness, and to create a culture of love – but it just seems too much. There are too many other commitments, so many urgent things to be seen to first, too much disruption to break the patterns of a lifetime, and the fear that one might just be thought a nutter! To take discipleship really seriously – when most people in our society think that religion is just a private affair for 'the religious', and indeed there will be several in our own families and immediate circle who take a similar view – seems just a little too 'over the top.'

2. Yet it can be done, and it has been done, and it is being done!

3. We can only have the energy, the strength, the joy to follow the path of discipleship if we ask the Father in prayer. For us alone, it is impossible to live as disciples; but if we ask for the Father's gifts of strength, and energy, and joy, then it is possible 'because everything is possible for God'.

4. Instead of going away sorrowful, we are called to stay and pray for the help we need to be disciples.

5. This 'help,' this 'strength,' this 'energy,' this 'joy' is what in traditional western jargon has been given the name 'grace' – but using that word is not helpful in preaching: it is religious jargon that has become so debased through controversy that it obscures more than it reveals to the average listener. So avoid the term 'grace' and use a series of words with a common meaning in its place.

6. This need for the Spirit's help and presence if we are to follow Jesus's path to the Father points out three other important truths:

    First, the life that the young man could not follow is not something that can be partitioned off from the rest of life: it is not something that is for a special group of devotees such as nuns or monks; nor for just one or two aspects of life.

Everyone is called to set out on this journey, what it involves is different for each of us. What is common is that it involves every aspect of our lives: every part of our lives can contribute to the kingdom, and every aspect can contribute to its frustration.

Second, following Jesus is not simply taking on a philosophy of life or picking a particular path towards self-improvement. It is the opposite of the lifestyle guides found under the heading of 'body-mind-spirit' in an airport bookshop. To set out on the pilgrimage of faith is to establish a relationship with God and with others. This life is impossible without the gifts of God's help, strength, energy, and joy that come within this relationship of prayer by which we respond to the invitation to follow Jesus.

Third, we tend to think of prayer as a only 'private' thing – indeed, some people abandon fasting and prayer saying they would rather do something 'positive' for others. This idea fails to appreciate our situation as human beings. The rich young man could not bring himself to care for the poor, and most of us today find it just as difficult. In order to serve other humans, we need to ask the Father for his help and strength. Prayer, far from removing us from concern for others, opens us up to God and God's energy opens us up to others.

7. This gospel's message is not an easy one. We have to accept our weaknesses and we have to turn towards the Father in prayer, and then embrace change with his strengthening help. We can make a fresh start in a few moments in the Prayer of the Faithful.

Twenty-ninth Sunday of the Year

Introduction to the Celebration

Today we reflect on how Jesus came among us. He came as the one sent by the Father to bring us new life, yet he came among us as seeking to serve rather than to be served. We reflect also that for us, his followers, his way of life sets us a pattern for how we should live. In a world filled with the suffering caused by power struggles Jesus reminds us that our community here must display a different way of being human: 'Anyone who wants to become great among you must be your servant, and anyone who wants to be first among you must be servant of all.'

Rite of Penance

Lord Jesus, Son of Man, you came among us not to be served but to serve and to give your life as a ransom for many. Lord have mercy.

Lord Jesus, for those times when we have not heeded your word that 'anyone who wants to become great among you must be your servant'. Christ have mercy.

Lord Jesus, for those times when we have not listened to your word that 'anyone who wants to be first among you must be servant to all'. Lord have mercy.

Headings for Readings
First Reading

The prophet announced that one will be sent by God who will renew the people. This promised one will be the servant of God who by his suffering will bring reconciliation to all.

Second Reading

This passage presents us with a way of imagining who Jesus is. He is the one who can enter into the very presence of God – this is the privilege of the High Priest – and the new life he gives us can be imagined as his bringing us into that presence with him.

Gospel

The community of Jesus must seek to live life in the new way of the kingdom, it must be a community of service and love towards one another, and it must reject the old ways of power-seeking and selfishness.

Prayer of the Faithful

President

Gathered as a community that seeks to serve one another, and all our sisters and brothers, let us humbly place our needs before the Father of mercies.

Reader (s)

1. For all who are called to ministries of leadership in the churches, that they may follow the way of being servants of all. Lord hear us.

2. For all who have positions of power and responsibility in the world, that they may discover the ways of peace, justice, and know that they must serve those in poverty and need. Lord hear us.

3. For all humanity, that in seeking peace and justice they may encounter the Son of Man who came not to be served but to serve and give his life as a ransom for many. Lord hear us.

4. For this community, that we will manifest the presence of God in our gentleness and service to those in need. Lord hear us.

5. Specific local needs and topics of the day.

6. For those called to a ministry of leadership in this church, that God will protect them, and grant them strength to be servants to their sisters and brothers. Lord hear us.

President

Father, gathered as the new community of the Son of Man we make these prayer to you. Hear us, and grant our needs in Christ Jesus, our Lord. Amen.

Eucharistic Prayer

Preface of Sundays in Ordinary Time I (P29) fits the theme of the gospel. None of the Eucharistic Prayers is particularly appropriate. However, the acclamation 'Dying you destroyed our death …' is appropriate.

Invitation to the Our Father

The Son of Man came not to be served but to serve, and he taught us how to pray to the Father.

Sign of Peace

Let us express our desire to love and serve each other by offering each other a sign of peace.

Invitation to Communion

The Son of Man came not to be served but to serve, and to give his life as a ransom for many; and now he bids each of us to drink of the cup from which he drank. Happy are we whom he has called to be his people.

Communion Reflection

The prayer 'Soul of Christ' (Missal, p 1020) is appropriate.

Conclusion

The mention of two of The Twelve, James and John, in today's gospel makes the use of Solemn Blessing 17: Apostles (Missal, p 375) suitable. Both names can be added in the first intercession, and the second intercession's final word 'men' can be dropped without affecting the meaning.

Notes

1. Sending out mixed messages

Given the emphasis on the leader of the community being the servant of all, presidents have to be careful today about ritual displays whose built-in message is that the priest is actually 'The Important One' who is set over the people. Many of our rituals are variants on more elaborate rituals whose function was to show 'where the power lay'. Therefore, this is not a day for an entrance procession with the president taking the place of honour at its end. Nor is it a day to use incense with its implied message that the priest is a unique person more special than the community. Likewise, in reading notices be careful about honorific titles which set people on a ladder of importance but always with the ordinary people, the community, on the bottom rung.

2. The gospel

If one reads the shorter form today one is given a little bit of teaching abstracted from its context. However, part of the nature of the good news is that Jesus teaches in response to situations he encountered. That dynamic should be respected; therefore, the long form should be read.

COMMENTARY

First Reading: Isa 53:10-11

This is the conclusion of the Prayer of Thanksgiving of the Servant-Prophet (Isa 52:13-53:12) from Second-Isaiah. Victory is the reward of the prophet, but he does not see victory in his lifetime, and as a result of his victory through suffering he is able to share that victory with all those who look to him.

By accident today the first reading is thematically closer to the second reading than it is to the gospel, but this similarity should not be dwelt upon as it could foster the notion that all three readings on Sundays share some common themes.

Psalm: 32 (33)

This psalm is an expression of the Lord's faithfulness to his people; it is not clear how it is a meditation on the first reading or a prayerful preparation for the gospel.

Second Reading: Heb 4:14-16

What was distinctive about the High Priest (e.g. Caiaphas or Annas) was that he could, once a year, enter into the very presence of God in the Holy of Holies and there intercede for the whole people. This piece of information is the basis for the theology of Jesus being developed here by the author of Hebrews. Jesus is both like and unlike this High Priest. Like the High Priest when he entered the temple, Jesus is now in the presence of the Father and interceding for his people. Unlike the High

Priest, Jesus is not one of a succession or one who stands in the presence of God periodically: he is the unique High Priest – the title, which has passed into our liturgy, used in this passage (but nowhere else) is that he is the 'Great High Priest' or the 'Supreme High Priest'. As the Great High Priest he makes perfect intercession for us, and so he is the uniquely merciful High Priest where we find mercy and grace.

First Reading > Gospel Links
The first reading is focused on one verse in the gospel: 'For the Son of man also came not to be served but to serve, and to give his life as a ransom for many' (Mk 10:45). It sees this as the fulfilment of the Suffering Servant promised in Isaiah.

Gospel: Mk 10:35-45; shorter form: 10:42-45
This incident with the sons of Zebedee is found in its fullest form in Mark. No doubt the reason the event became part of the gospel was that jockeying for position was a source of strife in the churches in which Mark preached, and recalling this story – and then supplying a piece of formal teaching derived from it – was intended to offer the Christian antidote to such desires for positions of honour.

HOMILY NOTES

1. The values of the kingdom are exactly opposite to those of the world of power politics, social climbing, and vain display. We all know this, yet generations come and generations go by, and we still import titles of honour, displays of prestige, and even the jargon of imperial Rome, the *cursus honorum*, into the church. The pope may take the title 'servant of the servants', but a look at the pomp and circumstance surrounding the papal ceremonies suggests that the need for a power display outweighs theology. Bishops are to be servants, but 'for the people's sake' they wear the last remnants of imperial purple. Clergy are called to take on extra ministry over and above the ministry of the baptised, but in exchange

they get a range of titles all suitably graded so that everyone from a newly ordained deacon to Vicar General knows exactly which rung each is on. Reading this gospel should make us all mightily embarrassed!

2. When John in his gospel wanted to convey the same message he did not have a little teaching scene like this one we read today; rather he had Jesus get up and wash the feet of his disciples with all the messiness and embarrassment that goes with such an act of service. Moreover, we know that foot washing was one of the ways that Christians in the early churches learned how they should see one another as brothers and sisters in Christ (e.g. 1 Tim 5:10). Indeed, it survived as a rite used regularly in some monasteries and by bishops on Holy Thursday. Now it has a formal place in the liturgy of the Lord's Supper on Holy Thursday – although it is still such a shocking message that it is always in danger of being simply skipped or turned into a token affair.

3. Given that the gospel should make any cleric uncomfortable, and anything one says about the gospel is likely to be taken as hypocritical self-justification, a better commentary on the gospel is to actually perform the action Jesus carried out and wished us to carry out in imitation of him.

   Therefore, introduce the actual practice of foot washing – many in any average congregation will never have seen it or will not remember it from Holy Thursday – and then wash the feet of a group of the community.

   Meanwhile, have these words from John read as a commentary on the action taking place:

   When he had washed their feet, and taken his garments, and resumed his place, he said to them, 'Do you know what I have done to you? You call me Teacher and Lord; and you are right, for so I am. If I then, your Lord and Teacher, have washed your feet, you also ought to wash one another's feet. For I have given you an example, that you also should do as I have done to you.

   Truly, truly, I say to you, a servant is not greater than his master; nor is he who is sent greater than he who sent him. If you know these things, blessed are you if you do them' (Jn 13:12-17).

Then, while the action of foot washing continues, have the shorter form of today's gospel re-read.

4. Apart from one action being worth several thousand words, by making a community more familiar with the action of foot washing one is enriching the repertoire of the community's liturgical experience and helping the community appreciate the action on Holy Thursday more fully.

Many people grumble that no matter how short a homily is, it is still too long – words have become cheap. An action like foot washing will make people sit up – no doubt you reading this think the idea daunting (so too did St Peter) – and hear today's gospel on its second reading in a way they did not when it was first read!

Thirtieth Sunday of Ordinary Time

Introduction to the Celebration

Rather than give an introduction, say something like this:

We are gathered here as people called to share in the Lord's supper. As such, it is appropriate that we should be at least on speaking terms with each other, so let us introduce ourselves to each other by way of preparing for this celebration.

Rite of Penance

With the blind man, we call on you: O Son of David, have pity on us. Lord have mercy.

With the blind man, we call on you: O Son of David, have pity on us. Christ have mercy.

With the blind man, we call on you: O Son of David, have pity on us. Lord have mercy.

Headings for Readings
First Reading

The prophet prays for the time when the Lord's Anointed One will gather together a scattered people: the blind will be given sight, the lame healed, and all led to a new land of joy.

Second Reading

Who is Jesus: he is the perfect High Priest who leads us into the presence of the Father; and transforms us into his priestly people.

Gospel

St Mark picks on a single blind man calling on Jesus to represent each and every one of us. As disciples of Jesus we call out for mercy and acknowledge Jesus as our teacher. We receive the gift of sight and we set out after Jesus. But Jesus is going up toward Jerusalem and the cross.

Prayer of the Faithful

President

As we heard in the second reading, Jesus is the new, perfect and eternal priest, and because we have become his people in baptism we can stand now with him and make our prayers to the Father.

Reader (s)

1. With Jesus our high priest we pray for all our sisters and brothers that we may have the gift of sight to see the way to true life. Lord hear us.

2. With Jesus our high priest we pray for this church that we will have the strength to bring the gift of light to those we meet during this week. Lord hear us.

3. With Jesus our high priest we pray for all the world's leaders that they may be given sight to act with wisdom and the foresight to see the ways of co-operation and peace. Lord hear us.

4. With Jesus our high priest we pray for our society that our blind spots may be removed, that we may overcome our prejudices, and work for a more just society. Lord hear us.

5. With Jesus our high priest we pray for ourselves as individuals that we may overcome any blindness to loving our neighbours. Lord hear us.

6. With Jesus our high priest we pray for all who are suffering, fearful, oppressed, that they may be comforted by God's grace. Lord hear us

7. Specific local needs and topics of the day.

8. With Jesus our high priest we pray for those who have died that they may see God face to face. Lord hear us.

President

Father, recalling that Jesus restored sight to Bartimaeus, we pray today that our blindness may be removed, through that same Christ, our Lord. Amen.

Eucharistic Prayer

The Preface of the Fourth Sunday of Lent (P15) – which is for the gospel of the man born blind – fits today very well; the notion of the Christ gathering in the scattered people – the Christian reading of the passage from Jeremiah – fits the christology of Eucharistic Prayer III.

Invitation to the Our Father

In union with our great High Priest, let us stand as a priestly people before the Father and pray:

Sign of Peace

The Lord has gathered us around his table and offered us his peace. Let us offer peace to one another.

Invitation to Communion

The Lord restored sight to the blind man, he enlightens all who call upon him, and he beckons us towards the fullness of life; happy are we who are called to his supper.

Communion Reflection

Have a structured silence.

Conclusion

Prayer over the People 7 (Missal, p 381).

COMMENTARY

First Reading: Jer 31:7-9

This is part of Jeremiah's prophecy of the restoration of Israel when the people will be delivered from captivity by the people in 'the north' (=Assyria). He deliberately presents this new gathering in terms of the original exodus: a people are led triumphantly through the desert from captivity into a land of lush meadows and flowing streams. The captives are restored, healed, and set in clover!

The notion of Jesus as the new Moses, who leads the people

on the new exodus out of captivity, and the one who gathers and restores scattered Israel, saw in prophecies such as this the divine promise of what was happening in Jesus.

Psalm: 125 (126)
The Lord is the deliverer of the people from bondage and the bringer of new joy. The psalm is a perfect reflection on the hope expressed in the first reading. In the case of the original audiences of both the first reading and psalm that hope was messianic hope; in the case of the Christian community at their liturgy it is our eschatological hope.

Second Reading: Heb 5:1-6
This reading continues on from last week's, but as it stands it lacks the context within which these verses make sense. The unit of text is 4:14-5:10 and seeks to make sense of who Jesus is in terms of him not only being our High Priest, but our merciful High Priest. Every High Priest had to be appointed by God to perform his sacrifices, but in the case of the High Priests of the Old Covenant, they were acting as sinners on behalf of sinners, and so were in the same boat as those they represented. Jesus, by contrast, was without sin, and so his priesthood was of a wholly different sort: of the order of Melchizedek. He did not need to do this priestly service for himself, and so his action is wholly one of merciful love for us sinners.

This way of approaching the mystery of Christ has two resonances for western Catholics: first, the notion of the work of Jesus as mercy for sinners has continued in the form of the language of the cult of the Sacred Heart of Jesus (see Preface 45 for an outline of that approach) – so this is a christology with which we are far more familiar than we might suspect, albeit using a different language; second, seeing how the author of Hebrews uses the notion of the Melchizedek-style priesthood as referring uniquely to the action of Jesus – his whole point in naming Jesus's priesthood with that of Melchizedek was that it could not be shared with any other on whose behalf Jesus suffered – it should be obvious how inappropriate were/are references to presbyteral ministry as belonging to 'the order of Melchizedek'.

First Reading > Gospel Links

The link is seen as one of prophesy and fulfilment: one of the signs of the messianic times is that the blind have their sight restored as part of the great re-gathering of Israel; now Jesus healing Bartimaeus is a fulfilment of this for an individual. In so far as Bartimaeus is intended by Mark to be a token/promise of the eschatological healing, he intended his story to be read against such prophetic statements as we find in Jeremiah today.

For the sake of giving people something more than lapidary phrases, it is worth reading the remaining four verses of this section of the letter: up to the end of 5:10.

Gospel: Mk 10:46-52

This story, apparently simply another healing miracle, is only found with the man named, Bartimaeus, in Mark – here again we have an example of a story that we think of as common to all three synoptic gospels but where Mark offers the most complete form of the story, and where that complete form has its own distinctive theology.

We should first note how the story occurs at a turning point in the gospel. This is the second healing of a blind man, but at Bethsaida the blind man recovered sight slowly and is told to tell no one (8:22-6); now the restoration is immediate and the form of the messianic secret is abandoned: the end is now in sight as Jesus turns to Jerusalem. So this healing brings the earlier progressive revelation of Jesus's identity to a conclusion. Up to this only the inner circle – represented by Peter – and demons have recognised Jesus's true identity; now a blind beggar on the roadside can call out the messianic royal title to attract attention. This healing is also the beginning of the work of Jesus in Jerusalem: being hailed as 'Son of David' anticipates the shouts of the crowd on his entry to the city.

However, Mark clearly thinks of this as a call-story as much as a healing. The blind Bartimaeus sees the true identity of Jesus and calls for mercy. He then leaves his garments – a pointer to the ritual of baptism within the churches where Mark preached where the old life was seen as old garments and Christian faith seen as new garments – is healed, and is told that it is his faith that has saved him. Receiving his sight is almost incidental: he has called for mercy and is told that he is saved. Then to complete the theme of the call story, he joined the throng (*ékolouthei*) who are accompanying Jesus on his momentous journey up to Jerusalem. Whereas the healing stories are understood as relating to individuals who are healed and then told to tell no one, in this story the individual then becomes a fellow traveller with the community of Jesus, and so its baptismal echoes are here understood in terms of the church.

HOMILY NOTES

1. Blindness is terrifying. Darkness brings before us all our terrors. Not being able to see where we are going is the stuff of most human fears. The poverty and blindness of Bartimaeus speak to any human being of feeling – and, indeed, if there is someone to whom it does not speak, then that person probably would have no time for religion or things of the spirit as she/he would be insensitive to promptings in our imagination that lead us to faith.

2. But thinking of poor, blind, ignored Bartimaeus can distract us. We can listen to this gospel but only hear it in the way we hear a 'news item': another detail, a bit of information about someone far away which we might simply believe, or refuse to believe, or simply note that we know it. 'Oh yes, Bartimaeus, is that not the guy Jesus healed near Jericho?' or 'Yes, wasn't he a lucky guy: right place, right time!' or 'That story of Bartimaeus: shows how gullible people were in those days and the power of religious preachers to get their followers to accept accidents or falsehoods as miracles!'

3. Much as these are interesting approaches, all three miss the point, for Mark's story of the incident of sight being restored

is intended to alert every one who hears the gospel to the nature of the work of Jesus.

4. Recall the proverb: 'There is none so blind as him who will not see.' Likewise we say that 'Greed is at the root of all evil,' but we could also say that blindness is there as well. We have all met people who are blind to the crassness of their actions or statements. We have all met people who are blind to the consequences of the actions or blind to their bigotry or blind to their prejudices. Dare we admit it: our own eyesight might just be a little dim also!

5. We live in a world of blindness. There is the blindness of world leaders who press forward policies that are so short-term that we have whole regions that simmer with unrest. We have blindness that prevents us seeing how policies create injustice and stop development. We have the blindness that sees global warming yet refuses to take action in time.

   Closer to our localities we have blind spots about what is really of value in society: we may prefer a motorway to our heritage or we may prefer our holidays to a just wage for workers. Greed finds blindness a steadfast ally.

   Then in our lives we can find blindness to those around us, blindness to the community, blindness to the needs of those who need us. Blindness can be a great help in avoiding awkward questions of conscience.

6. Asked would we like to leave our blindness behind, to become aware of our prejudices, to have our blind spots treated, we all respond with an emphatic 'yes' – few of us willingly seek darkness, carelessness, destruction. But it is not as simple as opening our eyes: we need also the gift of new sight. This gift is the 'enlightenment of faith', it is the 'grace of God', it is the gift of the Spirit.

7. If we would see our lives, see those around us, and see our world, we must cry out: 'Master, let me see.' Then in the face of our need of forgiveness, we have to cry out: 'Master, let me see again.' Then knowing that we must grow in our discipleship, we cry out: 'Master, let me see more.'

8. We want the Lord's gift of sight and enlightenment – this is our prayer every Sunday. We want to follow the Master along the road – we are a pilgrim people. But it is worth remembering that when Mark said that Bartimaeus set out along the road following Jesus, that road led towards the cross.

Lectionary Unit III.II

This stage consists of three Sundays (Sundays 31 to 33 inclusive) when we read of the final revelation of the identity of the Son of Man in Jerusalem.

Thirty-first Sunday of Ordinary Time

Introduction to the Celebration

We have gathered in the Holy Spirit, here, to offer loving thanks to the Father in union with Jesus, his Son. But we cannot love God whom we cannot see, if we do not love our neighbour whom we can see.

Likewise, we cannot thank God for all his gifts, most of which we cannot see, if we do not value and care for the creation around us which we can see.

It is this mystery that we serve the God who is greater than all by caring for the visible world, this mystery that we know the God who is love by loving our neighbours, that we recall in today's gathering.

Rite of Penance

For those times when we have not loved the Lord our God with all our hearts, and our neighbours as ourselves. Lord have mercy.

For those times when we have not loved the Lord our God with all our minds, and our neighbours as ourselves. Christ have mercy.

For those times when we have not loved the Lord our God with all our strength, and our neighbours as ourselves. Lord have mercy.

Headings for Readings

First Reading

This reading reminds us that the Lord has placed us within the wonder of his creation – a land flowing with milk and honey – and we can there discover the Lord and his love for us.

Second Reading

Jesus is our priest, the king of all creation; he stands before the

Father and presents us and all creation to the Father. Jesus, the high priest, our king, presents to the Father an eternal and universal kingdom, a kingdom of truth and life, a kingdom of holiness and grace, a kingdom of justice, love and peace.

Gospel

This gospel presents us with a new vision of the universe, and a new way of viewing all creation: we must love God, but we love the God we cannot see through loving our neighbour whom we can see, and we praise the Creator whom we cannot see through valuing the creation we can see.

Prayer of the Faithful
President

As creatures within God's creation, let us stand and pray in union with Jesus Christ, our High Priest and the King of all creation.
Reader (s)

1. That we, and all humanity, will respect the integrity of the creation which God has given us as our earthly home. Lord in your mercy, hear our prayer.

2. That we will learn to use wisely the resources of God's creation, recalling that all these resources are God's gifts. Lord in your mercy, hear our prayer.

3. That we will live in a way that does not abuse the environment that God has created around us. Lord in your mercy, hear our prayer.

4. That the world's resources may be used for the benefit of all humanity and may be used in a sustainable way. Lord in your mercy, hear our prayer.

5. That we will recognise the new responsibilities that our technological abilities place on us with regard to the creation. Lord in your mercy, hear our prayer.

6. That just as we have grown in technical skills in using the creation, so we might grow in wisdom in using what God has given us. Lord in your mercy, hear our prayer.

7. That we may listen to the groans of the creation and respond as individuals and communities in the way we live. Lord in your mercy, hear our prayer.

8. That we commit ourselves to protecting life and all creation, be it water, earth, or air, and know the limits set by wisdom. Lord in your mercy, hear our prayer.

President

Father, you are the beginning and the end of all that is; hear us, and answer us in Christ Jesus, our Lord. Amen.

Preparation of the Gifts

The procession can often become an affair of tokens: books, tools, toys, along with an equally token amount of wine and pre-cut roundels that we claim are 'bread'. The overall impression is that sacramentality is a matter of tokens, play-acting, and that it is radically separate from the rest of life and reality. Indeed, we often make a juxtaposition between reality and 'mere' symbolism – forgetting that all reality is symbolic/sacramental of the divine reality. So, if we want to value the creation and present it as sacramental, then today dispense with the temptation to present 'tokens' and concentrate on presenting real food and real drink so that the God of all creation can be thanked. This means having a large real loaf – remember that unleavened bread came into use in the tenth century simply because it could be stored without going stale – and a large jug of wine.

If you do this – and it will need preparation, for instance, in the form of training ministers to help with the fraction – then it can become visible that the created things of this world can be the location of our encounter with the Lord of all creation.

Eucharistic Prayer

Preface of Sunday in Ordinary Time V (P33) is suitable; it works particularly well with Eucharistic Prayer II.

Invitation to the Our Father

Let us thank the Father for our daily bread as we say:

Sign of Peace

Rejoicing in the presence of the Christ in our gathering, let us greet one another as sisters and brothers.

Invitation to Communion

He has called us to gather in his presence, he welcomes us around this table, now he calls us to become one with one another and with him in sharing this loaf and this cup.

Communion Reflection

Our God is the God of all humans.
The God of heaven and earth.
The God of the sea and the rivers.
The God of the sun and moon.
The God of all the heavenly bodies.
The God of the lofty mountains.
The God of the lowly valleys.
God is above the heavens;
and he is in the heavens;
and he is beneath the heavens.
Heaven and earth and sea,
and everything that is in them,
such he has as his abode.
He inspires all things,
he gives life to all things,
he stands above all things,
and he stands beneath all things.
He enlightens the light of the sun,
he strengthens the light of the night and the stars,
he makes wells in the arid land and dry islands in the sea,
and he places the stars in the service of the greater lights.
He has a Son who is co-eternal with himself,
and similar in all respects to himself;
and neither is the Son younger than the Father,
nor is the Father older than the Son;
and the Holy Spirit breathes in them.
And the Father and the Son and Holy Spirit are inseparable.
Amen.   *Tirechán the Bishop*

Conclusion

There is no Solemn Blessing that highlights the gift of the creation, however, that for the Beginning of the New Year (Solemn Blessing 3, Missal, p 368) can be adapted by changing the last line of the first invocation from '... keep you safe throughout the coming year' to '... keep you safe throughout the coming week'. With that small alteration it is most appropriate for today.

Notes

We are all aware of the environmental agenda – global warming, the destruction of the planet's resources, the damage that is done by excessive desires of some societies – and know that this is also a Christian agenda because of our belief in the absolute given-ness of all. However, it is often difficult for this concern to find expression within the liturgy except by it being imposed upon the liturgy as a theme. While such themes may be of great importance (e.g. Communications Sunday, Prisoners Sunday, and what not) they run the risk of making the liturgy simply into being an occasion for the conveyance of something else, and silently a message that is destructive of liturgy is transmitted: liturgy is about getting something (e.g. communion) and a place where we can be got at (e.g. someone sends us their message). However, it is better to think of liturgy as, somehow, an end in itself. We are there because there we are who we are: brothers and sisters in the Lord. And, there we are who we are going to be in the fullness of the heavenly kingdom. We are not there for some reason other than being there, any more than we are with our loved ones for any reason other than being with them. Liturgy is the centre of Christian life because it is really life, indeed the foretaste of eternal life.

However, the liturgy is, *de facto*, the primary place where Christians learn of the implications of their commitment to Jesus and to one another and, as such, it is the place where they hear the Christian vision on the environmental crisis that confronts humanity. Today is one of the days when this theme can be introduced in a way that seem to well up out of the liturgy rather than being imposed upon it – and, therefore, it figures prominently in these notes.

If one is going to dwell on the environmental crisis within the liturgy, then there are some important factors that have to be taken into account.

First, it would be untrue to our tradition to see care for the environment simply in terms of divine commands ('Do this!' 'Why?' 'Because God orders it!') as this ignores the sacramentality of the whole creation in the human quest for God.

Second, it would be untrue to our tradition to see care for the environment simply in terms of impending disaster ('Do this!' 'Why?' 'Because otherwise we will be destroyed by global warming!'). This may make sense to an environmental group or a politician, but it does not take account of our vision, as Christians, of the environment as 'creation'. Threats may have their place in the current human debate, but we have something far richer to concern ourselves with in the liturgy.

Third, we cannot preach about the environment without relating this to the sacramental nature of the universe. Just as we cannot speak of 'sacraments' – pre-eminently the Eucharist – without speaking of the Christ as the primordial sacrament; likewise, we cannot speak of the creation without seeing it as coming through the Logos – 'through whom all things were made'. And, therefore, speaking of the creation as sacramental cannot be done without speaking of the sacrament of the Logos, the Christ, and so of the 'sacraments' within the church.

Fourth, when we speak at the Eucharist about sacramentality, then it has to inform our practice: it must be a genuine celebration of the gifts of food 'which earth has given and human hands have made' which becomes our encounter with the food of life. Tokenism in liturgy sends the signal that really the creation does not matter!

Lastly, we must bear in mind that many of the most vocal forms of Christianity today – fundamentalist evangelicalism – have such an impoverished view of the sacramentality of the creation, that many people, Christians included, do not even recognise the notion of the sacramentality of creation as part of the good news.

First Reading: Deut 6:2-6

This text links the affirmation of the uniqueness of Yahweh with presenting the fundamental religious law by which the people are to live in the Lord's Land. By the time of Jesus these verses had taken on the status of being a summary of the whole law and were recited daily as a statement of commitment. It was this text that was written out and placed in phylacteries, and which was repeatedly used in liturgy as a credal statement.

Psalm: 17 (18)

The choice is determined by the command to love God with all our strength, and now God is loved because he is the strength of humanity. The first reading and the psalm form a couplet picking up the complex nature of all references to God: our 'strength' is only ours in so far as it is the gift of God who is the source, 'the strength', of the creation.

Second Reading: Heb 7:23-28

The author of Hebrews seeks to understand the Christ-event by seeing Jesus as a priest, indeed as a high priest. The role of the high priest was set out in the annual liturgy by which sin was removed from the people and they were restored to being his loyal subjects and, therefore, those who received his love and protection. The presence of sin, demons, and the drudgery of day-to-day living meant that each year that relationship became 'strained' and needed overhaul and renewal. This was done by the liturgy of atonement: the camp and the people were purified by being smeared with blood; and the effect was a new beginning. Now, for this author, that liturgy and its chief actor, the high priest, are compared and contrasted with the death and resurrection of Jesus. In both cases the people are renewed, the relationship with God overhauled, and a fresh start made. By contrast, that which the other high priests did was only a temporary fix for it lasted but a year and they themselves were less than perfect. Jesus, however, is perfect and the renewal which he effects does not pass away.

When reading the Letter to the Hebrews one must always remember that it is an imaginary metaphorical language based on a particular imaginary recollection of an actual liturgy. It is, therefore, theological imagination in its most pictorial form. Failure, however, to recall this fact has made this reading one of the most fought over passages in the scriptures since the Reformation. Hebrews is not a set of instructions in a 'theology of the atonement' but poetry to try to express the wonder of Jesus to a people steeped in the collective memories of Second Temple Judaism.

First Reading > Gospel Links

The continuity between the covenants: what is mandated in the first reading is repeated as part of the teaching of the messiah in the gospel.

Gospel: Mk 12:28-34

This passage, given the title 'the great commandment,' is one of the few places where Mark's episode is longer than that found in either Matthew or Luke (both of which only parallel vv 28-31).

In Mark the questioner is presented as a genuine seeker after the truth and not some cute word-spinner seeking either to trap Jesus or engage in fanciful display of legal skill. The scribe comes and asks a basic question, and is given the basic teaching in response.

Both commandments are taken from the Law: the first is taken from Deut 6:4 (see the first reading), while the second is taken from Lev 19:18. In presenting the teaching in this way, Mark wishes to present Jesus as both the continuation and the fulfilment of the Law.

Lastly, we have vv 32-4 which form the scribe's reply and which are, fundamentally, a repetition of what Jesus has just said, prefaced by the word 'Teacher'. This is more than a rhetorical device: the role of the disciple in every master-disciple exchange was to be able to repeat the master's teaching and praise his wisdom while doing so (it is a form preserved in many ancient texts), and it is used here to show not only that the scribe has become a model disciple, but that here we have the formal teaching of Jesus as Teacher, and as such each person hearing the story is placed in the position that s/he should say: 'You are right, Teacher; you have truly said that he is one, and there is no other but he; and to love him with all the heart, and with all the understanding, and with all the strength, and to love one's neighbour as oneself, is much more than all whole burnt offerings and sacrifices.'

And, then, as a reward for having become a disciple, hear: 'You are not far from the kingdom of God.'

HOMILY NOTES

1. Christians are often blamed for being so concerned for the next life that they ignore the value and beauty of the world around them. Christians are blamed for being so interested in being saved from the world, that they do not care for saving the planet. Christians are blamed for being so interested in their 'souls' that they do not take sufficient interest the practicalities of life.

2. This caricature is unjust, but we have to admit that many Christians have adopted such a strange attitude to the material world that it is easy to see how the caricature has arisen. Indeed, there are many people who preach a version of Christianity that runs like this: God made the world as a testing-ground for human beings. The time in the testing-ground is only a transitory stage and the testing-ground is only a background. What counts is saving one's soul and this is really a private matter that has little to do with other people and precious little to do with the material creation. In short, Christianity is about getting rescued from the world by Jesus.

3. It is very hard to say just how this 'Christianity' conflicts with

the Catholic vision of creation in terms of a list of points; rather it conflicts with a whole vision of the universe as somehow pointing towards a source that is greater than it, and of the whole creation displaying a purpose that embraces the whole of reality while still being greater than it.

4. Ours is a sacramental vision of the creation: all comes from God, all somehow bears the imprint of its divine origin, it all comes into being through the Son, it all speaks to us of its origin, we come to appreciate its plan through our faith in the Son who has entered the creation as one of us, and we look forward not to the creation being abandoned but brought to its perfection in Christ the king of the universe.

5. What do we mean by a sacramental vision? Let's begin with what we are doing now: here we are gathered as a group of people for a meal, we are using words to speak of realities that are beyond words, we are using food and drink to experience being united with one another and with Christ. The realities of this creation – a gathering, words, food – are not just speaking to us about this life, but the whole of life uniting us to all the Christians here on earth, with the saints in heaven, with the Lord who died and rose.

   Unless we engage with the physical realities of other people in the assembly, unless we hear stories like those in the scriptures, unless we eat and drink in this meal – that larger world remains hidden to us. This world reveals the divine world to us and enables us to encounter it.

6. Let's now think about our lives and the people we love. Anyone who loves another person knows that that love transforms the whole of life, it gives purpose and energy, and brightens up every moment. When love or commitment goes sour or is taken away, then it sucks the joy, the light, and the energy from life. It is through human loving and being loved that we discover that there is love in the universe. In discovering that love we discover purpose and providence, and can learn to love God and to accept God's love. It is in the intimacy of human, earthly, love that we know that love is more than

an earthly reality. This world's love reveals the divine love to us and enables us to encounter it.

7. Now let's think about the creation: the universe, our planet with all its wonders, the environment that enables us to live. We profess that all of it, heaven and earth, is the work of the creator. 'We believe in one God, the Father, almighty, the creator of heaven and earth, of all that is' whether it is visible or invisible. This all comes from God and in 'doing its thing' it sings his praises. It is through discovering the wonder around us that we realise that there is a wonder beyond these wonders. It is in relating to the creation that we discover more about who we are and the vastness of God's majesty and love. This universe reveals the divine to us and enables us to encounter it.

8. It is when we love others and through loving the creation that we express our love for God. It is through caring for others with all our mind and heart and strength that we come to know the love of God and to love God. We embrace each other and we embrace the creation because this is how we learn to be embraced by God.

9. We often say we are the People of God. But to be the people of God we have, first, to become the people of love. To be the people of God we have, first, to become the people of the Creation.

Thirty-second Sunday of Ordinary Time

Introduction to the Celebration

We can gather here because each of us has heard, in some way or another, the divine invitation to become beloved daughters and son of the Father. The Spirit has moved our hearts to set out to follow the Lord, and we have started on a journey towards the Father in the way we live our lives. However, as we gather today to celebrate this journey, we are also conscious that we often fail to live life in accordance with this invitation. The gospel recalls Jesus seeing a poor widow in the temple treasury and his way of looking at this woman is a challenge to all of us who accept his invitation to follow him.

Rite of Penance

Lord Jesus, you call us to show mercy to the poor. Lord have mercy.

Lord Jesus, you call us to use our skills to help any who are in need. Christ have mercy.

Lord Jesus, you call us to protect those who are oppressed. Lord have mercy.

Headings for Readings
First Reading

In pre-modern societies the widow was the commonplace example of the person of no importance, the irrelevant, the no-body. Yet in this reading we hear how a widow has been chosen by God to have a special place in God's caring plan for his people.

Second Reading

Jesus Christ is our great high priest, and in union with him through the Holy Spirit, our prayers are brought into the very presence of the Father. That is why we look to his coming with hope and joy rather than with fear, as the last line of this reading put it: 'when he appears a second time, it will not be to deal with sin but to reward with salvation those who are waiting for him.'

Gospel

Jesus sees a widow making what is but a small offering in monetary terms, but he sees here differently from others who were standing around. He sees her with dignity; and his respect for her as a person allows him to see that she has actually given more than all the rich.

Prayer of the Faithful
President

Jesus Christ is our great High Priest, and in union with him, we enter now into the presence of the Father and present to him our needs.

Reader (s)

1. Let us pray for ourselves gathered here, that we will learn to see the world more and more with the eyes of Christ. Lord hear us.

2. Let us pray for all the members of this community, that we will be a people who respect others, work for justice, and acknowledge human dignity. Lord hear us.

3. Let us pray that this church, gathered before our heavenly Father, may be one that exudes his welcome, embrace, and care to all around us. Lord hear us.

4. Let us pray for those in authority, that they may recognise the dignity and respect to which every human being is entitled. Lord hear us.

5. Let us pray for the whole church of God, that in our dealings with each other as the church we will respect human dignity. Lord hear us.

6. Let us pray that we all will recognise the new responsibilities that our technological abilities place on us with regard to the creation. Lord hear us.

7. Specific local needs and topics of the day.

8. Let us pray for the dead that they may encounter Christ with his reward of salvation for all those who are waiting for him. Lord hear us.

President

Father, in your love you have called each of us into existence, you have sent your Son to us to make us your daughters and sons, and have implanted the Spirit in our hearts to enable us to respond to your love. Hear us now as we seek to love our sisters and brothers in a way that reflects your love for us. We ask this in union with our High Priest who stands in your presence, Jesus Christ, your Son, our Lord. Amen.

Eucharistic Prayer

Eucharistic Prayer IV picks up the theme of the Christ proclaiming the good news of salvation to the poor.

Invitation to the Our Father

Gathered as his daughters and sons, let us pray:

Sign of Peace

The Lord Jesus wants his disciples to have a new way of looking at those around them; let us express our willingness to view our neighbours with forgiveness and peace.

Invitation to Communion

Each of us has been called by name to be present at this banquet, to stand around this table and through sharing in this loaf and cup to offer thanks to the Father. Happy are we who are called to be here.

Communion Reflection

To become one with the Body of the Lord means that we should also be capable of recognising the Lord in the bodies of anyone who is poor or marginalised: one cannot appreciate participating in the Eucharist and not also be growing in appreciation of the love we owe to those in need.

With that thought as an introduction – and we must remember that many people view the Eucharist in individualistic terms of his/her personal relationship with God or, indeed, the obtaining of a sacral commodity – this is a day when some group within the community which cares for the poor should be asked to give an account of their work. Such accounts usually have the style of the 'sales pitch', but rather it should be requested that they witness to how they see their work as taking up the challenge posed by Jesus in today's gospel. In other words, how is their work with the poor a communion with the work of Jesus.

Conclusion
Solemn Blessing 12 (Ordinary Time III), Missal p 372, is suitable.

Notes
The Second Reading
Once again we confront the problem that the Letter to the Hebrews can appear to be just a jumble of words adding confusion to the Liturgy of the Word. Hebrews is always a difficult text, and even more so when it is approached in little pieces and without any real possibility of giving any proper guidance to it. This is not simply because the gospel takes priority, but because to do it justice one would need to devote the whole homily to it over the seven Sundays on which it is read. Yet, Hebrews is a key part of our theology of liturgy – indeed it was disputes over the very passage read today that was at the centre of Reformation-Counter Reformation disputes over whether or not 'the Mass is a sacrifice' (although neither side stopped to ask what 'sacrifice' meant within the image-driven theology of Hebrews) – and so should be heard. There is no simple solution, but certainly today is not the day to drop the second reading as it presents the mainstream Christian view of eschatology (the great party rather than final crunch) in contrast to the millenarians who seem to hog the media.

The Gospel

There seems little to recommend the shorter version as the discourse element is used by Mark as its introduction and should be respected as such. However, the force of the excerpt is clearly in the second element (vv 41-44): Jesus's actual teaching from the case of this widow.

COMMENTARY

First Reading: 1 Kgs 17:10-16

The stories about Elijah the Tishbite run from 17:1 to 19:21 and by being placed one after the other in the final form of 1 Kgs have been given by the editor a certain narrative quality. The power of Elijah as a prophet is shown in that he can decree a drought over the whole land – which is why the widow is on the brink of giving up – and this drought story runs from 17:1-24. Today we are reading a sub-plot within that story which shows the prophet with other powers: he can extend divine favour and divine protection to those whom he chooses. So what 'message' are we to draw from this? For the editor of 1 Kgs, this is obvious: Elijah is one of the great prophets of the tradition in that he knows the mind of God and God acts through him.

Psalm: 145 (146)

The choice is determined by the line that the Lord 'upholds the widow and orphan' which can be seen as a prayerful thanksgiving for the divine care and interest in the marginalised such as it presents as being demonstrated in the first reading.

Second Reading: Heb 9:24-28

Notwithstanding that this passage has been at the centre of Catholic-Protestant disputes about the nature of the sacrifice of the Mass and as such has generated an enormous theological literature that is supposedly based on this passage, this a relatively clear passage within the Letter. Its message is that Jesus has definitively replaced the annual ritual of the Day of Atonement in his own death. The people of whom he is the priest have been reconciled, sin has been put away, harmony restored. Therefore, we look forward to the final coming with joy: it will be the time of complete and final salvation.

If you can read this passage against the imagery of the ritual of the Day of Atonement (e.g. Lev 16), rather than against a backdrop of arguments over the theological description of the Eucharist or the 'final cause' of the Sacrament of Order, then its statement about the nature of Christ as the great High Priest becomes clear and elegant.

First Reading > Gospel Links

One suspects that the compilers of the lectionary were hard pressed to find an Old Testament passage that would link up with today's gospel; while there are many mentions of widows, they all belong to passages (e.g. Isa 1:17) that make very different points to that in the gospel. So the only link appears to be similarity of setting: the prophet takes notice of a widow, so too does the Christ. However, the first reading does not help us in any way to draw out the gospel.

Gospel: Mk 12:38-44 (shorter version: 41-44)

These two pieces of tradition, one a teaching on religious ostentation, the other an object lesson drawn from life, are connected by Mark as a unit in that they both mention widows – the very image of poverty and marginality in ancient patriarchal societies. In the first part of the pericope the summit of offence is that these religious people abuse widows and swallow up their life-support; in the second part of the pericope we are presented with an ideal of righteousness: the widow is greater than the wealthy and the ostentatious. The real devotee is the person who shares their little rather than the great donor whose name is then held in honour. As arranged by Mark this pericope is like a diptych: two joined pictures facing each other and we are invited to compare, indeed contrast, the characters in each. On the one hand, a scene that is visible to the whole public, while on the other a private scene that goes unnoticed except by Jesus. The first character belongs to the world of ostentation and display, the widow to gritty reality and there her great offering places her in the presence of God.

This short crisp unit is only found in Mark. Several bits of this pericope survive in Luke but they are far less focused, while Matthew has mutilated the first section out of recognition and omitted the actual woman.

HOMILY NOTES

1. When we stand and recite the creed we affirm our belief in the events surrounding our salvation: the life, death and resurrection of Jesus and in what he has revealed to us about the Father and the Spirit. Because we solemnly affirm this faith each Sunday, it is all too easy to slip into thinking that to be a Christian is simply a matter of accepting that creed. The argument runs like this: I profess the creed, therefore I am a 'Christian'. That is fine if you think of being a 'Christian' in terms of accepting a particular set of religious beliefs. But one might be described as a 'Christian', and yet not be a follower of the Christ.

2. To be a follower of Jesus is far more engaging than just accepting a creed: it is a whole way of thinking about life, a way of acting, and an alternative vision of the world. Following Christ involves us as social beings – how we relate to other human beings, economic actors in society – what constitutes our values for success and what we believe to be worthy economic goals, and how we work to build up the society around us – how we relate to the larger problems such as peace-making, global poverty, the destruction of the environment.

3. Being a Christian involves seeing the whole of the universe as the creation of a loving God.

4. We glimpse this new vision of life in the tiny incident that is recalled today. It seems so banal: a tiny incident by an anonymous poor woman and a comment by Jesus upon it – can that really indicate a wholly different vision of the world from that which is our society's common 'default option'?

5. The widow, the proverbial image for the most marginalised in ancient society, is a person of no importance whatsoever. She is just one of the mass of people who need to be processed through this particular system – namely people wanting to make an offering to God at the temple – as fast as possible. She is indistinguishable from thousands of others and what she actually contributed is, equally, viewed as insignificant. She is not a person, but a biological entity. She is the type of person that can be left queuing indefinitely without being spoken to or given a sign of fellow human recognition. She can be brusquely pushed aside by clearly uniformed minor officials when a VIP has to be given special treatment and impressed. She is, if she dared to speak to one of those officials, just a problem. In terms of her economic significance, she is nothing. And the frightening reality is that we view so much of the world using that optic. If an individual, a group, a country does not impact on us economically, then it and its problems do not matter. We are more interested in countries whose land has oil than carrots!

6. The wealthy making a carefully calculated donation to the temple, and getting VIP treatment while they do so, are a familiar group: they would love to be alive today in 'the age of celebrity' and would be happy to volunteer to participate in some glitzy event. But we also see the widow. One might even experience her plight while waiting in casualty in a hospital, trying to obtain justice from some vast bureaucracy, or even at a large religious gathering when it is clear to the stewards that some are more united to Christ than others.

7. Jesus's view of the situation is radically different. Each person is to be viewed as an individual. And each individual is worthy of respect for each is to be understood from within her or his own circumstances. This woman, her situation, her intention: these form the framework of how Jesus her. Only within this framework can it be seen that she has given more than the rich.

8. To learn to view others with dignity and respect is no easy

task: it goes right against the grain. To relate to individuals rather than mobs is also counter-cultural and flies against the fundamentals of mass consumption. To appreciate that each person is a beloved of God can only be known by those who themselves have responded to divine invitation to become beloved themselves.

Thirty-third Sunday of Ordinary Time

Introduction to the Celebration

Autumn is turning into winter, the leaves have fallen, the cold darkness seems to be ever more present – and for us, Christians, our thoughts turn to the end of time. But rather than the end of time being an apocalyptic prospect, we journey onwards with the confidence that the Lord who is the judge of the living and the dead is also the one who is the healer, the reconciler, the one who forgives, the prince of peace. It is in his presence that we have gathered, rejoicing that this meal is the anticipation of the heavenly banquet.

Rite of Penance

Lord Jesus, you came to show us the way to the Father. Lord have mercy.

Lord Jesus, you come to us now bringing reconciliation and peace. Christ have mercy.

Lord Jesus, you will come to judge the living and the dead. Lord have mercy.

Headings for Readings

First Reading

Even when the future looks apocalyptic, there is always God's saving will that his people should enter into everlasting life.

Second Reading

Jesus is our Great High Priest: he has conquered sin and death, and his sacrifice has made all of us acceptable to the Father.

Gospel

In the midst of all of life's trials we trust that the Christ who has conquered death will conquer every other evil, and in the end bring us into his glorious presence. The universe does not end in futility, but in the glory of God.

The gospel reminds us that we are not people who engage in useless speculations about 'the end of the world' – because only the Father knows about times – but we press onwards building up the creation knowing that the Lord will bring it to perfection.

Profession of Faith
Use the Nicene Creed (see Homily Notes)

Prayer of the Faithful
President
We have been made acceptable to the Father by Jesus our great High Priest, so now we can stand before the Father as his priestly people asking him for our needs.
Reader (s)
1. That we, and all humanity, will respect the integrity of the creation which God has given us as our earthly home. Lord hear us.
2. That we will learn to use wisely the resources of God's creation, recalling that all these resources are God's gifts. Lord hear us.
3. That we will live in a way that does not abuse the environment that God has created around us. Lord hear us.
4. That the world's resources may be used for the benefit of all humanity and may be used in a sustainable way. Lord hear us.
5. That we will recognise the new responsibilities that our technological abilities place on us with regard to the creation. Lord hear us.
6. That just as we have grown in technical skills in using the creation, so we might grow in wisdom in using what God has given us. Lord hear us.
7. That we may listen to the groans of the creation and respond as individuals and communities in the way we live. Lord hear us.
8. That we commit ourselves to protecting life and all creation, be it water, earth, or air, and know the limits set by wisdom. Lord hear us.

President
Father, among all life's difficulties we journey onwards in faith, hope and love because we know your love and care through Jesus Christ. Hear us now for we make these prayers in union with Christ Jesus, our Lord. Amen.

Eucharistic Prayer
Preface of Sundays in Ordinary Times V (P33) with Eucharistic Prayer II or III.

Invitation to the Our Father
On behalf of all creation, as a priestly people let us stand before the Father and pray:

Sign of Peace
To build up the creation involves building peace; let us express now to one another that desire for peace.

Invitation to Communion
The Son of Man will come at the end of time bringing all to the perfection of the heavenly banquet; meanwhile he is with us now and bids us to join him in this meal at this table.

Communion Reflection
Our God is the God of all humans.
The God of heaven and earth.
The God of the sea and the rivers.
The God of the sun and moon.
The God of all the heavenly bodies.
The God of the lofty mountains.
The God of the lowly valleys.
God is above the heavens;
and he is in the heavens;
and he is beneath the heavens.
Heaven and earth and sea,
and everything that is in them,

such he has as his abode.
He inspires all things,
he gives life to all things,
he stands above all things,
and he stands beneath all things.
He enlightens the light of the sun,
he strengthens the light of the night and the stars,
he makes wells in the arid land and dry islands in the sea,
and he places the stars in the service of the greater lights.
He has a Son who is co-eternal with himself,
and similar in all respects to himself;
and neither is the Son younger than the Father,
nor is the Father older than the Son;
and the Holy Spirit breathes in them.
And the Father and the Son and Holy Spirit are inseparable.
Amen.

(This creedal statement is found in the writings of Tirechán – an Irish bishop of the early eighth century).

Conclusion

Solemn Blessing 13 (Ordinary Time IV), Missal, p 373, is suitable.

Notes

There is an emphasis on eschatology in the final weeks of the liturgical year, and in the Year of Mark we have his version of the synoptic apocalypse as the gospel and one of the more vivid apocalyptic visions from Daniel as the first reading: the combination brings with it a special set of problems.

Apocalypticism is that strand of Jewish and Christian thought – and it has been there from the beginning and is still alive and vibrant today – that thinks of what is happening in the world's history as if God were running a computer programme: they happen to be living at the moment when the programme is coming to its climax which involves all the terrible sufferings of the good people who are faithful to God and this 'time of tribu-

lation' – to use a stock apocalyptic phrase – will then be followed
by the end of the world and then the evil doers will get their reward: damnation. Apocalypticism can be characterised by:

- fearfulness by a group who see themselves as God's people
  in opposition to the people linked with the wicked one;
- the terrible times are almost upon them;
- they know the plan of the future that is laid down;
- there is a black-and-white clash between 'the forces of good'
  and those of evil;
- they see their predicament in the most dramatic terms: earth-
  quakes, evil monsters, angels with shining swords;
- they think of God as the stern master who lets his own people suffer and then who rejoices in punishing the wicked one;
- strife rather than love is the most significant reality within the
  creation;
- a suspicion that the normal means of grace – be it the temple in
  Jerusalem or the sacramental system in Catholicism – are not
  really working any more either because they have become
  corrupt or are not fit for this special time of crisis: either way,
  people have to take drastic action for themselves in their own
  specially aware groups.

In contrast to this approach – very clearly visible in today's
first reading – we know from our overall reading of the gospels
that Jesus separated himself from this movement (indeed it is
probably the reason he left John the Baptist). Moreover, while
many apocalyptically inclined people joined the church without
abandoning their apocalypticism, we see constant efforts among
the evangelists to include them while taming this trend. Today's
gospel provides a very clear example: after the apocalyptic section – which brings those apocalyptically inclined followers of
Jesus within the ambit of the preaching – we are then told that
no one knows, no angel knows, not even the Son knows, when
the day will come. But if you do not know when the programme
will end, you cannot decide where you are now within it! In effect, today's gospel engaged with apocalyptic to try to under-
mine its basic ideas – and, indeed, to root it out of the church.

However, when read as a lone passage, and linked with the apocalyptic dynamite that is Daniel, this can have serious consequences. First, it can enflame those who are disposed to this approach within the congregation. Second, it can create the spirit of distrust of God's love that characterised many contemporary apocalyptic movements in the United States of America: if you do not think that this is a dangerous phenomenon within contemporary Christianity, do a web search using the search-string 'end times'. Third, it can provoke much useless questioning about 'the end' rather than focus people on discipleship where faith is seen as a pilgrimage.

When these readings were selected in the late 1960s, these problems were not foreseen, so today we need a workaround. One solution is to note that the gospel speaks about the creation – at some time in the future that only the Father knows – when the Lord will return. The question is then, how will we have performed in our stewardship of the creation? This gives an opening to address the theology of creation, and ecology as a Christian concern in today's homily – a topic that is of great importance in itself, but one which is often hard to find space for within the dynamic of the liturgical year.

COMMENTARY

First Reading: Dan 12:1-3

Written, shortly before 164 BC, by someone who saw the conquest of Palestine by the Greeks under Antiochus Epiphanes as the beginning of the final crisis when God would finally punish the world and his enemies, this passage expresses the hope that a few, the elect, will be saved. Michael – the great avenger of God – will do the sorting: the wicked will enter everlasting punishment, but the ones who have remained true will be awoken to everlasting life.

The teachers are those who have accepted the special apocalyptic knowledge and communicated it to the elect.

Psalm: 15 (16)

The Lord, and resting in the Lord, is the end point of human existence; without God we as creatures are incomplete. It is the insight of this psalm that inspired the opening line of Augustine's *Confessions*: 'You, O Lord, have made us for yourself and our hearts are not at rest until they rest in you.' The psalm fits perfectly with the eschatological motif of today's liturgy, but we should note that it is wholly free of apocalypticism.

Second Reading: Heb 10:11-14, 18

The letter seeks to make sense of what happened to Jesus – the chosen one of God but also the one who suffered and died on the cross – by seeing him as in the tradition of the priesthood. But if he is in that tradition, he must also be outside it – for he is the unique Son. This is done by contrasting the many priests of the Old Covenant with the single priest of the New Covenant: they had to offer many sacrifices for their priestly work was imperfect; he, by contrast, only needs to offer a single sacrifice for his sacrifice is perfect and complete. It is worth noting that the notion of priesthood used in Hebrews – as a theological motif – is absolutely unique to Jesus: it not only could not be shared by any of his brothers or sisters, but there would be no need to share it. This point has practical importance for the liturgy and any attempt to extrapolate from this reading to an understanding of the Eucharist. The Eucharist is the sacrifice of thanksgiving that is pleasing to the Father for it is offered in the Son present as the church's head; it is an abuse of theological language to see our gathering in terms of ' sacrifice' as that notion is elaborated by the author of Hebrews.

First Reading > Gospel Links

At face value this choice was no doubt made on the assumption that the gospel is a piece of apocalypticism from the New Testament, so having a passage from the more notorious example of apocalypticism from the Old Testament is somehow a case of balance. If the compilers recognised that Mark is deeply opposed to apocalypticism – and this is not a widely held view — then the relationship would be one of type (i.e. here is an example of how many people thought about God and the end times) and anti-type (i.e. here is how Jesus thought about the same issues and note that his thinking is the exact opposite). However, this relationship of type and anti-type is not one that normally attracted the compilers of the lectionary, so probably here is a case where they just opted for what they thought was a passage belonging to the same genre as the gospel.

Gospel: Mk 13:24-32

One of the underlying themes running right through Mark's record of his preaching is the need to cope with groups who have entered the church but who have not really abandoned aspects of their earlier spirituality that do not really fit with Jesus's message. We see it in the clashes at the beginning of the gospel where opinions held by members of the church – probably ex-disciples of John the Baptist who did not really appreciate how different Jesus's view was – are subtly undermined by having them expressed by 'pharisees' and others only to be rejected by Jesus. Here we see the same process at work with regard to apocalypticism – which again may be a legacy of John the Baptist brought into the church by some who were originally his followers.

The fundamental element in all apocalyptic preaching is that the end is a great crunch – fire, brimstone, the great battle from which a little band will be rescued – and that it is coming soon: indeed, so soon, that you had better hurry up and join the elect who will be saved. We know that this approach to religion was widespread within Judaism at the time (e.g. the Book of Daniel), and that there were groups getting ready for the end (Qumran), and that John the Baptist preached his baptism as a sort of 'last chance saloon'. Jesus, by contrast, preached a kingdom that is coming, but it comes in gentleness, the end is the heavenly banquet, and God is characterised as forgiving love rather than avenging justice. For Mark, the Son of Man has come (Mk 2:10), but his coming has not brought a catastrophe for the world, but only for Jesus himself: 'And he began to teach them that the Son of man must suffer many things, and be rejected by the elders and the chief priests and the scribes, and be killed, and after three days rise again' (8:31).

So how does Mark challenge apocalypticism here? On the one hand he has Jesus use the language of apocalypticism, but then negate its very basis: 'but as for that day or hour,' nobody, not even himself, knows. An apocalypticism where no one but the Father knows when the programme will have run its course is a contradiction. It is as if Mark is saying to his audience: of course you can engage with apocalyptic language, but it is all quite irrelevant to Christian discipleship. Mark's subtlety was no doubt inspired by the desire to keep his congregations together – apocalyptic followers are inherently sectarian for it essential to their spirituality that they split off to form the 'true,' 'pure remnant' – but, alas, this section of his gospel (and its parallels) have been understood down the centuries by many Christians as Jesus's approbation of an apocalyptic approach to faith.

HOMILY NOTES

1. The gospel puts before us the great image of the Son of Man returning to the earth and gathering his people. This dramatic image – the stuff of many a religious nightmare – arrests our attention and focuses us, at this time each year, on one little line in the creed:

   He will come again in glory to judge the living and the dead, and his kingdom will have no end.

   Unfortunately, the image of today's gospel is so striking that down the centuries generations of Christians have become so excited about the 'apocalypse', that they have forgotten that proclaiming that the Lord will come at the end of time is only the second half of the equation. So what is the first half?

2. Whenever we think about the end when the Lord, the Son of

the Father will come again; we must also think that the Lord, the Son of the Father, is the one through whom the universe came in existence at the very beginning. This is what we profess earlier in the creed:

Through him all things were made.

And the Lord, the Son of the Father, who was there at the beginning and will be there at the End, is also the one who is with humanity as our source of light and life:

For us and for our salvation
he came down from heaven:
by the power of the Holy Spirit
he became incarnate from the Virgin Mary,
and was made man.

3. To profess to be a follower of Jesus is to assert that he is the Alpha – there at the beginning – and the Omega – there at the End – and with us now.

4. But what does this mean? It means that we have to think of ourselves, all living creatures, and all creation as in a situation between God's love at the Alpha, the beginning, and God's love at the Omega, the end. Between these times we have been entrusted with the creation: we hold all creation, all life, on trust from God.

5. Jesus makes it very clear that we do not know when the end will come: 'But of that day or that hour no one knows, not even the angels in heaven, nor the Son, but only the Father.' Our task is to act as the people who have been given responsibility to use the creation well, to act as good stewards, and to remember that when we abuse it we are breaking God's fundamental loving trust in us.

6. We are all on a journey from the Alpha towards the Omega. How we make the journey — how we behave along that road, how we act as pilgrims who have no notion when they will arrive – is all-important.

7. During the coming week we shall hear many reports in the media about climate change. We will hear of a new initiative to cut down on energy use. We may take a load of bottles to

the bottle bank for recycling, or we might just switch off some lights or gadgets that are running on stand-by. When we hear these reports or do these things, we might think that all this has little do with religion or faith or waiting for the Lord to return to judge the living and the dead: we could not be more wrong. We, as the people who have professed the universe to have been made through the Son and who believe he will come again, are the people who can set all ecological concerns in context. The creation is God's; we have been entrusted with it; we are called to be good stewards.

Lectionary Unit III.III

This stage consists of the last Sunday of Ordinary Time, when the Feast of Christ the King is seen as the liturgical celebration of the fulfilment of the mystery of the Son of Man.

Although this is seen as the culmination of the Year of Mark, the end of the year's reflection on the eschaton is taken from John.

The Feast of Christ the King

Introduction to the Celebration

Last January we began a cycle of readings from the gospels of Mark and John. We read them between January and Ash Wednesday, and then again from Pentecost until today: they have been laying before us one way of recounting the mystery of Jesus, our teacher, our brother, and our God. Now today we come to the end of this year-long recollection. Today we are thinking of Jesus, not as someone who came among us in the past, but as the King of all creation who will come again among us. When he comes at the end of time, he will gather all of us into his kingdom, and present that kingdom to the Father.

Rite of Penance

Your kingdom is a kingdom of truth and life. Lord have mercy.

Your kingdom is a kingdom of holiness and grace. Christ have mercy.

Your kingdom is a kingdom of justice, love, and peace. Lord have mercy.

Headings for Readings
First Reading

This reading reminds us that the Lord, Christ the King, stands beyond human time and gathers all together, making all things new, forming the kingdom that he presents to the Father.

Second Reading

This reading describes Jesus, the Anointed of the Father, as the Alpha and the Omega. We confess he is the Alpha when we say in the Creed: 'through him all things were made'; we confess he is the Omega on this feast: he stands at the end of all human endeavour and gathers it together to form the kingdom which he then returns to the Father.

Gospel

Today we acclaim Jesus as our king: but he is not a king in the earthly sense. This gospel challenges all Christians, just as it challenged Pontius Pilate, to reflect on what it means to call Christ our king and to see in him the fulfilment of human destiny.

Prayer of the Faithful
President

As we look for the coming of the kingdom in its fullness, let us unite ourselves with Christ the eternal priest, and standing before the Father present him with our needs.

Reader (s)

1. For the whole church of God, Christians everywhere, that we may live in a manner that is consistent with the universe being God's creation, which comes into existence through the Word and which will be brought to its completion in Christ the King. Lord hear us.

2. For all people of good will, the whole human family, that we all will become more conscious of the divine presence in the universe and grow to be more in harmony with it. Lord hear us.

3. For those for whom the universe is a riddle and not a mystery, who do not acknowledge the reality of creation, that the Lord of creation may give new sight to their eyes. Lord hear us.

4. For this community, each of us and the whole group, that we will continue on the path of discipleship and look forward to all our efforts being gathered together into the kingdom of the Father by Christ. Lord hear us.

5. Specific local needs and topics of the day.

6. For all who have died, that they may be brought to the banquet prepared for us in the fullness of the kingdom. Lord hear us.

President

Father, your Son is the Alpha and the Omega, the beginning and the end; hear the prayer we make in union with him. Amen.

Eucharistic Prayer

The Preface of Christ the King (P51); and Eucharistic Prayer III is appropriate as it contains the notion of the universal priest: a perfect offering rising to the Father from one end of the creation to the other.

Invitation to the Our Father

Christ has gathered us and called us to grow to become the fullness of the Father's kingdom; let us now pray for that growth among ourselves, all Christians, all humanity, and in the whole creation:

Sign of Peace

The Lord calls us to become the kingdom of justice, love and peace: let us celebrate now the presence of this kingdom among us.

Invitation to Communion

We come now to this table at the Lord's bidding, looking forward to being called to the banquet of the kingdom when Christ is all in all.

Communion Reflection

The Preface can be adapted into a reflection on Christ as King/High Priest in this way:
The Father anointed Jesus Christ, his only Son, with the oil of gladness,
as the eternal priest and universal king.
As priest he offered his life on the altar of the cross
and redeemed the human race
by this one perfect sacrifice of praise.
As King he claims dominion over all creation,
that he may present to his almighty Father,
an eternal and universal kingdom:
a kingdom of truth and life,
a kingdom of holiness and grace,
a kingdom of justice, love, and peace.

Re-using the preface in this way has much to recommend it. In many ways this preface is the best liturgical summary of the significance of this feast, and when heard only once today – at a time when concentration is often difficult – it does not have time to sink in.

Conclusion

May Christ the universal King guide your steps in the way of justice, guide your words with his wisdom, and guide your hearts towards his holiness. Amen.

May Christ the universal King be your leader, your light, and your peace both now and always. Amen.

May Christ the universal King grant this church a place in the kingdom he presents to the Father. Amen.

Notes

1. The task today is to rejoice in our good news. Our good news is our vision of the eschaton. How different is our feast of Christ the King from the Day of Doom of fundamentalist evangelicals! And, it is appropriate to think of the eschaton at the end of the liturgical year. But it only happens at the end of the year, and hence this feast and it is the feast we are celebrating. It is not a case that we are celebrating the end of the year, and so this feast will do as a kind of liturgical 'full stop'. Getting this logic of this sequence clear is essential if we are to strike the right note in today's liturgy. In a nutshell:

- This is the last Sunday in this liturgical year.
- The end of a human year is a fitting occasion to think of the end of all.
- We have a very distinct vision of the end summed up in the image of Christ, King of the Universe.
- This vision of the eschaton is what we are celebrating.
- Given our vision of the eschaton, it is a day of great hope and joy.

2. One of the most basic aspects of all human celebrations is the alternation in the 'tone' of each day: there are ordinary days and

special days. There are times which have a special stress of solemnity and those which have not; the special days make us appreciate the ordinary, and it is only by contrast with the ordinary that the special stands out. Without the alternation of ordinary time and stressed time, life becomes monotonous, the wearying tick-tock, tick-tock of the clock. And human time is far more varied than clock time. One of the unintended consequences of the more informal style of liturgy that accompanies the use of the vernacular has been that most Sundays are very much like most other Sundays: it always feels the same. This is a great pity and, because we are celebrating our glorious vision of the eschaton, today is a day when we should invoke the more solemn liturgical register.

This is a day for a formal procession with incense, cross, acolytes carrying lights, the Book of the Gospels, other ministers. Then incense and lights at the proclamation of the gospel, and then again once the gifts have been placed on the Eucharistic table.

This feast must not be a dull whimper, nor is it a day on which to flag up next Sunday as the first Sunday of Advent; rather we must make a joyful solemn splash about how we view the final future of all humanity and the universe.

3. In the notices and in the newsletter it is worth pointing out that:

> Today marks the end of reading the gospel of Mark; and next year we will be recalling the mystery of Jesus our Saviour through listening to the gospel of Luke.

Little nuggets of information like this increase the community's awareness of the richness of the structure of the lectionary.

COMMENTARY

First Reading: Dan 7:13-14

Second Reading: Apoc 1:5-8

Both these readings have been selected not because of some relationship with the gospel (usual rationale for selecting first readings) nor because they fit within a sequence of reading from a

particular book (the usual rationale for selecting second readings), but because they can both be read by Christians from the
perspective of today's feast and the mystery that feast celebrates.

Both these readings are closely related in genre: the first is a
late Jewish apocalyptic work; the second a Jewish-Christian
apocalyptic work that dates from the later first century. As such
they both tap into forms of Judaism at the time of Jesus: the
world is a place corrupted, the Evil One, Satan, is active there
persecuting the holy ones who follow the Lord despite their sufferings, and God will soon intervene and punish the wicked, defeat the Evil One, and rescue and reward the saints. Not only is
this great crunch going to happen soon, but it is now foretold in
visions and, indeed, its timings can be calculated and future
events predicted. This was a minority strand within Judaism
(this can be seen in that out of the many such books written only
Daniel made it into the canon), but many of these apocalypticists
became Christians, probably having first become followers of
John the Baptist, and so this has become a strand of Christian
thought and spirituality. Within Christianity it is also a minority
strand (out of the many such books, only the Apocalypse of John
made it into the canon), but has been influential (there are apocalyptic sections in three of the four gospels: Mk 13:5-37; Mt 24:4-
36; Lk 21:8-36). In fact this whole approach simply does not fit
with the rest of the Christian message except when it is ham-
mered in like the proverbial square peg in the round hole, and
there has been a continual effort to marginalise it (e.g. the
Orthodox do not read Apoc in the liturgy; in the west we have
evolved sophisticated strategies to re-integrate the wilder forms
within the broader whole), but it keeps cropping up:
Priscillianism in the West; Chiliasm in the East; Millenarianism
in the West; the messages of Fatima; contemporary American
'evangelists'; and the list goes on and on.

Today we read both readings with Jesus, the incarnate Son,
as the subject about whom the readings speaks. He is the 'son of
man' and the one of great age is the Father. Christ is establish-

ing, by the Father's will, the entirety of the kingdom and he is its sovereign, and his kingdom will endure because as High Priest he offers it to Father. The incarnate Son, is also the Alpha and the Omega, and as such is true God and true man and so can be addressed with the title 'Almighty' which we usually reserve for the Father, and the Son is he who is, was and will be: Christ the Eternal and Universal King.

These readings are problematic if we seek to read them within their original context. Not only are they part of the whole terror-eschatology of apocalyptic but, as is clear from the final verse of the second reading, because they are doctrinally confusing: the person who wrote the Apocalypse of John had no notion of the divinity of Jesus but saw him as a kind of cosmic final agent/ hero – much like the author of Daniel imagined the 'son of man'. However, if read within the firmly established focus of today's liturgy, they can be seen as imaginative poems in praise of Jesus whom today we address using the metaphors of High Priest and Universal King.

In a nutshell: we start with the theology expressed in today's preface and from that starting point we see these two readings as liturgical poetry. If, however, we were to start with these readings and try to distill from them a view of Jesus, we would end up very far from the faith we would then stand and acclaim in the creed.

Psalm: Ps 92 (93)

This psalm invokes the imagery of 'the eternal king' – a king with all the glory but not the limitations of an earthy king – for God. It is especially suited to today's liturgy; and in the liturgy we hear the psalm christologically: the Lord who is king is Jesus the Lord, it is the Christ who is the eternal king.

First Readings > Gospel Links

There is no link. All three readings are chosen as they can be used within the overall theme of the eschatological kingship of the Christ which the liturgy celebrates.

We should note that while there is an apocalyptic strand in the synoptics, John's gospel is resolutely anti-apocalyptic.

Gospel: Jn 18:33-37

This scene from the passion is rich in irony: Jesus is about to prevail over sin and death, but he does so from the cross. Pilate who serves an earthly king, writes the truth – about which he could not care less – when he writes the title that is placed above the cross. However, here this reading serves not the agenda of·its author within the passion narrative, but the needs of today's liturgy.

There are three aspects to this liturgical reading of this gospel:

(1) Here Jesus accepts for himself the title of 'king'. But (2) declares that what this means in his case is not to be confused with an earthly king, nor his kingdom with an earthly kingdom (and so, incidentally, counters a basic notion of apocalyptic that the final establishment of divine justice will take effect within the terrestrial-historical order). And (3) that as this unique kind of king, Jesus gathers all that is true to himself: 'All who are on the side of truth listen to my voice.'

As with the other readings, we begin with the picture of the mystery as we celebrate it under the heading of 'Christ the King' and then explore this in the gospel. An attempt to arrive at the feast by exegesis of the text would simply leave everyone thoroughly confused.

HOMILY NOTES

1. When we listen to the voices of those advocating concern for the environment, care for the planet, or care for the quality of human life, we hear certain themes recurring. We find these themes whether the promoters of these concerns are Christians (viewing the universe as a creation with a plan and providence within it) or theists (who see ecological concern as somehow a sacred activity) or people who ignore the sacred dimension as if it were irrelevant.

2. Some of these themes are:

- The importance of recognising that humans can act constructively or destructively in the way we live.
- The importance of recycling: we must not behave as if anything can simply be used and thrown away as waste; we must see every object as having its own value.
- That we must recognise that everything we do as individuals or small groups becomes part of a larger pattern that can have far greater consequences.
- We must keep our eyes fixed on the longer-term picture: 'Now', 'Today' are such fleeing moments!

3. For us who believe that God is the creator, the beginning and end of all that is, seen and unseen, these four themes of ecologists are not simply 'human wisdom' but part of our whole understanding of this mystery of why we are here. And the imagery we use to express this very complex set of beliefs is that Jesus, the Anointed of the Father, is the King of All Creation. It is in him that all creation comes to its perfection, and then through him that it is presented to his Father.

4. On Holy Saturday night we welcomed the risen Christ by inscribing the Paschal Candle (that actual candle, now a worn down butt, can be a visual at this point) with these words:

> Christ yesterday and today,
> The beginning and the end
> Alpha and Omega
> All time belongs to him
> And all the ages
> To him be glory and power through every age forever.

5. We often think of God the Son at the beginning of the creation: as we say in the creed: he is 'begotten not made, of one Being with the Father. Through him all things were made' and St John adds: 'and without him was not anything made that was made.' This is recognising Christ at the beginning, the Alpha of all.

6. Today we think of Christ as the end, the final point, the goal of all creation, the Omega of all.

7. And for us, this is the future of hope, not a great catastrophe, not a great crunch, but when all that is good and noble is brought to perfection. The figure of the Christ stands at the end of time like someone gathering the harvest, and then presenting it in its completed state to the Father.

8. So how do we Christians understand those four themes:

- *The importance of recognising that humans can act constructively or destructively in the way we live.*

   Our actions are not simply random activity: we are called to act with justice and honesty, with care and respect, not from self-interest but because this is part of God's loving plan. We want to be in harmony with nature, but we also want to be in harmony with the Love that brought nature into existence and which draws it towards its goal.

- *The importance of recycling: we must not behave as if anything can simply be used and thrown away as waste; we must see every object as having its own value.*

   Everything exists because of God's loving will in giving it existence, and each thing has unique value because it is brought into being through the Son. To see anything as useless, waste, rubbish, is to ignore the Alpha of the creation and its Omega.

- *That we must recognise that everything we do as individuals or small groups becomes part of a larger pattern that can have far greater consequences.*

   We recognise that we are called to behave responsibly as individuals and as groups. We know we must have an intimate relationship with God as individuals in prayer and action, but we must also have a group relationship with Christ as his body, the church. The Lord, who calls each of us by name, is also the Lord who calls us to become the kingdom, and it is that kingdom, embracing all creation, that is presented to the Father.

- *We must keep our eyes fixed on the longer-term picture: 'Now', 'Today' are such fleeing moments!*

   Just as we must think long-term about the material universe – both forwards and backwards – if we are to act with understanding, so we have to remember the Alpha of the universe – that all comes into being through the Son – and its Omega – when the Son presents it to the Father – if we are to act wisely within God's creation.

9. For us these are not bits of human wisdom, rather they are fragments of the divine plan that we can see around us and which point us to the incompleteness of any understanding of the universe that does not acknowledge it as a creation – a creation that comes from God and which returns to God, and which is suffused with the divine love through the presence of Christ, the Alpha and the Omega.